BUREAU OF SPIES

BUREAU

OF

SPIES

THE SECRET CONNECTIONS BETWEEN
ESPIONAGE AND JOURNALISM
IN WASHINGTON

STEVEN T. USDIN

Prometheus Books

59 John Glenn Drive
Amherst, New York 14228

Published 2018 by Prometheus Books

Cover design by Liz Mills
Cover image © Eric Nathan / Alamy Stock Photo
Cover design © Prometheus Books

Trademarked names appear throughout this book. Prometheus Books recognizes all registered trademarks, trademarks, and service marks mentioned in the text.

The internet addresses listed in the text were accurate at the time of publication. The inclusion of a website does not indicate an endorsement by the author or by Prometheus Books, and Prometheus Books does not guarantee the accuracy of the information presented at these sites.

Inquiries should be addressed to
Prometheus Books
59 John Glenn Drive
Amherst, New York 14228
VOICE: 716–691–0133 • FAX: 716–691–0137
WWW.PROMETHEUSBOOKS.COM

22 21 20 19 18   5 4 3 2 1

Library of Congress Cataloging-in-Publication Data

Identifiers: LCCN 2018016005 (print) |
ISBN 978-1-63388-476-2 (hardcover) | 978-1-63388-477-9 (ebook)

Printed in the United States of America

For Elena, Maxime, and Anton, and Mesfin Mekonen,
the heart and soul of the National Press Club

CONTENTS

CONTENTS

NOTE FROM THE AUTHOR

This book is a history of the connections between intelligence and journalism, of spies who pretended to be reporters and reporters who dabbled as spies, told by examining covert activities that occurred in a building four blocks from the White House, the National Press Building.

Conducted properly, spying leaves few traces. Some of the stories in *Bureau of Spies* have been revealed because governments no longer feel compelled to keep them secret. Others were revealed when Nazi Germany and imperial Japan found themselves on the wrong side of history and were forced to disgorge their secrets. Post-Watergate attempts to rein in government abuses of power led to revelations about collaboration between American news media and the CIA, as well as the CIA's illegal surveillance of reporters. A few brave Russians took advantage of the turmoil swirling around the collapse of the Soviet Union to smuggle secrets from the KGB's archives that have been released to the public. And some old spies are willing to tell war stories.

Along with espionage, notable instances of subversion, including subversive propaganda, are described in this book. These are important because, like stealing secrets, they raise questions about the boundaries between reporting and making news, cultivating sources and seducing recruits—and between building up and tearing down democracy.

While the intelligence exploits of some of the journalists who operated in the National Press Building are spectacular, their activities are in no way representative of the profession. The vast majority of the tens of thousands of men and women who worked in or visited the Press Building in the eight decades covered in this book had no association with spying. Revelations about the connections between a small number of journalists and intelligence agencies have coated all reporters with an undeserved

9

layer of suspicion. American reporters who have worked overseas or taken an interest in uncovering government secrets are routinely and usually falsely accused of being, or collaborating with, spies. Such accusations are insidious because efforts to disprove them are interpreted as evidence of the quality or depth of an individual's "cover," while shrugging off or joking about unfounded rumors can be misinterpreted as acknowledgment of their veracity. Labeling reporters as spies can tarnish or destroy reputations and provoke threats to innocent persons' liberty or safety. To avoid causing harm, I have taken care in this book to avoid associating any individual with espionage unless they have acknowledged the connection or there is strong documentary evidence.

In writing this book I've benefited greatly from the assistance of Ken Jacobson, who helped shape its form and substance, the perceptive comments of Carl Feldbaum, who challenged me to do better, the critical comments of John Haynes and Mark Kramer, the confidence of my agent, Kathi Patton, and editorial assistance from Barbara Egbert. I'd like to thank Gil Klein, chair of the National Press Club's History and Heritage Committee, Jeffrey Schlosberg, the NPC's archivist, and John Powers of the National Archives for their generous help. Of course, any mistakes are entirely my responsibility.

SPYING BETWEEN THE LINES IN THE NATIONAL PRESS BUILDING

During the winter of 1925 sledge hammers smashed into the last remnants of Washington's Newspaper Row, a string of ramshackle buildings dating to the 1840s that staggered like the often-inebriated reporters who worked in them up the east side of 14th Street from Pennsylvania Avenue to F Street. The blows crashed into offices bearing the names of newspapers from around the country, along with the Ebbitt House Hotel and its beloved bar—all demolished to make way for the National Press Building, the new home for Washington's press corps and the National Press Club. Reporters who scurried into temporary quarters had witnessed the improbable trajectory of the club from its origins as a boozy poker parlor in rented rooms into an organization that would own an office building around the corner from the White House.[1]

A fourteen-story human beehive rose from the rubble, humming with men and women collecting, organizing, and disseminating news—and providing perfect cover for espionage, subversion, and propaganda. Over the decades, an assortment of professional spooks and freelance spies have hidden there in plain sight, blending in with the legions of reporters who used the Press Building as a base for informing, misinforming, entertaining, and enraging the public through the craft of journalism. Those spying between the lines from the Press Building's offices, corridors, and bar stools have included homegrown and German fascists, spies for imperial Japan, British intelligence operatives, representatives of Soviet civilian and military intelligence agencies, and CIA officers.

Like all great spy stories, tales of espionage rooted in the Press Building are filled with colorful characters performing tense dramas against a backdrop of world-changing events. While they are interesting in isolation, assembling these stories serves a larger purpose: showing how intelligence and news organizations have used and shaped each other, and revealing the roots of phenomena that continue to influence events around the globe today. The history of espionage in Washington's National Press Building reveals that there's nothing new about industrial-scale dissemination of fake news, foreign governments covertly influencing American elections, or massive disclosures of government secrets.

Four decades before Edward Snowden's birth, a reporter working from a Press Building office plastered the War Department's most closely held secrets across the front pages of the *Chicago Tribune* and the *Washington Times Herald*, giving Hitler's generals a roadmap to America's war plans. President Franklin Roosevelt, like many of his successors who faced similar leaks, considered prosecuting the reporter and his publisher for espionage—and ultimately decided to do nothing.

Long before the internet made the production of fake news child's play, offices in the Press Building served as conduits for a foreign government to plant rumors and lies in American newspapers.

Years before he organized the Watergate burglary as part of a program of espionage and dirty tricks supporting the campaign to reelect President Richard Nixon, a CIA officer used a front company based in the Press Building to spy on the presidential campaign of Barry Goldwater.

WikiLeaks wasn't the first anti-secrecy group to dump huge quantities of classified data into the public domain. In the late 1970s, comrades of a rogue CIA officer published a magazine from a Press Club office that revealed intelligence secrets with the explicit goal of shutting down American covert operations.

The chain of events that led to construction of a building dedicated to journalism, which was also a uniquely fertile ground for espionage, was set in motion by the yearning for a warm, comfortable place to drink and play poker.

The National Press Club's origins, and by extension the roots of the Press Building, can be traced to a conversation between Graham Nichol, a one-legged *Washington Times* police reporter, and James Hay Jr., White House reporter for the *Baltimore Sun*. The discussion took place a block north of the intersection of Newspaper Row and Rum Row, a collection of taverns that started at 14th Street and dribbled several blocks down Pennsylvania Avenue toward the Capitol. Hay recalled the event a quarter century later:

> On a wet and windy day near the end of February, 1908, I was standing at the corner of Fourteenth and F Streets—about ten feet from the northwest angle of the National Press Building of the present—when I saw, approaching on crutches against the gale that always howled about that particular locality on breezy days, the tall and broad-shouldered figure of the [Press Club] founder, the late Graham Bright Nichol, red as to hair and altogether satisfactory as to personality.... [Nichol] in his Big Bertha voice made this statement, confession and prophecy: "I'm getting damned tired of having to hunt a stuffy, ill-ventilated little ballroom in a cheap boarding house every time I want to play a game of poker! Hell's Bells! Why don't we get up a press club? A place where the fellows can take a drink or turn a card when they feel like it?"[2]

Hay explained how dream was turned into deed:

> That night the determined Mr. Nichol betook himself to Number One Police Station, then on Twelfth Street, a short distance below Pennsylvania Avenue, the rendezvous, loafing ground and pseudo-club of the city's police reporters and their friends.... [The reporters] immediately confessed to the same yearning for the luxury of a "few upstairs rooms" that had so upset and agitated the soul of Mr. Nichol.[3]

Nichol gathered pledges of ten dollars apiece from the enthusiastic crowd, held a meeting three weeks later in the F Street Parlor of the Willard Hotel, and officiated on May 2, 1908, when the National Press Club opened its doors as a going concern, occupying the second and third floors over a jeweler's shop at 1206 F Street.

The surroundings were far from palatial—the steep staircase to the card room on the third floor "might have disheartened an Alpine goat," Hay complained—but from the start the National Press Club was a magnet for reporters, government officials, diplomats and celebrities. Buffalo Bill Cody, the British and Japanese ambassadors, a handful of actors, and a bevy of minor luminaries joined publishers, correspondents, and reporters at the club's official housewarming on May 18.[4]

In its earliest days, Press Club leaders established a rule that reflected their deep understanding of reporters' psyches and laid the foundation for the institution's longevity: All bills were due on presentation. This simple, practical decision ensured the NPC's viability even as press clubs around the country faltered and collapsed under the burden of unpaid bar tabs from fiscally improvident hacks.[5]

The Club prospered and outgrew its modest quarters, moving three times to larger, plusher rented rooms. In 1925 a handful of members came up with a bold idea that would have seemed a drunken fantasy just a few years earlier. They envisioned a massive office building on one of the most valuable real estate parcels in the city. It would be large enough to accommodate Washington's entire press corps, with space set aside as a permanent home for the club, and an income stream from rents to fund the club's operations into perpetuity.

Conceived in the middle of a decade of unrivaled optimism and economic growth, the Press Building seemed destined to succeed. A bond prospectus solicited investments in an edifice "designed to be the national headquarters of the Press and to consolidate under one roof offices for the Washington representatives of practically every publication of importance in the country."[6] It boasted that the National Press Club's Board of

Governors had already approved over 150 lease applications, representing "most of the metropolitan newspapers of the United States."

From the start, the project was meant to be more than an office building. Its scale and location made the Press Building a steel and concrete expression of the importance and power of the American news industry, and of Washington's role as the capital of an emerging world power. The most modern building in the nation's capital, with more than five hundred miles of wiring and enough electricity to power a city of ten thousand, it was also Washington's largest private office building. Press Building superlatives included housing the 3,500-seat Fox Theater, the largest theater south of Philadelphia.[7]

A full page advertisement in Washington's *Evening Star* in August 1927 touting the building's unique features highlighted a free twenty-four-hour answering service "equivalent to an attendant in your office day and night. . . . This service, the first of its kind, is one of the many innovations for the comfort and convenience of the National Press Building."[8]

The *Washington Post* hailed the Press Building's completion as a "dream come true," and a "monument to journalism." It was, a *Post* editorial asserted, "less a mark of the accomplishments of the members of the press than evidence of the power of the profession they represent."[9] The paper also acknowledged that in gaining prestige and gravitas, the Washington press corps was also losing some of its rough-edged charm—a lament that has been repeated over the years as journalism has become ever more professional and respectable, and the behavior of journalists more restrained. "The press, more especially in the United States, has attained a new dignity within the last few decades," the *Post* proclaimed pompously. "It has lost, possibly, some of its picturesqueness, but it has gained in worth and stability."

At fourteen floors, the NPB exceeded the city's height limit, which was modified to permit its construction. Coming to life at a time when Washington was starting its long, slow transition from sleepy, stagnant southern backwater to semi-sophisticated city, it also strained the boundaries of contemporary manners. This tension was on display in the building's elevators, where young female operators posed a quandary in a city that clung to old ideas of decorum long after they'd been abandoned in more modern metropolises like New York and Chicago. "Going up and down certain male tenants doff their hats for the charming operators. Others keep on their Kellys until some other woman enters the car, and they uncover the old bean, although the passenger may be half as good looking or gracious as the elevator operator," a *Washington Post* columnist informed readers in October 1927. "Indeed, the woman passenger may be in the building distributing propaganda for more equal rights for women, or for the suppression of tobacco, or the repeal of the inalienable right of a married man to get out at least one night a week. There is a third class of men who lift their hats neither for the female operator nor the woman passenger."[10]

The Press Building management made special accommodations for newspapermen who refused to bow to convention, reserving an elevator for the exclusive use of men, shielding them from obligations to remove hats or extinguish cigars in the presence of the fairer sex.[11]

National Press Building, 1930s.

While women operated its elevators, and there were a handful of female reporters working in the building, very few of them got off on the top floor, which was occupied by the Press Club. Women weren't admitted to, or with the exception of special events, even allowed to set foot in the National Press Club until 1971. This was sixteen years after a hotly contested referendum resulted in a decision to admit the first African American member. Prior to 1955, the only black men to step inside the Press Club were employees or entertainers, like the "Negro members of the CCC camp at Alexandria, Va." who, according to a *Washington Post* report, sang spirituals for Press Club members, Vice President John Nance Garner, and other dignitaries in April 1935.[12]

From its creation in 1908 through the 1970s, bourbon and poker were at least as important as press conferences to reporters at the National Press Club.
    Credit: National Press Club archives

Pretty elevator operators and a prestigious address were selling points, but they weren't the main reasons the National Press Building became a magnet for reporters—and intelligence operatives. Easy access to the Press Club's meeting and card rooms, home away from home for all but the most reclusive reporters, was at least as enticing as the building's central location and modern amenities. The Press Club was an informal guild hall and a venue for press conferences and formal dinners. Above all it was a drinking club, home to an unending series of poker games, and the best place in Washington to pick up gossip that was too juicy to print.[13]

CHAPTER ONE
WASHINGTON MERRY-GO-ROUND

Reports from the first known spy in Washington's National Press Building started flowing into the Lubyanka, the headquarters of Soviet intelligence, in 1933. There was a symmetry and an invisible connection between the buildings. The elegant Lubyanka, originally built as the headquarters of a Czarist-era insurance company, dominated one side of a square in central Moscow a few blocks from the headquarters of the Communist Party of the Soviet Union, while the Press Building is four short blocks from the White House. It took five minutes to drive from the Lubyanka to the Kremlin. In the '30s a reporter could pick up a Coke in the lobby of the Press Building, hop into a taxi on 14th Street, and finish it in the Capitol rotunda before it warmed up. The Lubyanka and the Press Building were wired with state-of-the-art telecommunications technology; both buildings buzzed around the clock as their inhabitants struggled to stay on top of news streaming in from around the globe.

The parallels between the headquarters of the *Obyedinyonnoye gosudarstvennoye politicheskoye upravleniye* (OGPU), as Soviet intelligence was called at the time, and the home base for the Washington press corps echo the real affinities as well as the misleading resemblances between journalism and espionage. A glance inside the two buildings revealed the essential differences. In 1933 there was a newsstand in the lobby of the Press Building, the National Press Club occupied its top floors, and the dozen floors in the middle contained the largest concentration of reporters in the United States, probably the world. In the Lubyanka's basement cells the innocent were starved, beaten, and shot, while above them thousands of employees worked for the world's largest, and arguably most ruthless, intelligence organization.

In contrast to the heavily guarded Lubyanka, the Press Building, designed and built to provide modern offices in the nation's capital for the world's news media, has always been open to the public. This accessibility created a constant flow of humanity that provided excellent cover for espionage. The tens of thousands of journalists who have worked and played in the Press Building over the last nine decades camouflaged a sprinkling of professional spies who pretended to be reporters and of real reporters who, motivated by ideology, patriotism, a longing for adventure, or greed, collaborated with foreign and domestic intelligence agencies.

The OGPU's first known operative in the building was Robert S. Allen, an American reporter who dabbled in espionage but was not a professional spy. He worked from an office on the 12th floor and was identified in an initial report to OGPU headquarters in January 1933 by the codename Sh/147. Subsequent reports used the cover name George Parker. A fixture at the Press Club, at Washington dinner parties, and on the pages of America's most prestigious newspapers, Allen produced a continuous stream of information and gossip that was essential reading for anyone interested in American politics, whether they were in Minneapolis or Moscow. Equally important to the almost infinitely patient Soviet spymasters, he was well positioned both to gain access over time to tightly guarded secrets and to identify other potential agents.[1]

Allen's Soviet handler provided his superiors in Moscow a thumbnail sketch of the new recruit's career, starting with a description of *Washington Merry-Go-Round*, a book Allen co-wrote in 1931. The OGPU officer penned a summary that would have made a great dust-jacket blurb: "The characters he depicts in the book are a reflection of the pettiness and emptiness of many of Washington's current Republican congressmen and Cabinet members."[2] The book's actual dust jacket promised, and *Washington Merry-Go-Round* did a good job of delivering, access to "what the newspapers do not print about the politicians of this country and what the Washington correspondents write only between the lines: the inner realms of politics, society, the diplomatic corps, the White House and the press itself."[3]

Allen "knows most of the lawmakers and cabinet members, and also has extensive contacts in all of the departments" of the US government, the OGPU report noted. It highlighted his friendship with Raymond Moley, the head of Roosevelt's brain trust. Moley coined the term "New Deal" and served during the transition as FDR's de facto chief of staff. Allen, his Soviet handler stated, also "knows Roosevelt himself, as well as the House majority leader" and "is a valuable contact, especially bearing in mind Roosevelt's future administration."[4]

As in most real spy stories, many of the details of Allen's espionage career are unknown and will probably never be uncovered. The name of his OGPU handler isn't revealed in the fragmentary records about Allen that have leaked out of the KGB's archives. Not clear are how Allen linked up with the OGPU, the full scope of his espionage, and what motivated him to spy for the Soviet Union.

A parenthetical comment at the bottom of an OGPU memo— "(For now the payment is 100 American Dollars a month)"—shows that Allen's involvement with Soviet intelligence went beyond the legitimate give-and-take of a reporter with a source.[5] It may explain why a journalist like Allen with no ideological or familial ties to communism or the USSR agreed to spy for Stalin's secret intelligence service. On the other hand, money may not have been the only, or the primary, reason Allen provided information to the OGPU. He wasn't a communist, but he was, in the 1930s, a man of the Left and an ardent antifascist.

Whatever his motivation, there can be no doubt that Allen was acting as a witting agent of a foreign intelligence service. Relationships between reporters and sources are sometimes ambiguous; Allen's collaboration with the OGPU wasn't close to the gray zone. Allen had seen enough of the world to recognize the boundary between journalism and spying, and to know he'd stepped over it by accepting money from a foreign intelligence agency to hand over confidential information obtained from American government officials.

A short, red-haired man with an impulsive, incendiary temperament, by 1933 Allen had already had enough adventure to last most people a lifetime. In 1916, as a sixteen-year-old, he quit his job as a copy boy at the *Louisville Courier Journal*, lied about his age to join the Army, and rode into Mexico as a private in General John J. Pershing's expedition against Pancho Villa. Two years later, Allen followed Pershing to Europe, sailing home in 1918 as a boy lieutenant. Soon after returning to the Midwest, he hung up his uniform and enrolled in the University of Wisconsin to study journalism.[6]

Most journalism students ease into the profession, but Allen wasn't satisfied covering football rivalries or school board meetings. Working as a police reporter for the Madison *Capital Times*, he risked his neck infiltrating and writing exposés of the Ku Klux Klan. The stories earned Allen a scholarship to study abroad. He picked the University of Munich, arriving in time to write freelance accounts for the *Christian Science Monitor* of Adolph Hitler's November 1923 Munich Beer Hall Putsch—a failed attempt to take control of Bavaria and use it as a springboard to Berlin—and the future Führer's subsequent trial.[7]

When Hitler entered a makeshift courtroom on February 27, 1924, to defend himself against a charge of treason, Allen was close enough to report that the prisoner "laughed and joked and shook hands with a number of friends and supporters who rushed up to him and encouraged him to keep his head up, whereupon Hitler replied. '*Ach! Wir werden schon siegen*' (We shall win all right)."[8]

Like other foreign journalists at the trial, Allen was befriended by an avuncular Nazi—and future American intelligence operative—named Ernst Hanfstaengl. Speaking in fluent English, Hanfstaengl tried to smooth the rough edges off Nazism. He failed to charm Allen, who claimed the honor of being the first American journalist to despise Hitler.[9]

Allen's reporting from Germany led to a job in Washington reporting from an office in the National Press Building for the *Christian Science Monitor*, an influential paper with a national readership.

Ironically, at the time when he was recruited as a paid covert informant for the Soviet Union, Allen was viewed by his peers as a *victim* of espionage. President Herbert Hoover, incensed by his portrayal in *Washington Merry-Go-Round*, had demanded that the Secret Service identify its author or authors. They quickly homed in on Allen. As the OGPU file noted, "Hoover insisted that he be fired."[10]

The *Monitor* immediately sacked Allen, bringing tensions between the Washington press corps and the White House, which had been simmering for years, to a boil. From the moment he stepped into the White House, Hoover had barely tolerated the press. Relations between the Fourth Estate and the leader of the executive branch dimmed as the Depression cast an ever-darker cloud over America, and Hoover's name became a synonym for misery. Shantytowns came to be called "Hoovervilles;" newspapers were dubbed "Hoover blankets." A president once celebrated by the press as "The Great Humanitarian" seethed as his reputation withered. Enraged by stories he considered defamatory, Hoover struck back, encouraging his personal secretary, a former private investigator, to spy on and intimidate reporters. Allen's unmasking and rapid dismissal, rare victories during a period when almost nothing went right for Hoover, were savored in the White House and lamented at the Press Club.

A *Washington Post* columnist wrote that Allen's firing "is of more than passing interest because of its possible bearing on the espionage atmosphere that has prevailed over the nation's capital for the past two years."[11] The columnist added, "Whether there is anything to it or not, it is amazing the number of people here, in our official life and on the fringe, who sincerely believe their telephones are being tapped. They know what they are talking about, they insist; they can hear the click. And they relate hair-raising instances of being shadowed." Reporters who felt the Hoover administration was terrorizing them petitioned the Press Club to form a committee to investigate White House censorship.

Fear of White House surveillance didn't stanch the flow of gossip or deter Allen and his co-author, Drew Pearson, from writing a sequel, *More Merry-Go-Round*. They didn't describe the scene at the Press Club—reporters drinking moonshine, playing poker and billiards, smoking cigars, spitting tobacco, and occasionally urinating into tall brass spittoons—but they did repeat stories told there that were far more colorful and truthful than those that made it into newspapers. "Washington probably boasts more small, independent bootleggers per capita than any other city in the country and has established a unique and universal system of liquor distribution," Allen and Pearson wrote.[12] Secreted among the city's monuments were "quiet unobtrusive places where, if the right word is spoken, one may enter a guarded door, place one's foot on a rail, and partake of Maryland rye, cut Scotch or beer, usually spiked, but sometimes the genuine article brought from Baltimore." The *Merry-Go-Round* sequel reported that one of the liveliest speakeasies, located in an alley across the street from the State Department, was forced to close when "an act between a Follies girl and a derelict newspaper man" brought unwanted attention.

The *Merry-Go-Round* books sold 180,000 copies, an impressive achievement in the depth of the Depression.

The success of the two books—and the fact that Allen and Pearson had been fired—prompted them to team up on a syndicated newspaper column, also called Washington Merry-Go-Round. The column took off slowly. When Allen started working for Soviet intelligence Washington Merry-Go-Round was earning its two authors a grand total of twenty-five dollars a week. Allen kept bread on the table by reporting for the *Philadelphia Record*. A hundred dollars a month from the Union of Soviet Socialist Republics must have been a welcome boost.[13]

Allen may have come to the OGPU's attention when he and Pearson reported in their column on December 8, 1932, that William Borah, an irascible Idaho Republican who chaired the Senate Foreign Relations Committee, "didn't support Governor Roosevelt, but he is eager to cooperate with him—on Soviet Russian recognition." Washington Merry-Go-Round followed up on December 19 with a report on a "steady drift towards Russian recognition."[14]

The next month, Allen disclosed a bit more information to his Soviet intelligence contact than he had provided to the public. Borah, one of the most powerful politicians in Washington, had informed Allen in confidence about a conversation with Senator Robert Bulkley, a Democrat from Ohio. Allen reported to the OGPU that after visiting Roosevelt, Bulkley told Borah, "You are going to win out on Russian recognition when Roosevelt takes office. He told me he was going to act promptly on that as soon as he takes over."[15]

The news must have been welcome in Moscow. Stalin viewed America as a counterweight to Japanese aggression in the Soviet Far East, a source for technology desperately needed to modernize Soviet industry, and a base for espionage against European nations and the Russian diaspora.[16]

Allen's report to the OGPU on Borah illustrates the asymmetry in US and Soviet intelligence capabilities. At a time when the United States had almost no capacity to collect or analyze foreign political intelligence and the Kremlin was a black box to American policymakers, men in the Lubyanka were privy to a private conversation between two US senators revealing a controversial, secret policy decision made by America's next president. It was the dawn of a golden age for Soviet intelligence in America, a period lasting more than a decade, during which Stalin's operatives, including a surprising number who were handled by officers based in the National Press Building, peered into every crevice of American society. From the mid-1930s to the late 1940s, spies reporting to Moscow penetrated the White House, the Justice and State departments, the military and its contractors, Congress, and Hollywood.[17]

Allen had good sources in the Office of Naval Intelligence (ONI), the only effective American foreign-intelligence organization in the decade leading up to World War II. They informed him that the United States wasn't going to make a fuss about communist subversion in Japan, and Allen passed the news to Soviet intelligence. "Roosevelt shares the general attitude of the admirals and Navy strategists that an uprising 'of any kind' is to be hoped for in Japan," Allen told the OGPU. Naval intelligence officers knew that radicals plotting against the Japanese government were communists, Allen said, but they "manifest no hostility because of this fact. What their attitude would be if a Communist regime were to be set up in Japan they do not say. But to start with they would view with 'friendly' interest internal turmoil in Japan."[18]

The ONI secrets Allen passed on included details about Japanese military preparations in the Mariana, Caroline, and Marshall Islands, specks on the map that Tokyo was administering under a League of Nations mandate. Japanese authorities had rebuffed American requests to visit, so in the summer of 1932, Allen reported, "Four American naval officers, speaking Malayan, disguised themselves by staining their skins, and reached the islands as native fishermen." They discovered extensive military fortifications.[19]

Allen's reports on Japan suggest he was actively responding to Soviet requests, not merely passing along scraps of information that he happened to come across. In the early 1930s, the US government and military were secondary targets for Soviet intelligence. The Lubyanka was far more interested in Washington as a source of information about the USSR's potential adversaries—and Japan topped the list. The information on Japan Allen provided to the OGPU never made it into Washington Merry-Go-Round columns.[20]

Perhaps to demonstrate that he had personal access to the highest ranks of government, Allen gave his OGPU handler a letter on Columbia University letterhead that he had received from FDR confidant Moley. It requested Allen to "in all confidence, go the Congressional Library and look up the files of *Wallace's Farmer* and give me your opinion of Wallace as (a) a Progressive and (b) a man of forceful expression. You will readily see why I am asking for this and I turn to you as a good judge of these questions."[21] Henry Wallace was appointed secretary of agriculture in the first Roosevelt administration, a critical position at a time when ameliorating conditions in the Dust Bowl and pumping up deflated commodity prices were prerequisites to pulling America out of the Great Depression.

Allen's work as a covert agent for the Soviet Union didn't last long. It isn't clear when or why he stopped feeding the OGPU confidential information. The last known report mentioning information from Allen was sent in February 1933. Maybe the Soviets tired of paying for slightly enhanced versions of stories that anyone with a nickel to spare could read in the *Merry-Go-Round* columns. Given Soviet intelligence agencies' penchant for developing sources over long periods of time, it is more likely that Allen broke off the relationship. Possessing a strong temper, a short fuse, and no patience for threats to his independence, it is easy to imagine that he chafed at requests to gather sensitive political or military information. Or perhaps he no longer needed the money. Washington Merry-Go-Round quickly became one of the nation's most widely distributed columns, and a profitable business.[22]

The records that have leaked out of the KGB's archives about Allen do not tell the whole story of his apparently brief collaboration with Soviet intelligence. He was privy to confidential information from FDR's brain trust, the War Department, and Congress that would have been of interest in Moscow. Few people knew as much as Allen about the peccadillos, secrets, and weaknesses of Washington's power elite—information of tremendous value to a foreign intelligence agency seeking to recruit spies.

Allen may not have broken any laws by passing information to Soviet intelligence. The Foreign Agents Registration Act, which requires anyone who works on behalf of a foreign government to publicly register with the Justice Department, wasn't enacted until 1938. He definitely violated confidences, both with men and women who wouldn't have shared their secrets with him if they'd had an inkling that their insights would be transmitted to the Kremlin, and with readers, who had no idea Washington

Merry-Go-Round's reporting was tainted: in its early days by a covert financial relationship with Stalin's secret police, and later by the specter of exposure that must have been in the back of Allen's mind whenever he reported on issues of interest to the USSR.

Allen spied for the OGPU for only a short time, but he remained entangled in the world of espionage for decades, including serving as an intelligence officer for General George Patton during World War II. Throughout the early decades of the Cold War, Allen was both predator and prey, ferreting out and publishing secrets from American intelligence agencies and becoming the subject of efforts to plug leaks, including an illegal CIA wiretap.

CHAPTER TWO

A POPULAR SPY

Robert S. Allen's peers had no idea that he had collaborated with Soviet intelligence, and if word had leaked out the resulting scandal could have ended his career. The men in the National Press Club felt quite differently about the second known foreign intelligence operative in the Press Building, Vladimir Romm. Reporters treated him as a representative of the Soviet state, and given the Bolsheviks' reputation for conspiracy many assumed he was a spy. This did not prevent even conservative anti-communists from admiring him. No other Soviet official—and few Americans—was as well liked or respected in Washington as Romm.

Vladimir Georgievich Romm was born in May 1896 into a world that has so thoroughly disappeared that it is difficult today to even imagine. In the Romanov Empire, ethnicity—an amalgamation of race, religion, and language—was all-encompassing, defining possibilities and determining how people were identified by others, thought of themselves, and perceived their surroundings. The overarching importance of ethnic identity extended even to the name of Romm's hometown. As Jews, the largest population in the city, Romm's family called it Vilna, as did Russians, the third-largest group. While Romm was growing up, Vilna was known as the "Jerusalem of the North," a description Napoleon, astonished by the sight of a Jewish city on the edge of Christian Europe, came up with in 1812. Poles, who ruled the city they called Wilno from the fourteenth century until Napoleon's defeat brought Russian rule, were the second-largest ethnic group. Lithuanians, less than three percent of the city's population when Romm was born, called it Vilnius.[1]

The Romms were a prominent family that had dominated and profited from Hebrew printing and publishing in Czarist Russia. Vladimir attended an elite private college in St. Petersburg, an opportunity that was generally denied to Jews. His father, George Romm, a physician, had been imprisoned for membership in the Bund, a Marxist Jewish organization, and as a boy Vladimir helped his two brothers run a clandestine cell of the underground Socialist Revolutionary Party.

Romm was conscripted into the Russian army in 1916, serving in the infantry and secretly preaching the merits of socialism to his comrades. After the Czar was deposed in March 1917, Romm served as a commissar, traveling in November 1917 to Petrograd as a delegate to the second All-Russian Congress of Soviets. He likely witnessed one of the more dramatic moments of the revolution when messengers burst into the Congress at three a.m. announcing that the Winter Palace had been stormed and that members of the provisional government had been arrested. Few realized at the time, but this was one of the defining moments of the twentieth century: the establishment of the Soviet Union.

Romm's life in 1918 reflected the tumultuous times. He started the year in Novgorod, near Petrograd (as St. Petersburg was called during the war), serving as an official of the local government. Spring and fall were a blur: back in Petrograd in May, working in the Popular Commissariat of Foreign Affairs; unemployed in June, living nine hundred miles north in Arkhangelsk, a bleak city on the coast of what Russians call the Northern Icy Ocean. By November Romm was a thousand miles south working for the provincial government in Voronezh. In December he washed up on the outskirts of his hometown, Vilna, and helped Soviet forces take control of the city.

By the end of this restless year, Romm found his life's calling. He had been recruited into the *Glavnoye Razvedyvatelnoye Upravlenie* (GRU), the Red Army's intelligence service. Romm became a member of the first, and most talented, generation of Soviet intelligence officers, an elite group of men, and a few women, born in the last years of the nineteenth century on the shifting edges of empires, who had experienced the downfall of the Hapsburgs and eagerly participated in the destruction of the Romanovs. They shared a passionate utopian vision of communism and, without exception, were ultimately consumed by the vicious reality of Stalinism. Americans and Europeans were impressed by their idealism, intelligence, and selflessness. Few of their Western acquaintances realized that these cultured patriots, who could discuss literature and art intelligently in three or more languages, were just as capable of stalking and brutally murdering "enemies of the people."

In April 1919 Polish troops pushed the Soviets out of Vilna. Romm was posted as assistant military attaché in the Soviet embassy in Kaunas, capital of the independent Lithuanian state that had been created in 1918. He stayed until May 1921, organizing a network of espionage agents, then was transferred to Kharkov, Ukraine, where he witnessed, and must have had a hand in implementing, a massive crime against humanity. Intelligence officers like Romm were on the front line of a deliberate manmade famine. They forced peasants in Ukraine onto collective farms, confiscated their grain, and prevented them from leaving, condemning a million Ukrainians to agonizing deaths from starvation.[2]

Romm was sent on his first posting to the West in August 1922, splitting his time between Berlin and Paris. In the City of Light, he was part of a network of agents who infiltrated the city's cafés and garrets to keep the GRU's eyes on thousands of Russian émigrés as they hatched innumerable plots and counterplots aimed at overthrowing or spreading, subverting, or promoting the newborn Bolshevik regime.

Romm acquired his cover as a journalist in December 1924 when he was appointed head of foreign operations for the Soviet newspaper *Trud* (Labor). Three years later he was fired from the GRU for "not being completely devoted to the line of the Central Committee."[3] Romm's deviation must not have been considered serious, because rather than suffering the fates typically experienced by Soviet spies who fell from grace—imprisonment in a labor camp, even execution—he was allowed to transfer from military intelligence to the rival OGPU. The OGPU gave him the kind of assignment that was offered only to the most trusted individuals.

Romm was sent to Tokyo. His cover job was working as a correspondent for the Telegraph Agency of the Soviet Union (TASS), the official Soviet government news service. Most Soviet citizens who traveled abroad were forced to leave their families behind as collateral against the temptation to defect. It is a mark of his superiors' trust that Romm was accompanied by his wife, Galena, and their infant son. Both Japanese and French intelligence services quickly determined that he was a spy and kept an eye on him.

Romm traveled widely, spending a great deal of time in China, especially in Manchuria. He or his superiors had correctly anticipated that Northern China would be the launching pad for the Japanese empire's expansion. His job was to answer a critical question: Which way would the Japanese leap, south to China or north to Siberia?

While posted to Tokyo, Romm signed the "Declaration of the 83," a critique of Stalin's foreign policy written by Leon Trotsky and other prominent Communists. Published just as the split between Stalin and Trotsky broke into the open, the declaration included extensive discussion of the situation in China, one of Romm's areas of expertise. After it became clear that Stalin had come out on top, Romm submitted a groveling letter to the Communist Party apologizing for signing the Declaration. He must have been valuable; he retained his life, freedom, party membership, and OGPU job.

In 1930, after spending two and a half years in Asia, Romm was sent back to Europe, reporting to OGPU *residents* (station chiefs) in Geneva and Paris. Since his previous European stint Soviet intelligence had woven intricate networks throughout Western Europe, penetrating government and industry. A well-oiled apparatus sent Moscow a stream of intelligence on defense strategies and military plans, diplomatic alliances and commercial secrets. Its top priority, however, reflected Stalin's obsession with enemies of the people. Russian emigre organizations were so saturated with Soviet intelligence agents that many would have collapsed if Moscow's provocateurs and informers had pulled out. Even as Mussolini and Hitler came to power, fascist dictators were secondary targets for the OGPU, as Stalin was fixated on gathering intelligence on, and plotting to kill, Trotsky.[4]

Romm maintained his cover as a journalist, working for TASS. He was treated by other foreign reporters both as a representative of the Soviet government and as an exemplar of the kind of men the regime was believed to be creating. John T. Whitaker, an American journalist who knew him in Geneva, where they both covered the League of Nations, later wrote that Romm "had come because Moscow anticipated the Japanese attack on Manchuria and believed that its success or failure would be decided by the diplomatic struggle in Geneva. Romm was one of their aces; they wanted a man of his ability and background on the spot in Geneva."[5]

Romm was a living embodiment of Americans' fantasy of Soviet Man: erudite, charming, and selfless. His demeanor in Geneva's Bavaria Hotel dining room, the unofficial nocturnal headquarters for international journalists and diplomats posted to the League of Nations, helped persuade influential men that the USSR could be integrated into the modern world. "Of the hundreds of correspondents of all nationalities at Geneva during this period, Vladimir Romm was among the most popular and widely known, especially among his American colleagues," an American foreign correspondent remembered. "And this popularity had its effect in the almost unanimous press support of the Soviet's application for entrance into the League." Romm's circle included Allen Dulles, a well-connected diplomat who returned to Geneva during the Second World War as an intelligence officer and went on to become the longest-serving director of the CIA.[6]

While Romm and his OGPU comrades were popular in the salons of the European elite, they were also engaged in less convivial activities. Soviet intelligence was very much a contact sport during Romm's second European posting. Well out of sight of the diplomatic receptions and dinners, GRU and OGPU officers and their agents operated with relative impunity, kidnapping and killing White Russians, even shooting their own agents who had come to be suspected of treachery.

On June 2, 1934, Romm stepped out of the small circle of diplomats and journalists who frequented Geneva's Bavaria Hotel and onto the pages of the *New York Times*. "One of the most significant visitors from the Soviet Union to the United States since the Bolshevist revolution will depart for Washington next Thursday," the *Times* reported. "He is Vladimir Romm of the newspaper *Izvestia*, who will be the first permanent correspondent of the Soviet press in the United States." Before Romm departed, American reporters were invited to a lunch in his honor at *Izvestia*'s headquarters on Pushkin Square in central Moscow. The boisterous group included *Izvestia* editor Karl Radek, the most colorful member of the Bolshevik inner circle and the only top Communist to socialize with American reporters. The Americans, enlivened by liberal quantities of vodka, wished Romm well and assured him his life in Washington would be far easier than theirs was in Moscow.[7]

Romm's arrival in Washington was noted in the *Goldfish Bowl*, the Press Club's irreverent newsletter, which reported in July 1934 that he was "Russia's first native contribution to the Washington press corps since we recognized the Soviet." It added that "Mr. Romm, ably introduced about town by our own Larry Todd, represents *Izvestia*, semi-official Soviet morning newspaper with 2,000,000 subscribers." Todd, a popular Press Club member, headed the TASS office on the thirteenth floor of the Press Building, which he shared with Romm.[8]

Romm attended State Department briefings, White House receptions, and society dinner parties. As the first Soviet journalist in the United States and one of a handful of Soviet citizens living in Washington, he was the object of intense curiosity. Curiosity quickly turned to respect as Romm tirelessly responded to endless questions about life in the Soviet Union, communism, and Stalin. In addition to reporting—

for *Izvestia* and for the OGPU's successor, the NKVD—Romm acted as an informal ambassador, giving speeches to university students, meeting with industrialists, and swapping stories with American reporters.[9]

Romm told his American friends that he'd taught himself English while living in Tokyo by listening to jazz phonograph records. He knew more popular American songs than most professional singers.[10]

The Washington press corps admired the somewhat reserved Romm. They were bowled over by his blond, vivacious wife, Galena, who told one and all that her name meant "chicken" in Italian, and by their eleven-year-old son, who was known by the very American nickname "Billy."

Ernie Pyle, a journalist whose stories about ordinary Americans made him one of the most loved and influential writers of the era, devoted an entire column to praising Romm in terms that would have made an *Izvestia* editor blush: "You could call Vladimir Romm a devout Communist. He feels that his life belongs to the party, and that giving it his complete devotion is little enough. I didn't get that from him, but from his friends. He doesn't try to propagandize you. He talks gently, in a low soft voice, about his paper and his American friends and about America. He doesn't try to sell Russia to you."[11]

Pyle continued: "He is courteous and affable. People like him. But nobody knows much about him. That is because of his deep feeling that the party, and not he, is of importance. It isn't even a conscious reticence about himself. It is sober preoccupation with the cause." Pyle noted that Romm spoke English, French, and German well, and "some Italian and Japanese."

Romm "expects to go back to Russia in a year or two, and probably stay there," Pyle reported. "He hasn't taken foreign assignments for pleasure or the adventure, but because he feels he should go out in the world and learn how people of other nations think and live. It gives him a broader and more accurate background for his future work back in Russia."

Pyle may have been right about Romm's motives, but in fact many of the Soviet spy's adventures in Washington were pleasant, and they certainly didn't prepare him for his future in Russia. The warm embrace of the Washington press corps gave Romm a front seat at events like the annual Founder's Day dinner at the National Press Club, held in 1936 on a warm evening in May. Romm watched President Franklin Roosevelt, the guest of honor, laugh as journalists lampooned him and his cabinet in a series of skits. The contrast with Moscow, where the penalty for joking about Stalin was imprisonment or death, must have been shocking.[12]

Romm traveled to Yosemite National Park in August 1936 to participate as one of two representatives of the Soviet government in a conference convened by the Institute of Pacific Relations (IPR), an international organization dedicated to fostering peaceful relationships among nations bordering the Pacific Ocean. Characteristically, he was remembered as one of the hardest-working participants. Inevitably, Americans who spent time hiking around the park and in roundtable discussions with Romm came to view him as a friend. As the only participant who could speak Russian, English and Japanese, Romm seemed to be everywhere and to know everything and everyone.[13]

There was, however, one important thing that Romm didn't know: he wasn't the only Soviet spy in Yosemite Park. In an extraordinary coincidence, Romm spent much of the meeting sparring with a member of the Japanese delegation, a young journalist who like Romm was an expert on China—and, unknown to Romm, a spy for Stalin. Ozaki Hotsumi was the most important member of an intelligence ring that operated in Tokyo under the direction of the legendary Soviet intelligence officer Richard Sorge. To preserve his cover, Hotsumi argued passionately at the Yosemite meeting against the Soviet position, rationalizing Japan's expansionist policy in China. Romm accused Hotsumi of defending an imperialist government led by warmongers.[14]

The conference marked a turning point in Hotsumi's career. His skillful justification of Japan's expansionist policy in China brought him to the attention of powerful politicians, and the friendships he forged in Yosemite with Japanese aristocrats put him on a path to penetrating the inner circle of Japan's political and military elites.[15] Five years later, these connections allowed Hotsumi to obtain precise information about the timing of the Nazi invasion of the USSR, intelligence that Stalin, at great cost to the Soviet Union, ignored.

Soon after Romm returned from California, he and Galena told their American friends that they had received instructions to pack up and return to Moscow. It was, they said, a temporary stop, as he'd been assigned to a prestigious new position as *Izvestia's* London correspondent. Soviet ambassador Alexander Antonovitch Troyanovsky hosted a farewell lunch at the Soviet embassy, mirroring the send-off Romm had received before leaving Moscow. Romm may have believed he was actually headed to London, but it is almost certain that as Troyanovsky toasted his long-time friend, the old Bolshevik knew or suspected the truth. As the OGPU defector Walter Krivitsky wrote, a "barbed-wire frontier separate[d] the old Bolshevik Party from the new. During the purge there was only one passport across this frontier. You had to present Stalin and his OGPU with the required quota of victims."[16]

Even if he chose to ignore it, Romm was aware of the danger. A number of his comrades had been recalled to Moscow with sugar-coated promises, only to be arrested, imprisoned, and, more often than not, executed. His former superiors in Berlin and Paris had already fallen victim to the madness. They were falsely accused—and, in an almost universal feature of Stalin's purges, had falsely confessed—to absurd charges of treasonous plots. Romm's fate was more dramatic, and grotesque.

Shortly after Romm's return to Moscow, foreign correspondents and international diplomats flocked to the Military Collegium of the Supreme Court of the Soviet Union to attend one of the show trials of prominent Communists that Stalin used to consolidate power. The audience heard Stalin's chief prosecutor, Andrei Vyshinsky, accuse Karl Radek, the former *Izvestia* editor, Lenin confidant, and central committee member, of plotting with Trotsky to commit an astounding range of crimes: assassinating the Leningrad Party chief Sergey Kirov, sabotaging the Russian railways, and plotting to overthrow Stalin and return capitalism to Russia. Even Walter Duranty, Moscow correspondent of the *New York Times* and a sycophantic apologist for Stalin, was shocked when Vyshinsky announced that the witnesses at the trial would include Romm, who had been arrested and had confessed his participation in the Trotskyist conspiracy.[17]

When word of Romm's arrest reached the National Press Club, his friends were stunned. Though their circumstances couldn't have been more different, members of the Washington press corps reacted just as countless loyal communists did when, after answering a late-night knock on their apartment doors, they found themselves in one of the NKVD's "black raven" police vans speeding through Moscow to the Lubyanka: "There must be some kind of misunderstanding. If only someone can get word to comrade Stalin, everything will be sorted out."

Charles O. Gridley, a *Denver Post* reporter who was president of the National Press Club, immediately launched a campaign to convince the Soviet government that they'd made a terrible mistake. Gridley and a Who's Who of the Washington press, including editors and reporters representing the *New York Times*, *Washington Post*, and Associated Press, sent a cable to Duranty, asking him to present it to the American ambassador for delivery to Soviet authorities. The former OGPU operative Robert Allen was among the signers.

"All members of the Washington newspaper corps have read with anxiety of the arrest of our colleague, Vladimir Romm," the telegram stated. "In our dealings with Romm we found him a true friend and advocate of the USSR. Never once did he even faintly indicate lack of sympathy for or disloyalty toward the existing government. He did more than any other Soviet envoy to popularize the Stalin regime in this country."[18]

When Romm was escorted, squeezed between two armed guards, into the courtroom the next day, it became clear why he'd been sucked into the madness. Previous show trials had depended on forced confessions, but the effect had been somewhat blunted by a lack of detail. In the absence of a storyline, it was difficult for some to follow or believe in the plot. Radek's prosecution opened the curtain on a new kind of Stalinist tragic opera, one in which fantastic confessions from the accused were rendered somewhat more credible by elaborate testimony from secondary characters.[19]

To weave together the story of a grand conspiracy between Radek and Trotsky, Vyshinsky needed a human link between the protagonists. Not only did Romm know Radek, Romm had been in France at precisely the time Trotsky was shuffling around the country trying to avoid Soviet assassins. Conveniently for the Soviet fabulists, Romm had also traveled between Paris and Geneva at exactly the times when Radek had visited the League of Nations. He was the perfect candidate for the role of counterrevolutionary vector. Adding icing to the cake, Romm's signature on the Declaration of the 83 was presented as evidence of his devotion to Trotsky.

Stalin's interrogators so ruthlessly broke the spirits of the accused with physical and psychological torture, and especially with entirely credible threats to their families, that witnesses eagerly admitted to terrible crimes. Perversely, some loyal Bolsheviks felt that by falsely testifying against themselves they were serving the cause they'd devoted their lives to advancing. The prosecutors who orchestrated the trials compensated for the absurdity of their accusations by providing compliant witnesses with piles of false facts, details that added an air of verisimilitude to what would otherwise have been farcical dramas. The descriptions of precise details of the crimes convinced gullible people around the world that the trials were fair, while the sight of dedicated Bolsheviks freely confessing to heinous crimes terrified those who knew they were lies.

"I had full knowledge of the terrorist plot against the Soviet Government," Romm testified, as he launched into an account of how he'd acted as a courier, conveying messages between Radek in Geneva and Trotsky in France. Romm described a meeting with Trotsky at the end of July 1933 in a dark alley in Paris near the Bois de Boulogne. Soviet intelligence apparently didn't realize that the French authorities hadn't permitted Trotsky to set foot in Paris and that he'd been sick in bed hundreds of miles away at the time Romm was supposed to have met him.[20]

Trotsky, Romm said, had steeled him for his mission, which was nothing less than destroying the Soviet Union, by quoting a Latin proverb: "What medicine cannot heal, iron will heal, and what iron cannot heal, fire will heal." Romm told the court that he had smuggled a letter from Trotsky to Radek pasted inside the cover of *Tsusima*, a Russian novel about Czarist Russia's humiliating naval defeat in the Russo-Japanese war. The letter, Romm and Radek told the court, described how Japan and Germany were poised to conquer the Soviet Union, as well as deals Trotsky had made to give the USSR's enemies territorial concessions in exchange for appointing him ruler of Russia. Radek testified that he had burned the letter.

Romm admitted that he'd agreed with Trotsky's son to serve as eyes and ears for the counterrevolution in Washington. "So!" Vyshinsky cried, "You were correspondent for *Izvestia* and special correspondent for Trotsky!"

"It is a sad and dreadful thing to see your friends on trial for their lives," Duranty wrote in the *New York Times*. "And it is sadder and more dreadful to hear them hang themselves with their own words." Duranty wrote that he had "known and liked" Romm since 1930. His old friend spoke in the courtroom "with the same charm and courage that made him popular among Washington newspaper men—one of the most exclusive and intelligent groups in the world and one that would never tolerate anyone shoddy or second rate." Incredibly, Duranty—who worked out of the two-room TASS office in the National Press Building when he visited Washington in preference to the well-appointed *New York Times* offices—seemed to believe that his old friends Romm and Radek were guilty as charged.[21]

Referring to the Russian journalist's signature on the Declaration of the 83, Duranty told his readers that "Mr. Romm declared he was a Trotskyist by conviction because he was not satisfied with the policy of Josef Stalin in China in 1926–27."

"It is still a mystery," Duranty wrote, that men like those on trial "could continue to follow Trotsky" when it had been obvious since 1923 that "Stalin was the man Russia needed and [was] Lenin's destined successor."[22] Of course, it is even more of a mystery how Western reporters like Duranty could continue to praise and tell lies on behalf of Stalin despite clear evidence of his crimes against humanity.

The *Times* reporter had no illusions about Romm's fate. "Mr. Romm is not on trial—not yet, at least. But he is not a good risk for life insurance."[23]

Duranty was a cynical Stalinist, but the American ambassador, Joseph Davies, was something worse: a complete fool who accepted the Moscow show trials at face value. He wrote to Arthur Krock, the *New York Times* Washington bureau chief, to assure him that Romm's testimony must be true because he provided so many details. "While his appearance on the stand was rather downcast, he looked physically well and as far as I could judge, his testimony bore the hallmarks of credibility," Davies wrote.[24]

Romm's friends in the National Press Building were naive about the Soviet Union, but they weren't as stupid as Davies. Press Club president Gridley led a delegation of editors and reporters to the Soviet embassy, located in an elegant mansion on 16th Street, a short walk from the Press Building, where they expressed their "shock and dismay at the news of Mr. Romm's arrest." *Washington Post* editor Felix Morley spoke for the group, telling Ambassador Troyanovsky that they knew Romm well and had often spoken with him about the Soviet Union, and that "he defended the policies of the Soviet government without qualification and with every indication that he believed in them wholeheartedly. Regardless of our views, we were compelled to recognize his brilliance and persuasiveness. In view of our experience with him, it will be extremely difficult for us to believe that he is guilty of any deliberate act of disloyalty to the Soviet government." A statement the reporters handed Troyanovsky noted that Romm had been "a member in good standing not only of the press gallery but also of the National Press Club," described him as "a journalist of unusual attainments and ability," and expressed "a lively professional and personal concern about Mr. Romm." The leaders of the Washington press corps were not sentimental men; their efforts on Romm's behalf were a testament to the extraordinary affinity they felt for him.[25]

The reporters apparently had no idea of the danger they were placing Troyanovsky in. The ambassador didn't want to remind anyone in Moscow about his close relationship with Romm, which stretched back to Tokyo and to his comrade's ill-advised decision to sign the Declaration of the 83. Countless men and women had been destroyed in the terror as a result of casual contacts with someone who was later purged. The Press Club delegation also failed to grasp the complete irrelevance of Romm's innocence. If Troyanovsky was touched by their naiveté, he kept his feelings to himself.

The ambassador tried to make the best of a bad situation, treating his visitors cordially and acknowledging that he shared their opinions of Romm's abilities. With a straight face, he also confided that Romm had been an outspoken Trotskyite prior to his posting to Washington. Describing Trotskyism as a kind of indecent addiction, Troyanovsky said that he'd helped wean his friend of the affliction, that while Romm was in Washington it seemed he'd been cured, but that, alas, it had been secretly lurking beneath the surface.[26]

Many of Romm's former friends in Washington were convinced of his innocence, but some influential American journalists—especially those who viewed Stalin and the USSR favorably—found it hard to believe that the Soviet government would present outrageous lies as truths, or that innocent men would confess to crimes. In an editorial published on January 26, 1937, the liberal *New York Post* posited,

> The Moscow trials require one to believe either (1) that Leon Trotzky [*sic*] is a monster or (2) that Joseph Stalin is a monster. And no ordinary monsters. For either Trotzky and some of his followers have plotted with German and Japanese emissaries to dismember the Soviet Union so that they might overthrow Stalin, or Stalin has staged the greatest frameup in world history to discredit Trotzky.... In all thirty-three

men have confessed. Almost all of them were old revolutionaries, men who had faced death and torture. One must believe either (1) that their confessions are true, or (2) that not one of the thirty-three had the courage to let out a protest before the assembled representatives of foreign powers and the foreign press. Not one.[27]

The editorial was written by Isidor Feinstein. In subsequent editorials, Feinstein, who is better known by the pen name he adopted the next year, I. F. Stone, made it clear he believed the official Soviet version of the show trials.[28] Even in those days, long before he became famous as a skeptic's skeptic, Stone was known as a muckraking gadfly who delighted in skewering the powerful, exposing mendacity and shaming politicians by publicizing their concealed conflicts of interest. Stone had accused the FBI of "carrying on OGPU tactics" against organized labor and written an editorial condemning the terror Stalin had unleashed after the assassination of his rival Sergey Kirov.[29]

Stone knew that the Soviet secret police employed brutal, immoral tactics, and he was acquainted with reporters who swore that Romm was innocent, but he never connected these thoughts. Stone traveled often to Washington in 1936, working out of the *Post*'s National Press Building office. Given his interest in the Soviet Union, as well as numerous common friends in the small circle of Washington reporters, it is almost certain that he met Romm at the Press Club or a social event.

Stone's editorial about the Radek trial is easier to understand in the light of a secret that he carried to his grave. While working to promote the New Deal, and writing sympathetically about Stalin, he had also sealed a secret bargain with representatives of the Soviet government.

Soviet intelligence files reveal that Stone was introduced to an officer of the NKVD in April 1936. The young journalist had been spotted as a possible recruit by a long-time Soviet intelligence agent, Frank Palmer, the head of Federated Press, a leftist news service that presented itself as an alternative to the middle-of-the-road Associated Press. Stone was assigned the cover name "Blin" (pancake). By mid-May Blin had entered the "channel of normal operational work"—meaning he had been recruited as a witting agent—according to a note in the NKVD files. Decades later, Oleg Kalugin, a retired KGB general, confirmed that Stone had been a Soviet agent in the 1930s.[30]

Stone probably didn't give the Soviets classified information—it is unlikely that he ever had access to any—but he was nonetheless a valuable and valued agent.

Unlike in novels and films, most espionage doesn't involve white-knuckle exploits of muscular secret agents. To support the work of spies who steal secrets, operatives are needed to serve as couriers, provide cover identities, and identify and help vet potential recruits.

To understand the utility of someone like Stone beyond his obvious ability to write stories that helped the USSR, it is helpful to imagine yourself in the shoes of a Russian intelligence officer posted in 1935 to the Soviet consulate in New York or the embassy in Washington. In contrast to elite operatives like Romm, you don't speak English well and don't have a nuanced understanding of American society. Yet your career, possibly your life, depends on your ability to persuade Americans to put themselves at tremendous risk by spying on their own country. To make the task even more harrowing, there is only one thing even more pressing than establishing and maintaining a network of informants who are willing and able to provide valuable information: doing so without getting caught. A single screw-up—a clumsy approach to an American who runs to the police or the newspapers, or a failure in tradecraft that alerts the FBI—will result in your expulsion.

Agents like Stone who could identify potential recruits and describe their motivations, weaknesses, and access to information were priceless to Soviet intelligence. This was especially true in the first few years after the establishment of diplomatic relations, when it became possible for intelligence officers to work under diplomatic cover in New York, Washington, and San Francisco.

In addition to his value as a talent spotter, Stone helped the Soviet cause through his writing. Soviet intelligence prioritized the recruitment of "agents of influence." These were typically individuals like journalists who penned editorials and who were in a position to shape public opinion or tweak government decisions in ways that favored the Soviet Union.

The May 20, 1936, NKVD report noting Stone's recruitment stated that "he went to Washington on assignment for his newspaper," has "connections in the State Department and Congress," and knows "Prince." Prince was Frank Prince, the nation's leading expert on anti-Semitism, an investigator who worked for the Anti-Defamation League as well as for congressional committees.[31]

Responding to a Soviet directive to provide derogatory information about the Hearst Corporation newspapers, a bastion of anti-Bolshevism, Stone reported that it had entered into a contract to supply Nazi Germany with a large consignment of copper.[32]

More important from the perspective of an intelligence agency desperate for recruits, Stone reported that Hearst's star reporter in Berlin, an American named Karl von Wiegand, was disillusioned by his employer's close ties to the Nazi regime. Von Wiegand had known Hitler since 1922, when he had hired the then-obscure rabble rouser to write commentaries for the Hearst newspapers about German politics. In the 1930s von Wiegand wrote stories praising the German dictator and suggesting that the Führer would never provoke or risk war with his neighbors. At the same time, von Wiegand privately opposed the Nazi regime and Hearst's pro-fascist editorial policy. He even met in secret with President Roosevelt in 1935 to express concerns about Hearst's support for Hitler.[33]

Stone reported that von Wiegand had traveled to the United States on the maiden voyage of the *Hindenburg* zeppelin. The NKVD, Stone suggested, could approach him through his son-in-law, Joseph Freeman— a friend to the USSR. Freeman's brother Harry worked for TASS in its Press Building office.[34] There is no evidence, however, that the NKVD recruited von Wiegand.

It is impossible to know whether Stone's writing about the USSR in general, and the Radek trial in particular, was shaped by his entanglement with the NKVD, or whether both Stone's covert work for Soviet intelligence and his editorial positions are better understood as reflections of his faith in Soviet Communism. What is certain is that Stone abused his readers' trust by claiming to present an objective account of the Soviet reality while secretly working for the NKVD. An accurate depiction of the show trials from a leftist like Stone would have convinced many Americans of Stalin's barbarity.

Stone and the *New York Post* may have been fooled by the Radek trial, but other American reporters understood what was happening in Moscow. A few days after Stone's pro-Stalin editorial hit the streets, the syndicated columnist Rodney Dutcher told his readers what the trial looked like to members of the National Press Club: "Few happenings abroad in late years have caused so much emotional disturbance—especially among the newspaper crowd, which is sure Romm was loyal to his government—as worry over the possibility that Romm might be shot."[35]

Stalin and his regime were savage, but they tried to present a human face to the world. Konstantine Aleksandr Oumansky, who had succeeded Troyanovsky as Soviet ambassador to Washington, told the credulous US ambassador Davies that pleas from the Press Club had led to a mitigation of Romm's sentence. He was, Oumansky claimed, "sent to do work in the interior."[36]

In fact, Romm was executed in the usual fashion, by a bullet fired into the back of his head, on March 8, 1937. Galena was forced to suffer the horrors of a Siberian labor camp, while their son was turned over to an orphanage and subjected to the cruelties imposed on children of enemies of the people.[37]

The execution was not announced, so reporters didn't know Romm's fate when, a few weeks later, Oumansky, speaking at a National Press Club luncheon, told them the USSR was "fundamentally on the side of democracy but is surrounded by enemies and we must defend ourselves."[38]

Romm wasn't the only former National Press Club member to suffer from the fatal embrace of the Soviet Union's intelligence services. Alexei Neimann, *chargé d'affaires* at the Soviet Embassy, had joined the club a month before Romm's arrival in Washington. Neimann returned to Moscow in 1935 and continued to work for the People's Commissariat of Foreign Affairs. In contrast to Romm, Neimann had not made much of an impression at the Press Club. None of the reporters who jumped to Romm's defense was in touch with him when the NKVD arrested him on August 9, 1937, and none was aware of Neimann's execution on April 8, 1938. Along with millions of other Soviet citizens who had been unjustly executed or imprisoned, Neimann and Romm were "rehabilitated" in 1956.[39]

Allen, Romm, and Stone were the first of a long line of Soviet intelligence operatives who used the National Press Building as a base for espionage, operating with relative impunity despite often-intense FBI surveillance. Soviet intelligence had a continuous presence in the building, but they were never alone. Over the decades, spies pretending to be journalists, and journalists moonlighting as spies, working to advance the interests of a number of governments—including that of the United States—have hidden in plain sight in the NPB's offices and corridors.

From the early 1930s to Pearl Harbor, German and homegrown fascists, American and Soviet Communists, British intelligence operatives, Japanese agents, and members of an unofficial, unnamed private intelligence network that reported to President Roosevelt all rubbed shoulders in Press Building elevators, jostled against each other in its narrow corridors and stood shoulder to shoulder at the Press Club bar. Mingling among the thousands of legitimate journalists, lawyers, and lobbyists who reported to the building every day, they pursued covert agendas: plotting to make America safe for plutocrats by overthrowing the government, inciting racial hatred in pursuit of an imaginary homogeneous past, giving Stalin's espionage networks a foothold in Washington, and conspiring with British intelligence officers to shape American public opinion and defeat politicians who advocated neutrality.

Governments didn't have a monopoly on espionage and subversion conducted in the Press Building. Especially during the long years of the Great Depression and the anxious months that culminated in the Japanese attack on Pearl Harbor, private citizens and corporations plotted behind Press Building doors to advance agendas that had a great deal in common with the fascism that was spreading across Europe.

CHAPTER THREE
"KIKE KILLER"

Army sharpshooters scanned the crowds from rooftops on the morning of March 5, 1933, as Herbert Hoover, his grim expression matching the foul weather, stepped into an open-topped limousine for his last ride as president of the United States. The dour Hoover and ebullient president-elect Franklin D. Roosevelt shared a lap blanket as the car traveled down the White House driveway, turned right onto Pennsylvania Avenue, dog-legged down 15th Street, and turned left back onto Pennsylvania Avenue past the National Press Building. Reporters who weren't on the Capitol grounds crowded into the Press Club lounge to listen, along with millions of Americans, to a radio broadcast of FDR delivering the most important inaugural address of the twentieth century. His assurance that "the only thing we have to fear is fear itself" was punctuated by the crackle of sleet hitting the microphone.

After the speech, Roosevelt retraced the path to the White House, this time as the thirty-second president of the United States. He was followed by an eighteen-thousand-person parade featuring brass bands, horse-mounted cavalry, and Indian chiefs in feathered headdresses. As the human river flowed past the White House, FDR watched from a chair on the lawn, behind bullet-proof glass—a reminder of how, on a sunnier, more carefree day three weeks earlier, he and the country had learned how vulnerable they were to the threat posed by even a single man determined to change history.[1]

Roosevelt owed his life, and America its salvation from the Depression, to a flimsy chair. The president-elect had been making jocular remarks from the backseat of a convertible to a crowd in Miami's Bayfront

Park on February 15 when Giuseppe Zangara, an Italian anarchist bedeviled by a decades-long stomachache, climbed onto a folding chair, raised his arm, and took aim. Just as his revolver discharged, the chair wobbled, jiggling Zangara's arm. The bullet missed Roosevelt, striking and killing the man seated next to him, Chicago mayor Anton Cermak. Paralyzed by polio, Roosevelt couldn't move. He didn't flinch in the sickening seconds after Cermak fell, seconds when a more accurate second shot could have found its mark. Before this could happen, Zangara toppled to the ground and civilians in the crowd pounced on him.[2]

Fears about the president's safety on Inauguration Day accentuated a terror that gripped and united the country, from the boardrooms of withering corporations to the kitchens of desiccated farms. Over four thousand banks failed in January and February 1933, wiping out the savings of millions and compounding the misery of Americans who were already struggling with massive unemployment, a drought that had turned Midwest farms into dust, and the near-total collapse of manufacturing. By Inauguration Day, the banking system had almost ceased functioning and the nation was on the brink of catastrophe. "The atmosphere which surrounded the change in government was comparable to that which might be found in a beleaguered capital in war time," the *New York Times* reported.[3]

The spirits of the "ten times ten thousand men, women and children" who had gathered in front of the Capitol to hear Roosevelt "were as somber as the grey sky above," *Time* reported.[4] The cover of the magazine, which hit the newsstands a week after the inauguration, featured a watercolor painting of a newly elected national leader sitting in a verdant garden, gazing serenely into the future, a friendly dog by his side. But it wasn't FDR with his Scottish terrier Fala (who wasn't born until 1940). *Time*'s cover story was dedicated to Adolf Hitler's election as chancellor of Germany and the founding of what would come to be known as the Third Reich.

When democracy failed them, millions of Europeans turned to strongmen, and there is no reason to believe Americans had been inoculated against autocracy. Roosevelt was being encouraged to emulate Hitler or Mussolini. A *Chicago Tribune* editorial on his inaugural address ran under the headline "For Dictatorship if Necessary."[5] Eminent Americans, including the country's most powerful newspaper publisher, William Randolph Hearst, urged the president to assume absolute power to save the country from disaster. Hearst even produced and distributed a film, *Gabriel Over the White House*, about a president who experienced an epiphany following a near-fatal accident that transformed him from a lightweight playboy into a dictator who brought prosperity to the United States and peace to the world.

It soon became clear that the new president's instincts veered more to the left than the right, and that the energetic steps taken in the weeks after he assumed power had averted the threat of revolution. Men at the top of the capitalist food chain found themselves aligned with rabble-rousers on the fringes of society in their quest for an American dictator, or at least a president more sympathetic to their interests.

It was from the National Press Building that, in the desperate years of the Depression, combatants in some of the bitterest battles for America's future planned and executed their campaigns. The Press Building was home to organizations promoting extremist social and political ideologies, some operating on shoestring budgets from hole-in-the-wall offices and others with almost unlimited funds occupying sprawling suites. Even as they exploited access to the nation's front pages to burnish their credibility and amplify their messages, these groups took pains to obscure their most unpalatable goals. Those with close ties to foreign interests tried to appear as American as the Fourth of July, while organizations dedicated to undermining the country's democratic institutions promoted themselves as patriots and defenders of the Constitution.

Hunger and anger brought strange, ugly characters out of the sewers, including some who hoped a National Press Building address would disguise their stench. James True was a prime example.

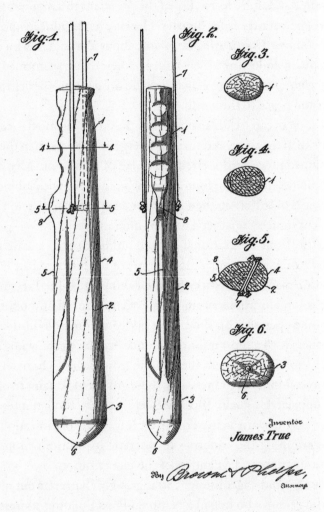

Dec. 31, 1935.　　　　　J. TRUE　　　　　2,026,077

POLICEMAN'S TRUNCHEON

Filed Sept. 30, 1935

Fig.1.　　*Fig.2.*　　*Fig.3.*

Fig.4.

Fig.5.

Fig.6.

Inventor

James True

By *Brown & Phelps,*

Attorneys

James True's patent for a policeman's truncheon. True marketed the truncheon as a "kike killer."

Although he had plenty of company on the fringe of the political spectrum, True stood out as the oddest, and most odious, character to ever occupy a National Press Building office. Operating behind locked doors on the tenth floor and from the comfort of Press Club armchairs, True cloaked his efforts to further Nazi ideals behind a nativist façade and seasoned his fascist social theories with pro-business bromides. But he made no secret of his animosity to the children of Israel and the descendants of African slaves.[6]

The newsletters and brochures emanating from True's office were as vile as any produced in Germany—in fact, many were translations of Nazi propaganda. True peddled more than hateful literature: his publications marketed the "kike killer," a wooden truncheon he had designed that featured one edge shaped like a cutlass, designed to crack a skull more efficiently than an old-fashioned Billy club. The Patent Office filed the invention under "Amusement Devices and Games." Ever the gentleman, True designed a smaller "ladies'" version.[7]

Six-foot-two with translucent skin covering a toothpick-thin body topped by alabaster hair, True looked like a septuagenarian minister. Visitors to his office quickly learned that the mild appearance was deceptive. A kike killer hung from a leather strap above his desk. He was afraid of the telephone, wrongly believing the FBI was listening, but wasn't shy about showing visitors the pistol in his desk's upper-right-hand drawer. Though True was ostensibly a journalist and publisher specializing in economics and business, somehow conversations in his office always turned to killing Jews and lynching blacks.[8]

True wasn't the first person in Washington to promote anti-Semitism or racism, but he was a leader in bringing prejudice that had once been shaded by euphemisms into the sunlight. Quiet forms of exclusion were woven into the fabric of American society, from the committees that guarded the purity of country-club membership rolls and vetted prospective medical students, to covenants that barred blacks, Jews, and Arabs from living in Washington's best neighborhoods, and a thousand other common forms of bigotry. For generations Jews had experienced discrimination, but there had been a tacit agreement to keep it under wraps, both by WASPs who sought to preserve their privilege and their peace of mind and by Jews who felt that publicly resisting prejudice would invite a violent backlash. True helped make the 1930s different. He and his admirers printed and shouted out loud their hatred of Jews, openly invoking the example of Nazi Germany as a model for America.[9]

Ardent anti-Semitism didn't disqualify True from enjoying the company of his peers at the National Press Club, where he was a member in good standing while working overtime to become one of the nation's leading purveyors of hate. True and his proclivities were well known to his colleagues. In a column that ran in newspapers around the country, a Press Club member, Charles Stewart, wrote about True's convictions as if they were an amusing sort of eccentricity. "He's a likeable chap—if you don't happen to be a Jew," Stewart, who clearly was not one, reported.[10]

The Press Club's relaxed attitude toward casual displays of rancid racism was proudly displayed on the pages of its newsletter, *The Goldfish Bowl*. More than a decade after True had joined the club, the publication, which had a habit of reprinting amusing squibs from newspapers, selected the following tidbit from the Clio, Mississippi, *Press* for the edification of its members: "The negro did not hang at Abbeyville last Friday. He was dressed and ready for the execution when a telegram from the Governor granted a respite for two weeks. The large crowd was very much disappointed." True must have chuckled when he read the headline crafted by the *Goldfish Bowl*'s editors: "Better Luck Next Time."[11]

True portrayed himself as pro-business and anti-communist, but he hated Jews and blacks more than Reds. His flagship publication, a weekly launched in July 1933 under the bland title *Industrial Control Reports*, was a mixture of real and imaginary news aimed at explicating and discrediting the New Deal, all the while promoting race hatred. One of the first American fascist periodicals, *Industrial Control Reports* used expressions like "Jew Deal," celebrated the formation of anti-Semitic vigilante groups, and informed its readers that what True considered biased foreign reporting in American newspapers should surprise no one because "you can safely state that 60 per cent of the New York Associated Press personnel is Jewish."[12] Communism and Judaism were fused in his mind, leading him to inform his readers that "Christian Nazism is the last bulwark against Jewish communism." True peddled the notion that blacks were allied with Jews as part of a vast conspiracy. He wrote about Jews hiring "big, buck niggers" to rape white women.[13]

Industrial Control Reports was aimed at businessmen and sold for twelve dollars a year, a steep price at the time. It was influential beyond its circulation, which never topped five thousand. The *Reports* served as a fascist guidepost because True often got the Nazi party line first, even scooping the German American Bund's *Deutscher Weckruf* newspaper. American fascists looked up to True as an elder statesman and leading thinker. Adding to the proceeds from subscriptions to his newsletter and sales of fascist tracts, secret funding for True's activities came from anti–New Deal organizations that were backed by some of the most powerful businessmen in America, including Pierre du Pont, a director of E. I. du Pont de Nemours and Company, and Alfred Sloan, chairman and president of General Motors.[14]

True coordinated closely with George Deatherge, a fascist who in the 1930s reconstituted and led the Knights of the White Camellia, a terrorist hate group similar to the Ku Klux Klan. One of Deatherge's innovations was an attempt to persuade his members to plant burning swastikas instead of crosses outside the houses of African Americans.[15]

True's activities aroused interest at the highest levels of government. In 1934 the White House ordered the Bureau of Investigation, which later became the FBI, to investigate the publisher of *Industrial Control Reports*. The Acting Attorney General concluded that it would be possible to try True for libel, but "prosecution would bring the most widespread publicity, and a failure to convict would bring an unfortunate result." FDR ordered another investigation in 1937 which again resulted in a recommendation against prosecution.[16]

The Office of Naval Intelligence (ONI) took an interest in True as part of an investigation of Nazi efforts to recruit American Indians. The Nazis wanted to persuade Native Americans that they were members of the Aryan race, and therefore superior to African Americans and Jews, as part of a propaganda effort aimed at building up support for Hitler in the United States. ONI learned that True was secretly funneling money from the German American Bund to Alice Lee Jemison, a pro-fascist Seneca Indian activist. He gave Jemison the code name Pocahontas, paying her to publish articles and tour the country giving speeches attacking the Bureau of Indian Affairs and the Roosevelt administration while urging support for American fascist organizations. Jemison lobbied for the Seneca tribe in Washington, testifying at congressional hearings alongside fascists.[17]

True had a number of admirers on Capitol Hill. His most vocal fan in Congress was Minnesota senator Thomas David Schall. Schall liked to ride horses and show off his prowess with a revolver despite having been rendered blind as a young man in a freak accident involving an electric cigar lighter.[18] He accused FDR of plotting to "Sovietize" the United States, drawing evidence from the pages of *Industrial Control Reports*. Schall arranged for True's fascist articles to be reproduced in the *Congressional Record* and disseminated at government expense.[19]

Seeking a broader audience, in 1934 True organized a new company, America First Incorporated, therewith coining a phrase that was to be adopted by American isolationists and brown shirts, and revived by twenty-first-century nationalists. The organization's mission statement attacked FDR and the New Deal as communist dupes and falsely asserted that "Soviet Russia is spending $6,000,000 this year in the United States on communist propaganda and the financing of riots."[20] True's publications equated the New Deal with Bolshevism, rooted Bolshevism in an international Jewish conspiracy, and urged the WASP majority, which he called "the real American patriots," to resist both—preferably with bullets and batons. In September 1934 newspapers across the country printed a public letter to FDR signed by "James True, President, America First!"

that accused New Deal officials of "following the theories of Karl Marx" and basing "their plans on the Soviet Russian system of regimentation and collectivism." Among other sins, True accused various government officials of belonging to an organization that advocated "negro equality."[21]

"America First is an extremely conservative organization headed by a group of individuals who are quite sure that most of Roosevelt's advisors are being subsidized by Stalin," the *Washington Post* informed its readers. "It is Mr. True's boast that he is the man who first informed industry that the Administration was heading straight down the road to Moscow." While the *Washington Post* handled True with thinly veiled sarcasm, *New Masses*, the literary bible of the Left, branded him an imminent threat to national security in a lurid article titled "Plotting American Pogroms." The exposé was written by John Spivak, a crusading investigative reporter.[22]

True often accused his opponents of being communists and Soviet agents—and when it came to Spivak, he was absolutely right. Spivak, who vehemently denied membership in the Communist Party, was not only a card-carrying member but also an official in its feared security apparatus that was charged with discovering and expelling ideological deviants.[23]

In addition, Spivak was a paid Soviet intelligence agent. In the 1930s, while leading a public crusade against fascists, he secretly worked with Jacob Golos, at the time the most talented and productive OGPU operative in the United States. Spivak gained the trust of congressional staff and of investigators at Jewish organizations, and he passed information he gleaned from them about Nazi propaganda and espionage activities to Golos for transmission to Moscow. He also used his contacts and investigative skills to track down Trotskyites.[24]

Whether he was writing for progressive publications or the OGPU's files, Spivak's reporting was colorful. For example, in a 1935 report to Moscow on the disappearance of a German named Count Alfred von Saurma-Douglas, Spivak noted that the aristocrat "had been castrated," and his wife "is a hermaphrodite."[25]

Spivak's sources, like his readers, had no idea he was an OGPU agent.

One of his most useful informants, an investigator in Washington for the Anti-Defamation League, slipped Spivak files from confidential congressional investigations about White Russians and Nazis. Another of Spivak's sources, a woman who worked on a congressional committee, provided him reports with details "about the chemical warfare industry, the division of the sphere of influence among the largest global arms producers, bribing methods, ties with intelligence agencies, purely technical military questions about individual types of weapons, etc.," according to a report in the KGB's archives.[26]

In his articles and books, Spivak attacked any and all public references to Soviet espionage as shameless Red-baiting. At the same time, his descriptions of the scale and sophistication of Nazi and Japanese espionage in the United States were wildly exaggerated. The only intelligence operation that matched the scope and accomplishments he attributed to Germany's infiltration of American government and business was headquartered a thousand miles to the east of Berlin, on Moscow's Lubyanka Square.

Industrial Control Reports and *New Masses* spent the summer of 1936 sounding alarms about imaginary communist subversion and equally improbable fascist pogroms. True kicked off the season by informing his readers that a Zionist conference had been held in Providence to "perfect plans to take over the nation starting Jewish New Year, September 15."[27]

A few weeks later, True gained national notoriety when *New Masses* published an explosive article about him under the headline "Pogrom in September!" The story recounted how the author had gained True's trust by claiming to be a representative of the Republican Party seeking educational materials about the Jewish conspiracy to take over America.

True's National Press Building "office is a key post in the anti-Semitic movement in America," *New Masses* told its readers. "From it literature is disseminated. From it come instructions in how to recruit Jew-baiters, how to spread the doctrine of intolerance, race hatred, persecution. From it James True has announced the first American pogrom will occur next month, September 1936." News of the planned "Jew shoot" prompted the Secret Service to assign guards to prominent Jewish government officials.[28]

True was one of a dozen Americans invited by a German Nazi agent in early 1939 to serve on a council that would "link together all patriotic movements in the United States for the purpose of recovering our country from control of the Jews." In May 1939 a prominent American fascist, Anna B. Sloane, wrote to Nazi propaganda minister Joseph Goebbels seeking money to create a newspaper to be called *The National Patriot.* Her letter named True as a member of the paper's advisory board.[29]

True often advocated splitting African American heads and shooting Jews, but all that he personally assaulted was truth and decency. He provided aid and comfort to Nazis in the years before World War II, served as a conduit for Nazi propaganda, and likely provided some assistance to the stream of emissaries from Berlin that passed through his office.

The Department of Justice indicted True in 1942 as part of a group of twenty-nine Axis propagandists charged with conspiring to destroy the morale of American soldiers. Much of the eight thousand pages of evidence the prosecution submitted to the court was secretly provided to the Justice Department by British intelligence, which had been shadowing and harassing American fascists for over a year. The trial was a circus, continually interrupted by defendants leaping to their feet to shout at the judge, each other, and their own attorneys. A mistrial was declared after several months when the judge died. In 1944 many of the same defendants, including True, were tried for conspiring with officials of the German Reich and leaders and members of the Nazi party to incite mutiny, otherwise sabotage the war, and set up a Nazi regime in the United States.[30]

True died during the trial.

CHAPTER FOUR
AMERICAN LIBERTY LEAGUE

Three floors below James True Associates and many steps closer to the center of the political spectrum and the top of the economic pyramid, a powerful organization fought Roosevelt's New Deal even more ferociously, and far more effectively, than True. The American Liberty League pioneered many of the practices that characterize American politics today: secretive funding of "grassroots" political groups with extreme agendas, massive expenditures on political campaigns by shadowy groups that are ostensibly independent of the candidates they support, and worship of interpretations of the Constitution that align with the financial interests of the wealthiest Americans while disregarding passages intended to check the powers of the privileged.

The Liberty League was also at the heart of a murky plot to replace FDR with a pro-business dictator.

The League was the direct descendent of an organization that fought for the right of Americans to drink legally, the Association Against the Prohibition Amendment (AAPA). Both the AAPA and Liberty League claimed to be dedicated to promoting liberty, and both were funded by a group of plutocrats who believed that the most important freedom was the freedom to avoid paying taxes. The AAPA was a decade-old in 1928 when Pierre du Pont took over its leadership.[1] He recruited John J. Raskob, a vice president at E. I. du Pont de Nemours and former Treasurer of General Motors, to lead the organization. At the time, Raskob had his hands full with two very different projects: building and managing the Empire State Building in New York and modernizing the Democratic Party in Washington.

Raskob provided more than $100,000 from his personal funds in 1930 to establish a permanent Democratic National Committee (DNC) headquarters with offices in the National Press Building. Previously, both political parties had operated temporary national offices only for about four months prior to presidential elections. Raskob, who had been chairman of the DNC since 1928, remained in New York, dedicating himself to marketing the world's tallest, and for years one of New York's emptiest, buildings. He left day-to-day operations at DNC headquarters in the hands of a savvy operator named Jouett Shouse, a man with two passions: politics and ponies. His bets about the former were far more often on the money.

Trying to match Raskob, the Republican National Committee also created a permanent headquarters office. Naturally, it was also located in the Press Building. This marked the start of the modern era of permanent campaigns waged by full-time professional political operatives.

Raskob fought bitterly to deny Roosevelt the presidential nomination, and having lost was forced to resign his DNC position in 1932. He turned his attention to the repeal of Prohibition, opening an AAPA office in the Press Building and putting Shouse in charge. The operation was funded by Pierre du Pont and his younger brothers, Irénée and Lammot; Raskob; Grayson Mallet Prevost Murphy, a banker who served on the boards of Anaconda Copper, Bethlehem Steel, and New York Trust; and other industrialists.[2]

The wealthiest men in America weren't investing their time and money to repeal Prohibition because they longed to order cocktails at the Plaza Hotel bar. While Prohibition offended the spirit of individualism they considered a hallmark of American society, and promoted lawlessness exemplified by thugs like Al Capone, these were minor inconveniences to the Robber Barons who backed the AAPA. If these had been the only drawbacks to banning alcohol, the du Ponts and their confederates could have waited for legislated temperance to die a natural death.

Raskob, the du Ponts, and their comrades detested and went to war against Prohibition because they blamed it for the one threat that kept them awake at night, a scourge that they feared would—and that ultimately did—destroy their way of life: income taxes.[3]

To keep the government afloat during World War I, Congress established a tax on the incomes of the wealthiest Americans. The du Ponts expected the affliction, like a similar tax imposed during the Civil War, to be temporary. Those hopes were dashed in January 1919 by ratification of the Eighteenth Amendment, which made Prohibition the law of the land. Revenue from taxes on alcohol sales evaporated, blowing a huge hole in the federal budget. This led Congress to expand rather than rescind the income tax.

Raskob and Shouse attracted donations to the AAPA with promises that the income tax would be washed away in a flood of beer if the saloon taps were reopened. The largest, most sophisticated American lobbying campaign up to that time was launched to support the unspoken proposition that government should be funded by taxing the drinking habits of millions of Americans rather than the incomes of a tiny elite.[4]

Working from his Press Building office, Shouse created front organizations and funded the campaigns of "wet" candidates for state legislatures and Congress. The AAPA intervened in fifty congressional races, winning 90 percent of them. It was so effective that even Utah, home to the teetotaling Mormon Church, approved the Twenty-First Amendment repealing Prohibition on December 3, 1933, sloshing the repeal movement over the threshold of the two-thirds of states needed to change the Constitution. Roosevelt tried to take credit for the deed, sending the first legal shipment of beer in Washington to the thirsty hacks at the Press Club, but Arthur Krock of the *New York Times* correctly attributed the success to Shouse and the AAPA. The association's efforts had shaved two years from the life of Prohibition, Krock estimated.[5]

Even as he raised a glass at a celebratory banquet held a few hours after Utah pounded the final nail into Prohibition's coffin, Shouse realized that the New Deal meant that he and his patrons had won a battle but not the war. Although Prohibition had been repealed, the income tax wasn't going away—and, even more than the tax, the Roosevelt administration's fiscal, regulatory, and social policies posed an existential threat to the lifestyles of the ultrarich. Three days after the celebration, the directors of the AAPA, in a more sober mood, passed a resolution calling on the board to consider forming a new group dedicated to defending "the principles of the Constitution."[6]

A letter to Raskob from Robert Ruliph Morgan Carpenter, a retired du Pont vice president and member of the company's board of directors, encapsulated the mindset of the AAPA's directors and the kinds of threats they were organizing to oppose. Writing in March 1934, Carpenter complained, "Five negroes on my place in South Carolina refused work this spring . . . saying they had easy jobs with the government. A cook on my houseboat at Fort Myers quit because the government was paying him a dollar an hour as a painter."[7] Carpenter asked Raskob to present his travails to Roosevelt as evidence of the need to scrap the New Deal before the country was ruined. Raskob wrote back without a hint of irony to suggest that Carpenter, who was married to Pierre du Pont's sister, "take the lead in trying to induce the du Pont and General Motors groups, followed by other big industries, to definitely organize to protect society from the sufferings which it is bound to endure if we allow communistic elements to lead the people to believe that all businessmen are crooks."

Realizing that no one else was going to do it, Raskob took the initiative, calling on his peers to join him to form an organization dedicated to unraveling the New Deal. When it came to organizing a massive effort to influence government and public opinion, Raskob had both a precedent and an energetic operative to run it. He recruited Shouse to crank up the apparatus he'd created to fight Prohibition. This time the goal wouldn't be amending the Constitution, it would be preserving the liberty—and fortunes—of the men who invented the modern corporation, men who had a great deal to lose if Roosevelt succeeded in creating a New Deal for American workers. Raskob and his comrades humbly envisioned the American Liberty League's mission as annihilating the "imported, autocratic, Asiatic Socialist party of Karl Marx and Franklin Delano Roosevelt."[8]

The roster of American Liberty League directors and funders read like a Who's Who of the American plutocracy. The men who ran US Steel, General Motors, the Chase Manhattan and JP Morgan banks, Standard Oil, and, until FDR's presidential nomination, the Democratic Party joined the du Pont brothers and Raskob in a crusade against what they viewed as populist tyranny.

On August 22, 1934, Shouse ushered a group of reporters into his office, suite 781 of the National Press Building—next door to the Democratic National Committee, where he'd been executive director—to announce formation of the American Liberty League. Sitting in his shirt sleeves, he said the League would "defend and protect the Constitution of the United States," and "teach respect for the rights of persons and property as fundamental to every successful form of government."[9]

At first its intended victim treated the Liberty League as a joke. President Roosevelt told reporters he'd "laughed for ten minutes" after reading in that morning's *New York Times* that "talk in Wall Street indicated that the announcement of the new American Liberty League was little short of an answer to a prayer." FDR criticized the League as a tool of the super-rich, quipping that one of its tenets was "love thy God but forget thy neighbor," and adding that its God was property.[10]

While FDR had shown amusement, news of the League's formation and of its powerful backers stunned and alarmed a retired Marine general named Smedley Darlington Butler. Reading newspaper stories about the organization persuaded Butler that attempts by a group of bankers and industrialists to recruit him to lead a coup that would take power from FDR had been real—and that the plotters must be stopped.

Butler was a strange candidate for right-wing generalissimo. As the most-admired soldier in America and a tireless advocate for veterans, it was plausible that Butler could recruit a mob of superannuated soldiers.

On the other hand, vilifying bankers and capitalists was his favorite pastime.

Butler had spent much of the first three decades of the twentieth century commanding Marines from China to the Philippines, and especially in Central America. He came to believe that America's muscular foreign policy benefited big business, hurt the people who found themselves on the wrong side of Yankee bayonets, and did nothing for regular Americans. Summing up his career in an August 1933 speech to the nation's largest veterans organization, the American Legion, Butler said he'd been a "high-class muscle man for Big Business."[11] He recounted that he'd "helped purify Nicaragua for the international banking house of Brown Brothers," had helped make Mexico "safe for American oil interests," and had flexed military muscle to help American business interests in the Dominican Republic, Haiti, and Cuba: "I helped the rape of half a dozen Central American republics for the benefit of Wall Street." Having spent fifty years in uniform and twice been awarded the Congressional Medal of Honor, Butler was drummed out of the service in October 1931 after causing a diplomatic incident by falsely accusing Benito Mussolini of running down and killing a child.

The same individuals who had financed the AAPA and later created the Liberty League tried to convince Butler to take over the American Legion and use it to mount a coup against President Roosevelt. Their models were the black-shirted veterans who put Mussolini in power and the *Croix de Feu* (Cross of Fire), a fascist paramilitary group recruited from French veterans. The idea was to keep FDR in office as a figurehead, much as King Victor Emmanuel III had stayed on when Mussolini took control of Italy.

Butler played along with the plotters, gathering evidence that he intended to use to disrupt the scheme. At one point, one of the conspirators told Butler that a new organization was being formed to support the putsch: "You watch; in two or three weeks you will see it come out in the papers. There will be big fellows in it. This is to be the background of it. These are to be the villagers in the opera." It would, Butler was told, be presented to the public as a society to maintain the Constitution. Butler later told congressional investigators that about two weeks later the "American Liberty League appeared, which was just about what he described it to be."[12]

Not only did the Liberty League appear when Butler had been told to expect it, spouting the kind of slogans about the Constitution and liberty that he'd been told to expect, but its principal officers included the men who had been pressing him to take over the American Legion. Butler became convinced that the plan to raise an army of veterans and wrest control of the country from Roosevelt wasn't just chatter from con men.

Determined to thwart the plot, and realizing that in the absence of evidence or witnesses he would be dismissed as a crank, Butler turned for help to a journalist at the *Philadelphia Record*, Paul Comly French, who had worked in the past as his personal secretary. Presenting himself as Butler's assistant, French visited Gerald MacGuire, an oleaginous bond salesman who had been the intermediary between the Liberty League and Butler. French rushed from the two-hour meeting to a nearby office where he typed a memo recording the bond salesman's remarks: "We need a Fascist government in this country to save the Nation from the communists who want to tear it down and wreck all that we have built in America. The only men who have the patriotism to do it are the soldiers and Smedley Butler is the ideal leader. He could organize a million men overnight."[13] MacGuire also suggested that arms and equipment could be obtained from the Remington Arms Co. on credit through one of the du Pont brothers who owned a controlling interest in Remington—and who were among the most enthusiastic backers of the Liberty League.

French broke the story of what came to be known as the Business Plot in identical articles published in the *Philadelphia Record* and the *New York Post* on November 30, 1934. The story quoted Butler as saying he had been asked by a group of "wealthy New York brokers to lead a Fascist movement to set up a dictatorship in the United States."[14] Other newspapers reported French's revelations with a combination of skepticism, incredulity, and scorn.

Editors were reluctant to give credence to the tale, but it piqued the interest of two members of Congress, John W. McCormack of Massachusetts and Samuel Dickstein of New York, publicity hounds who headed the House Special Committee on Un-American Activities Authorized to Investigate Nazi Propaganda and Certain Other Propaganda Activities. They deemed Butler's allegations credible enough—and the drama of uncovering a potential coup plot sufficiently likely to generate headlines—to merit an investigation. Butler, French, and MacGuire all testified to the committee in executive sessions.

In a report released in February 1935, the committee concluded: "Evidence was obtained showing that certain persons had made an attempt to establish a fascist organization in this country. There is no question that these attempts were discussed, were planned, and might have been placed in execution when and if the financial backers deemed it expedient."[15]

The report astounded Butler, not because of its revelations, but rather because of what wasn't revealed. There wasn't even a hint of the most explosive information he'd given the committee. The American Liberty League, the du Ponts and other powerful men Butler believed were behind the plot, weren't mentioned.

John Spivak, the crusading *New Masses* reporter and Soviet spy, got wind of the cover-up and traveled to Washington to investigate. A committee staffer inadvertently gave him unexpurgated transcripts of all of the testimony the committee had received in executive session. For Spivak, the suppressed testimony was irrefutable proof that the conspiracies he'd been writing about for decades were real: Wall Street bankers *were* plotting to destroy democracy; the threat of fascism wasn't a fantasy. He became intoxicated by the prospect of bringing down the nation's most powerful capitalists. Instead of simply reporting the facts, in two articles published in *New Masses* in January and February 1935, Spivak buried an accurate account of "Wall Street's fascist conspiracy" in a feverish, baroque, anti-Semitic conspiracy theory so complex that he had to publish a chart showing how the various players were allegedly connected. The stories were ignored or ridiculed.

Historians have shrugged off the Business Plot, but at the time it seemed real to many. FDR's secretary of Interior, Harold Ickes, believed the story was suppressed as a result of secret agreements between the American Liberty League and the country's major newspapers, which were owned by individuals who were members, or closely associated with members of the League. These connections, Ickes claimed, led publishers to ensure that their papers distorted and covered up the episode "in the interest of their advertisers and in defense of the capitalist class."[16] Four decades later, McCormack said he believed a dangerous plot had been disrupted: "If General Butler had not been the patriot he was, and if they had been able to maintain secrecy, the plot certainly might well have succeeded."

The Liberty League can be considered the Dr. Jekyll of the pro-business Far Right, which would make the Sentinels of the Republic, a spin-off from an older organization originally created to oppose women's suffrage, the Mr. Hyde. Operating with funding from the League—which at one time contemplated merging with the Sentinels—and from the same members of the du Pont, Pew, and Pitcairn families who funded the League, the Sentinels worked from an office on the Press Building's thirteenth floor. The group sent editorials on a regular basis to 1,300 newspapers denouncing as un-American progressive initiatives that put the interests of ordinary people above those of the rich. Child-labor laws, maternity benefits, unemployment insurance, and the distribution of birth-control information, were, according to the Sentinels, steps down the path to godless communism.

The tycoons who funded the Sentinels felt compelled to distance themselves from it in 1936 after an investigation by Senator Hugo Black revealed both their funding of the organization and its hateful nature. Black released a letter in which Sentinel representatives referred to FDR's policies as "Jewish Communism" and asserted both that middle-class Americans longed for an American Hitler and that the "fight for western Christian civilization can be won: but only if we recognize that the enemy is world-wide and that it is Jewish in origin."[17]

In addition to funding the Sentinels, the Liberty League and its leaders funneled money to another anti-Semitic group with a National Press Building Office, the Southern Committee to Uphold the Constitution, which shared members and goals with the Ku Klux Klan. This connection didn't faze the League. In fact, when it was being formed, the Liberty League's founders had contemplated aligning their organization with the KKK.

Starting in October 1934, Irénée du Pont and Shouse corresponded and held a series of meetings with KKK leaders, including Imperial Wizard Hiram Evans, about merging the two groups. The merger didn't happen because the businessmen believed the KKK's membership had dwindled to the point that it wouldn't be of much value; they weren't opposed to collaborating with hooded men who killed and terrorized African Americans. Even after the idea of a merger had been dropped, Pierre du Pont tried to enlist the KKK in the Liberty League's work. He wrote to Evans suggesting that the KKK emulate "vigilance committees" that had been formed on the West Coast to prevent government seizures of property, and argued that the time had come to reorient the KKK toward the protection of property.[18]

Although the Liberty League/KKK alliance was not consummated, the fact that some of the wealthiest men in America considered working with thugs who celebrated the lynching and terrorizing of innocent men, women, and children provides insight into their character and lends credence to the notion that the League backed the Business Plot.

Public disclosure of the Liberty League's ties to the Business Plot didn't diminish the enthusiasm of the organization's backers. The League poured over a million dollars, an unprecedented sum at the time, into defeating Roosevelt in the 1936 election. Its staff was three times larger than the Republican National Party's Press Building headquarters operation. Much of this money was spent creating one of the largest publishing enterprises in Washington, certainly the largest headquartered in the Press Building, where it had expanded from Shouse's desk to take up an entire floor. William C. Murphy Jr., quit his job as Washington correspondent for the *Philadelphia Evening Public Ledger* and resigned as president of the National Press Club to take on the task of running the League's publicity operation.

The League printed and distributed over five million pamphlets and leaflets during the campaign, and it bombarded newspapers with copy that generated thousands of anti-Roosevelt news stories and editorials.

Roosevelt branded the League a band of "economic royalists," but the recipients of its largesse were anything but aristocrats. The League's Southern strategy included secretly financing Gene Talmadge, the white-supremacist governor of Georgia. When Talmadge asked for help financing a national convention to offer himself as an alternative to Roosevelt, Raskob and Pierre du Pont each contributed $5,000 and General Motors president Sloan threw $1,000 into the pot. Their money helped Talmadge print a phony magazine, *Georgia Women's World*, and have it distributed at the convention.[19] The magazine featured a photo of Eleanor Roosevelt with two African American Howard University students above a caption describing the occasion as the first lady's "going to some nigger meeting, with two escorts, niggers, on each arm."[20]

Undisguised proselytizing for the rights of the rich, not reports of its role in the Business Plot or support for racist propaganda, led to the League's downfall. A dinner the League held at Washington's Mayflower Hotel in January 1936 was the beginning of the organization's end. The event was billed as a celebration of Al Smith, the Democratic Party's 1928 presidential candidate and a leader of the movement against FDR. Smith's contention that the New Deal was an attempt to replace the "clean clear air of America" with the "foul breath of Soviet Russia"[21] didn't disturb ordinary Americans nearly as much as the atmosphere in the room where he made these remarks. Newspapers described a saturnalian debauch at which two thousand raucous men in evening dress and soused women flashing diamond jewelry cavorted under crystal chandeliers. They were jammed "tailcoat to tailcoat, fluttery bouffant dress to sleek black velvet dress," the *Washington Post* informed those among its readers who were not fortunate enough to have secured an invitation. Coming at a time when millions of Americans were hungry, the detailed descriptions of the sumptuous food and drink were almost pornographic.[22]

"Al Smith chewed his cigar, discovered it was unlit, and unmindful of Arnold Bennett's maxim that 'Cigars and love affairs cannot be relit,' struck a match scratchily before the microphone for it," the *Post* reported.[23] The reporter didn't reveal whether Smith managed to reignite the butt; in any case the League's flame sputtered on that night and continued to dim until it was finally extinguished in 1940, when its Press Building office was closed.

CHAPTER FIVE
WE, THE PEOPLE

The largest and the most eccentric intelligence operation ever run out of the National Press Building had no name, didn't officially exist, and is little more than a footnote in histories of American intelligence. From 1941 to 1945 it operated in complete secrecy and in the open. Camouflaged by a newspaper column, it reported directly to President Franklin Roosevelt in the White House and deployed agents across the United States and to Mexico, the Caribbean, and the Soviet Union. Its agents included journalists, businessmen, wealthy socialites, Somerset Maugham's gay lover, and Hitler's piano player.

Headquartered in room 1210 of the National Press Building, this espionage agency was modeled on the legendary Bureau of Current Political Intelligence (CPI), a super-secret agency buried deep inside the State Department. According to an account of the CPI from the 1930s, "if you want to find out what is in Stalin's mind or are curious concerning the substance of the next Papal Encyclical, [the CPI] will find out for you. If you need a man to discover the source of the latest shipment of machine-guns to a Central American bandit, or the reason why a permit has been denied to a Central Asiatic 'scientific expedition,' it will serve you very well, even though the trail of evidence leads straight to Whitehall, Wall Street or the *Gaimusho* at Tokyo."[1]

The CPI's head, Dennis Tyler, was suave, debonair, unflappable, and, like the CPI, entirely fictional. Both were products of the imagination of a writer named John Franklin Carter, who signed some of his books "Diplomat." As the *New York Times* noted in an October 1932 review of Diplomat's first novel, *Murder in the Embassy*, the author displayed "a close knowledge of the diplomatic service and a sense of humor that is refreshing in the serious business of concocting successful mystery tales."[2]

Carter pulled off a remarkable feat: he created and led a *real* intelligence service that was modeled on the fictional CPI. He got his start when he wrote a nonfiction book profiling the leading contenders in the 1932 presidential election. The book didn't shy from describing Franklin Delano Roosevelt's physical disabilities, labeling him "the liveliest cripple in American politics."[3] Like many Americans, Carter misjudged FDR, predicting that as president, "when cornered he will play dead dog" because "he is not a fighter." Reflecting the frustration of reporters who found it impossible to goad the candidate into taking positions on controversial topics, Carter wrote that Roosevelt "is as hard to pin down as a live eel on a sheet of oilcloth." Despite these reservations, he concluded that "we could do far worse than elect as President a man who has been brought up to believe that privileges confer obligations and that life is not so serious that one can afford not to act like a gentleman."

Roosevelt was enough of a gentleman that he wasn't offended by the young author's lack of deference, and the two became friends. That friendship led, almost a decade later, to a secret collaboration between Roosevelt and Carter. Together, FDR and Carter created a real intelligence operation based on Diplomat's fantasy of an off-the-books, secret intelligence operation led by a cultured wisecracker who battled the forces of evil between cocktails.

While the organization Carter created didn't approach the omniscience of the imaginary CPI, it did have the ear of the president, who treated Carter's reports as seriously as those produced by formal intelligence agencies. Carter's network operated in total secrecy, a feat that is noteworthy because some of the world's most inquisitive minds walked past its headquarters in the Press Building every day. Carter and his operatives didn't hide behind locked doors; they often climbed a short flight of stairs to swap stories and lies with reporters at the Press Club bar. One of Carter's men had the habit of over-patronizing the club's Tap Room and sleeping off the consequences on a nearby sofa. Throughout his clandestine career Carter wrote newspaper columns, spoke on the radio, and sought public attention.[4]

When Carter and Roosevelt first met in the summer of 1932, neither the writer nor the candidate—an avid reader of mysteries and detective novels—could have devoted much attention to transforming the imaginary CPI into a real intelligence agency. Roosevelt had an election to win, and if successful he would have to steady the nerves of a nation teetering on the precipice of ruin, then try to make good on his promises to restore prosperity.

Carter had a very different priority: earning a living. The sober, humorless men who ran the State Department had solved the mystery of the identity of Diplomat and his alter ego Jay Franklin, the pseudonym Carter used for magazine articles. They gave Carter a choice: either stop writing—not even publish poetry—or clean out his desk in the State, War, and Navy Building. He picked prose over public service. Broke, eager for adventure, and anxious to avoid the constraints of conventional employment, the former diplomat sailed to Europe hoping to make his mark as an international freelance correspondent.[5]

In Budapest, Carter stayed with an old friend, Nick Roosevelt, a former *New York Times* reporter and diplomat, who was roughly halfway between Teddy and Franklin Roosevelt in the sprawling Roosevelt family tree. Roosevelt suggested that Carter travel to Germany and look up Ernst Hanfstaengl, an old acquaintance of the Roosevelt family who was serving as the gatekeeper for foreign journalists seeking access to Nazi leaders.[6] President-elect Roosevelt had also asked Carter to deliver a message to Hanfstaengl: If Hitler became too volatile "think of your piano-playing and try and use the soft pedal."[7]

By the time Carter left Germany a few weeks later, he and Hanfstaengl had formed a friendship that changed the course of both men's lives and years later, under Roosevelt's direction, formed the basis for a madcap intelligence operation.

Ernst Franz Sedgwick Hanfstaengl, Adolf Hitler, and others, 1933.
Credit: *Sueddeutsche Zeitung* Photo / Alamy Stock Photo

Carter and Roosevelt, like all of Hanfstaengl's friends, called him "Putzi," which roughly translates as "little tyke," a name he'd acquired as an infant and hadn't managed to shed even as he grew into a towering man with a head too large to fit in a standard-issue German army helmet. Hanfstaengl was raised in Germany in a bicultural home, the son of a Bavarian aristocrat who had married the daughter of a prominent New England family.

Hanfstaengl traveled to Boston and started classes at Harvard in 1905. His outgoing character, musical talents, and family connections ensured that he was one of the most prominent young men on campus. The aristocratic German barely satisfied the college's academic requirements, but he excelled in the social sphere, befriending scions of the Astor and Roosevelt clans, and landing invitations to White House parties, where he played the piano for Theodore Roosevelt. After graduating, Hanfstaengl managed the family's art business in New York and spent evenings in front of a Steinway at the city's Harvard Club, where he met Franklin Roosevelt.

Putzi's sweet life soured in 1914. Regardless of their social connections or bonhomie, German patriots were less than welcome in wartime America. The US government seized the Hanfstaengl family's art as alien property and auctioned it for pennies on the dollar. Decades after the war, government investigators uncovered evidence that Hanfstaengl had provided the dynamite to saboteurs who blew up an arsenal on Black Tom Island in New York Harbor in July 1916, igniting more than a million pounds of ammunition. The explosion, the equivalent of a 5.5 magnitude earthquake, caused $20 million in damage (equivalent to about $500 million in 2018) and denied valuable materiel to the British.[8]

Giving up on life in America, Hanfstaengl moved back to Germany in 1921. The next year, at the request of a Harvard alumnus who was studying the German political scene for the State Department, Hanfstaengl attended a speech by an obscure rabble-rouser. Recognizing Adolf Hitler's potential to exploit Germany's chaotic political and economic situation, he charmed his way into the Nazi inner circle, becoming the first wealthy aristocrat to embrace Hitler and Nazism.

Hanfstaengl was just a few steps behind Hitler at the Bürgerbräukeller beer hall on the night of November 8, 1923, pushing tables over, rushing to seize the stage and, with it, control of the government from the Bavarian prime minister. Putzi remembered the scene in a memoir: "Hitler clambered on a chair and fired a round at the ceiling. Hitler then told the audience: 'The national revolution has broken out! The hall is filled with 600 armed men. No one is allowed to leave. The Bavarian government and the government at Berlin are hereby deposed. A new government will be formed at once. The barracks of the *Reichswehr* and the police barracks are occupied. Both have rallied to the swastika!'"[9]

The poorly planned putsch was quickly suppressed. Hanfstaengl fled to Switzerland, while Hitler sought refuge in Putzi's home in the Bavarian Alps. When police arrived at the door, Hanfstaengl's American-born wife, Helene, persuaded her despondent houseguest to drop his revolver, along with his intention to commit suicide. The diminutive Hitler must have looked like a child playing dress-up when he met the authorities wearing Hanfstaengl's pajamas.

Following the trial that Robert S. Allen had covered, Hitler was sentenced to five years of confinement but served only nine months. After Hitler's release, Hanfstaengl became even closer to the Nazi leader, banging out Wagner operas on a piano for hours as the Führer worked himself into a frenzy and then flung himself onto stages at political rallies. Hanfstaengl's contributions to the Nazi cause included suggesting the *Sieg Heil* salutation and accompanying straight-arm salute, both inspired by his experiences as a cheerleader for the Harvard football team. Ironically, Hanfstaengl couldn't bring himself to salute Hitler.

Later dismissed as a court jester, Hanfstaengl did more to bring the Nazis to power than entertain its leader. He introduced the uncultured politician to members of the aristocracy, whose support was critical to his rise to power, financed a Nazi newspaper at a time when the party couldn't afford it, and, after the fascists gained control, served as the party's liaison to the foreign press.

When Hanfstaengl and Carter exchanged life stories they realized that Carter's parents had decades earlier been friends with Hanfstaengl's mother, the descendent of a famous Civil War general, John Sedgwick. Hanfstaengl arranged for Carter to observe Hitler delivering a speech and to interview the second-most powerful man in Nazi Germany, Herman Goering. Carter's friendship with Hanfstaengl did not make him sympathetic to the Nazi cause, but it did form the foundation for one of the oddest intelligence operations of World War II, a three-way partnership bringing together the German American aristocrat, Carter, and President Roosevelt.[10]

John Franklin Carter in 1936.
    Credit: Farm Security Administration—Office of War
Information Photograph Collection (Library of Congress)

Soon after Carter returned to the United States, just a few weeks before the election, FDR invited him for lunch at his Hyde Park, New York, estate. The wheelchair-bound Roosevelt, who relied on friends and relatives to travel and serve as his eyes and ears, must have appreciated Carter's impressions of Germany and his account of Putzi's rise to prominence in the Nazi hierarchy. FDR flattered the former diplomat by soliciting his ideas about reorganizing the State Department.[11]

Carter became a New Dealer, landing a job in 1934 as secretary of agriculture Henry Wallace's speechwriter and advisor. He also continued writing articles and books under various pseudonyms, including accounts of the activities of Dennis Tyler and the Bureau of Current Political Intelligence.

After two years Carter left Wallace's staff, rented an office on the twelfth floor of the National Press Building, and began a career as a journalist. His pro-Roosevelt syndicated column, We, the People, ran in hundreds of newspapers under the Jay Franklin byline, often alongside the Washington Merry-Go-Round column by Drew Pearson and Robert S. Allen, Eleanor Roosevelt's My Day column and Walter Winchell's On Broadway.

Carter's writings were more than partisan boosterism. He used access to editorial pages to advance agendas that he was pursuing behind closed doors. When he provided glimpses of Washington power struggles and inside dope on administration polices, the revelations were designed to affect the outcomes of the conflicts and shape policies. Although he had used the modest pseudonym "The Unofficial Observer" for *The New Dealers*, a book published in 1934 that billed itself as providing a Who's Who of the New Deal, Carter was not content with the role of observer. Nose pressed to the glass as some of the most momentous decisions of the era were made, he desperately wanted to be in the room making history, not just writing about it.

An incident in October 1939 illustrates Carter's close ties to the Roosevelt White House. It also demonstrates that although his column claimed to represent "the people," when he was forced to choose between informing readers and supporting the president, "the people" always came second. Carter had provided the White House an advance copy of a column describing a split within the Catholic Church between supporters of Father Charles Coughlin and Cardinal George Mundelein. Coughlin was using a popular radio program to preach anti-Semitism, race hatred, and disdain for FDR and the New Deal, while Mundelein, a friend and supporter of the president, was trying to steer Catholics into the mainstream of American society. If American Catholics failed to support Mundelein, Carter warned, Coughlin "may become either a Savonarola or a Martin Luther."[12]

Afraid that it would ignite a backlash against liberal church leaders, FDR asked Carter to kill the column. Carter responded immediately, scrambling to contact newspapers across the country. A note typed by one of FDR's personal secretaries, Grace Tully, and placed in the president's confidential files reported that the column had been "too dangerous" for Francis Spellman, a Roosevelt ally who had recently been appointed Archbishop of New York, and that it "was, therefore, 'pulled' from all papers except the 'Washington Star,'" which had already printed it. Tully's note added that FDR felt Carter's column "tells a desperate truth about the Church, Coughlin, and liberalism."[13]

By that time, Carter had devoted seven years to tireless promotion of the New Deal, mining his personal relationships with FDR and just about every political player of any consequence in Washington for insights and anecdotes that filled his books, radio broadcasts, and newspaper columns. While he may have convinced some of his readers, he had not convinced himself. The New Deal, Carter concluded, was a failure.

More important, Carter understood sooner than most of his peers that domestic policies were becoming irrelevant. The future, he realized, wouldn't be pounded out on government-issue typewriters but in dive bombers and tanks; America's fate would be shaped on European and Asian battlefields, not at Georgetown dinner parties. A president hobbled by Congress and the courts and harassed by powerful corporations couldn't meet the new challenges.

"The bitter time is at hand when we must speak and face the truth," Carter wrote in a book published in January 1940. "What we call democracy is not working to the general satisfaction of the American people. What we call capitalism is not succeeding in distributing sufficient goods and services to more than a third of our nation. What we call individualism is facing the critical competition of other social philosophies which rest on collective authority. We face the necessity of armed defense East and West, and the difficult problems of reform and reorganization at home, and we are hampered by a political system which puts a premium on evasion and delay."[14]

Carter argued in favor of strengthened authority for the president and told Americans that their prosperity and freedom required them to cast aside a defining characteristic of American democracy dating back to George Washington by electing FDR to a third term. He didn't inform his readers that he had been working for months out of the public eye to build support in the Democratic Party for a movement to nominate Roosevelt for an unprecedented third term.

As the calendar turned from 1939 to 1940, danger and deceit weren't confined to the pages of Diplomat's mystery novels. Nazi officers were reveling in Parisian nightclubs, the Luftwaffe was pounding London into a smoldering ruin in preparation for invasion, and FDR was simultaneously promising to keep America out of the war and desperately trying to equip the military with the men and weapons needed to win it.

Roosevelt was trying to steer the country through these crosswinds with one hand tied behind his back by an alliance of right- and left-wing isolationists, and with his vision obscured by an almost complete absence of foreign intelligence. At a time when Churchill, Stalin, Japanese leaders, and, to a lesser extent, Hitler could rely on large, sophisticated intelligence agencies with extensive networks of agents and skilled analysts, the American president's capacity for obtaining and assessing intelligence from abroad hadn't advanced much beyond Thomas Jefferson's. Like Jefferson, FDR relied on volunteers to travel abroad and report impressions, gossip, and undigested bits of news.

Carter summed up the situation in February 1941 when he told assistant secretary of state Sumner Welles that American intelligence was "pretty well loused up and floundering around."[15] The solution, the newspaper columnist said, was "a small and informal intelligence unit operating out of the White House without titles, without any bullshit." And he knew just the man to head it: himself. The assignment, Carter believed, would be a just reward for the hard work he'd done behind the scenes to help secure the president's unprecedented nomination for a third term.

Although his ability to provide the president the secret information and sophisticated analyses needed to support critical decisions was debatable, Carter's diagnosis of American intelligence weaknesses was accurate. Europe and Asia were at war, it was clear that the United States would be compelled to join the fighting, and the men in charge of the nation's meager intelligence resources were spending more energy pursuing turf battles than collecting and analyzing intelligence for the president. Carter didn't know it, but there was a single bright spot in the American intelligence firmament: a tiny, underfunded Army team had been startlingly successful in breaking Japanese codes, thereby providing real-time insights into Japanese military and diplomatic actions and intentions.

Lacking military or law-enforcement experience, the conventional gateways to running an intelligence organization, and having built a career from publicizing rather than protecting confidential information, Carter was an unlikely candidate to play the part of FDR's Francis Walsingham, Queen Elizabeth I's swashbuckling spymaster. With characteristic immodesty, Carter presented the traits that appeared to disqualify him as assets. Professionals in formal intelligence agencies were not and could not get the job done, he said. The president, Carter suggested, needed a nimble organization staffed by outsiders who were fast on their feet and unencumbered by legal niceties or a bureaucratic mentality. His work as a columnist was the perfect cover, providing opportunities to frequent the White House without attracting attention and a license to speak with almost anyone about almost anything.

Welles knew Carter's idea would captivate Roosevelt, who had long been fascinated by intrigue, plots, and conspiracies. The president was convinced that espionage and intelligence were too important—and far too much fun—to be left to professionals.

During World War I, while serving as assistant secretary of the Navy, Roosevelt had tried to organize a Naval Reserve Force consisting of private yachts that would travel the seven seas gathering intelligence. He was a voracious consumer of spy and detective novels, and he liked to dabble at code making and breaking. Roosevelt even took the time from his hectic White House schedule to dictate the plot for a detective story and allowed a friend to commission six prominent authors to write chapters based on the plot. They were serialized in a magazine and collected into a book, *The President's Mystery*.[16]

Roosevelt approached espionage as a game, and like all games he believed it was best played with friends. FDR's closest friends, the four men with whom he had escaped for a bachelor's cruise on the yacht *Nourmahal* in 1931 just after a failed assassination attempt, had since 1927 run a secret club called "The Room" that met in a Manhattan townhouse fitted out with globes, maps, and comfortable chairs. The Room could be dismissed as men acting like boys, except that its wealthy, aristocratic members had ready access to prominent politicians, tycoons, explorers, and real intelligence operatives. The Room was run by FDR's friend Vincent Astor, who had inherited fantastic wealth and an international business empire when his father, John Jacob Astor IV, went down with the *Titanic*. Astor and FDR shared a love of the sea and a passion for intrigue.[17]

Carter was banking on Roosevelt's appetite for adventure on the afternoon of February 13, 1941, as he walked the four blocks from his office in the National Press Building to 1600 Pennsylvania Avenue. Carter entered the White House a successful novelist, columnist, and political operative.

He emerged from a meeting with FDR with an additional occupation: leader and, for the time being, sole member of a new intelligence operation that would work exclusively for the president under the strictest secrecy.[18]

Carter had in essence become Dennis Tyler, the "diplomatic detective," and the president had blessed his plan to create a real version of the fictional Bureau of Current Political Intelligence. Carter and Roosevelt were well aware of the tradition, dating back to Christopher Marlowe and more recently practiced by Somerset Maugham (a visitor to the Room), of secret agents' writing novels that titillated the public with fictional and embroidered versions of the covert lives they had previously sworn to keep secret. As they met in the White House, the president and the creator of the fictional Dennis Tyler must have relished the irony: Carter was the only person in history to reverse the sequence, *first* creating an imaginary master spy, along with a fictional intelligence agency, and then, with the help of the president of the United States, turning himself into a facsimile of that character and establishing a real organization modeled on the fictional entity.

FDR gave Carter's plan the green light on the condition that it be kept secret and with the understanding that if any hint of Carter's covert activities leaked to the public, the White House would deny any connection to him. The operation was off the books and lacked an organizational structure or official budget—even a name.

The president financed Carter's work from a slush fund Congress had provided to deal with unspecified "emergencies." Money for Carter's operation, starting at $64,000 for the remainder of 1941 and growing to $120,000 for 1943 (equivalent to about $2 million in 2016), was laundered by the State Department. Assistant secretary of state Adolph Berle signed the checks, but Carter did not inform Berle about most of his activities. Berle took a dim view of those he learned about and quietly tried to undermine the amateur spy.[19]

Carter's first report to FDR, dated March 1, 1941—"Raw Material Situation in Belgium, as reported by Antwerp factory manufacturing electrical equipment for the Occupying Authorities"—consisted of three pages of lists of materials, from benzene to zinc, and notations about whether they were readily available, scarce, or unobtainable in the German-occupied country. Like hundreds of memos Carter sent to the president over the next four years, it was typed on stationery under the letterhead: *JOHN FRANKLIN CARTER, "We, the People," 1210 National Press Building, Washington, D.C.*

The president replied in writing, instructing Carter to show his information to "the Army, Navy and State Department—and also to the British Embassy."[20] FDR's many notes to Carter, always terse and sometimes humorous, were typed on White House stationery by one of his personal secretaries, Grace Tully. They were addressed to "Jack Carter" and closed with the typed initials "F.D.R."

The Belgian economic intelligence report was the first of a deluge of similar accounts Carter sent FDR based on interviews he and his agents conducted with a random assortment of individuals such as the chief dental officer of the Iraq Petroleum Company, who had fresh knowledge of situation on the ground. The descriptions of economic, political, and social conditions in Germany, Nazi-occupied Europe, Asia, and Latin America lacked context, and little effort was made to distinguish fact from rumor.

A March 8, 1941, memo from Carter on "Nazi Activities in the Union of South Africa" shows one reason why FDR looked forward to the novelist's reports while those from government bureaucrats gathered Oval Office dust. Carter told FDR that Nazi supporters in South Africa "number a quarter of a million of all sexes, shapes, ages and sizes," and that soldiers on their way to England "are set upon and beaten up in dark alleys, they are spat at by foul-breathed women . . ."[21] It is a safe bet that Roosevelt didn't receive any other reports that day with images as evocative as "foul-breathed women" spitting on soldiers.

In April, Carter forwarded to FDR a report written in confidence by a reporter for *Time* and *Life* magazines that painted an alarming, and accurate, picture of Japanese infiltration, subversion, and espionage in the Philippines. The Japanese, FDR was informed, had deployed agents under a variety of covers, especially as the owners of photography studios, to every corner of the archipelago, had blanketed the country with propaganda, and corrupted members of parliament, all in preparation for invasion and occupation.

To cope with an expanding covert workload, Carter decided that he needed a second-in-command. He had three criteria: The candidate must be acceptable to the president, have social standing and/or wealth, and be on friendly terms with the Brits. The last qualification stemmed from Carter's understanding that because of the centuries of experience and vast global reach of British intelligence, an upstart American intelligence operation couldn't hope to succeed without at least tacit support from London. Carter was in bad odor with the UK Foreign Office because at the State Department he'd been in charge of the British Empire Desk, which meant that his job often involved saying no to requests from his majesty's servants.[22]

Carter decided that Henry Field, whom he had met while canvassing for FDR's third term, fit the bill. Field was a great nephew and the financial beneficiary of the wealthy Chicago merchant Marshall Field, had grown up in England, had been educated at Eton and Oxford, and was as anglophilic as an American can be. He was also the black sheep of the Field family. Just before Carter met him in 1940, Field's uncle, who ran the Field Museum, had been forced to recall a book Henry had written about folklore in western Asia after it was discovered he'd plagiarized much of it. It wasn't an isolated incident: throughout his career Henry Field had a slippery relationship with the truth and a penchant for self-aggrandizement.[23]

Field had decided to redeem himself by joining the Navy. He was sitting in a hotel room in Washington preparing for an appointment to finalize paperwork to join the Office of Naval Intelligence when Carter knocked on the door and informed Field that he could not accept the commission because he'd been assigned to other duties "on higher authority." Field balked, saying he was determined to join the Navy. Carter, with typical overstatement replied, "I don't think you quite understand. The President has *ordered* you to work for him. I am head of a small team working for the White House. You are now part of this team."[24]

FDR kept Carter and his agents immensely busy. In the months before Pearl Harbor they spent as least as much time and energy on domestic as on foreign intelligence—though a great deal of their work stretched the boundaries of the concept of intelligence. Today it would be called "opposition research," and it wouldn't be legal to finance it with funds entrusted to the president for "emergencies."

Roosevelt sought Carter's assistance in dealing with a crisis in April 1941. He needed ammunition to attack a potent political opponent: the most admired man in America, Charles Lindbergh. "Lucky Lindy," at the time a colonel in the Army Air Corps reserve, had been the first man to fly solo across the Atlantic, a feat that made him one of the original American celluloid celebrities. He had parlayed fame into access to political and business leaders around the world, including Nazi military leaders who boasted to Lindbergh about their progress in creating the world's largest, most powerful air force. The American aviation hero became convinced that the neither the United States nor England could win a war against Germany. This view meshed with his anti-Semitism, as well as his complete confidence in the cultural and moral superiority of Northern Europeans.

Americans looked up to Lindbergh not for his ideas, which until 1941 most had never heard, but for his exploits and persona. When he began to speak out against intervention, halls were packed and radio audiences swelled with people eager to see and hear the man who had captured the world's imagination. Lindbergh proclaimed German victory inevitable and American intervention folly, legitimizing a broad popular movement to keep America out of a war that Roosevelt had privately determined the nation must enter and win. Roosevelt desperately wanted to knock the wind from Lindbergh's sails.

FDR's strategy for neutralizing Lindbergh was typically indirect. He asked Carter to prepare a detailed study of the "Copperheads," a term of derision that had been applied during the Civil War to Southern sympathizers and defeatists in the North. Carter gave Roosevelt a fifty-five-page report on April 22 and was in the Oval Office three days later for a typically raucous White House press conference. FDR began by railing against reporters who for a year and a half had been calling the aggressive patrols by US Navy ships in Atlantic and Pacific shipping lanes "convoys." This was like calling a cow a horse, the president said, repeating the simile several times and congratulating himself on his wit. He then dropped a bombshell, revealing that he intended to expand the patrols, which many Americans believed were provocations intended to drag the country into war. US Navy ships would travel "as far on the waters of the seven seas as may be necessary for the defense of the American hemisphere," Roosevelt said. He refused to say what they would do if and when they encountered the German navy.[25]

Near the end of the press conference, Constantine Brown, a reporter for the *Washington Star*, asked, seemingly out of the blue, "How is it that the Army, which needs now distinguished fliers, etc., has not asked Colonel Lindbergh to rejoin?"[26]

Thanks to Carter's report, FDR was armed with a response to the discreetly planted question. The president launched into a Civil War history lesson, noting that while there were "liberty-loving people on both sides" of the conflict, the Union and the Confederacy also had to deal with defeatists. "The Confederacy and the North let certain people go. In other words, in both armies there were—what shall I call them?—there were Vallandighams." It must have been the first time a president had uttered the name Vallandigham since 1863, when the Copperhead had been court-martialed and exiled from Washington to Richmond, the Confederate capital. Driving the point home, FDR continued, "Well, Vallandigham, as you know, was an appeaser. He wanted to make peace from 1863 on because the North 'couldn't win.'" The president made it clear that he considered Lindbergh a contemporary version of a Vallandigham Copperhead.[27]

An Associated Press story, which ran on April 25 in the *New York Times* and other newspapers across the country, reported, "Asserting that it was dumb to consider a Nazi victory inevitable, President Roosevelt classed Colonel Lindbergh today with appeasers who urged peace in the Revolutionary and Civil Wars on the ground that those wars could not be won."[28] The story also noted that just a few days before Lindbergh had said in a speech that the "United States cannot win this war for England, regardless of how much assistance we extend."

It seemed at first that Roosevelt had overplayed his hand. Newspaper columns portrayed his attack on Lindbergh's patriotism as unfair. If the aviator had remained silent, he could have emerged from the incident stronger. But FDR had astutely judged his adversary.

Lindbergh took the bait. Three days after newspapers reported FDR's comparison of Lindbergh to Vallandigham, the aviator released a public letter resigning his military commission, citing the president's remarks about "my loyalty to my country, my character, and my motives."[29] Coming as Americans were being drafted under the recently enacted Selective Service Act, Lindbergh's resignation was viewed by the public as proof that Roosevelt's accusations were on target—as if Lindbergh was resigning to avoid putting himself in harm's way. One of the president's fiercest and most credible critics was discredited. Neither Lindbergh nor his reputation ever recovered.[30]

As Carter expanded his network and began producing more, and more interesting, reports, Roosevelt started forwarding them to other players in similar informal intelligence networks he had created or encouraged. For example, on May 19, 1941, FDR sent Nelson Rockefeller copies of two of Carter's memorandums about Nazi activities in South America. Rockefeller, head of the blandly named "Office of the Coordinator of Inter-American Affairs," was leading a covert effort to push the Nazis out of South America. He was also providing financial and logistical support to British intelligence operatives who were waging a covert war in the United States to counter German interests. FDR's cover letter was marked "Private" and instructed Rockefeller, "Please show this to nobody. You might speak with me about this at your convenience."[31]

About this time Carter added his voice to the chorus of those predicting a German invasion of the Soviet Union. It would come, he stated in a May 16 report to FDR, "about June 1."[32] Although accurate, the intelligence wasn't startling: Drew Pearson and Robert Allen had published a similar prediction a month earlier, and Roosevelt, Churchill, and Stalin had received numerous secret reports pointing to a June attack. Stalin disregarded over a hundred specific, accurate warnings. When the NKVD forwarded from its spy in Tokyo a precise description of the planned invasion Stalin denounced the report as lies from a "shit who has set himself up with some small factories and brothels in Japan."[33]

In June FDR passed a report to Carter indicating that the situation in Martinique, a French colony in the Caribbean, was deteriorating. Pro-US mayors had been imprisoned by the Vichy government and the island had stockpiled a two-year food supply that would allow it to survive an embargo or siege. The president asked Carter to send one of his agents to assess the potential for the Caribbean island to become a base for hostile military operations against the United States.

Carter jumped on the task, informing Roosevelt that he had selected a Chicago businessman named Curtis Munson to travel to Martinique. Munson, Carter reported, was an old friend of undersecretary of commerce and FDR confidant Wayne Taylor, had visited Martinique in the past, and had military experience, having served as an aviator in the French Army during World War I. "He is a competent, level-headed business man, untainted by politics and without a record which could embarrass him," Carter wrote.[34]

Carter arranged for Munson to travel to Martinique as a representative of the Department of Agriculture to compile a report on the food security situation. The French government held up Munson's visa for two months. In the interim, Carter sent FDR reports about Martinique from European Jewish refugees, including one from the anthropologist Claude Levi-Strauss, who, fleeing the Nazis, had stopped there en route to Brazil. Levi-Strauss told one of Carter's agents that the "colored people of Martinique have been persuaded that if the US takes over the island, instead of having complete equality with the whites as they do under the French, they will revert to the position of the negro in the American south."[35]

Roosevelt held a typical press conference on August 26, 1941, treating the assembled reporters to an amusing story—the punchline involved Mongolian ponies—and criticizing unnamed columnists for spreading "falsehoods" that originated with "certain forces [seeking] to sabotage the program of aid to opponents of Hitlerism."[36] As the reporters were filtering out of the room, Roosevelt casually asked Carter to stay behind. Munson, who had slipped into the White House by the side door and wasn't listed on the appointment calendar, joined Carter and delivered a verbal report on the political, economic, and military situation in Martinique. He had determined that fears about Martinique's military preparations were overblown.

While Munson was investigating Martinique, Roosevelt was looking north, to Iceland, where the British feared their small garrison was in danger of being overwhelmed by the Germans. A Nazi naval base could have imperiled the convoys that were keeping Britain alive. The *New York Times* had reported on July 4, 1941, that Montana senator Burton Wheeler, the most ardent isolationist in Congress, said American troops were preparing to take over Iceland. Wheeler was trying to mobilize public opinion to head off military action; he was also putting American troops and national security at risk by tipping off the Germans. The leak alarmed FDR, prompting him to cut short a trip to Hyde Park for urgent meetings with Navy and State Department officials. Three days later, the White House announced that US Marines had landed in Iceland.[37]

White House spokesman Stephen Early went out of his way to express support for British newspaper reports slamming Wheeler for providing advance warning that the Germans could have exploited to disrupt the operation. FDR asked Carter to find out how Wheeler had learned of the secret plans.[38]

Carter had been digging up dirt on Wheeler for months and sending it to Roosevelt, who passed it on to political operatives working to engineer Wheeler's defeat in the upcoming elections. Carter learned from an informant he'd recruited on Wheeler's staff that the senator had been tipped off about the Iceland expedition from Boston mothers who wrote Wheeler protesting that their sons were being loaded on ships along with equipment for a Polar expedition.

Carter often found that to obtain information Roosevelt had requested, he needed cooperation from government agencies, especially the FBI. This was problematic because he lacked any official standing. Some government officials, especially law enforcement and intelligence professionals, thought he was a crank, and seized on his informal status to justify ignoring Carter. Carter and his operation exemplified characteristics FBI director J. Edgar Hoover detested. A fanatic about discipline and order—he'd turned the FBI into a world-class law-enforcement agency in part by creating one of the world's most efficient filing systems—Hoover despised loose cannons and dilettantes. Even worse for Carter, the FBI director hated criticism. He rarely forgot or forgave a slight, real or imagined, public or private. Carter had a record of insulting the FBI director in ways both real and public.

That record was on Hoover's mind on September 5, 1941, when Carter telephoned his office saying he had just met with the president, who had asked him to bring Munson to meet with the director. To prepare for the meeting, Hoover's staff pulled the columnist's file. The first item was a January 7, 1937, *New York Post* story under the Jay Franklin byline poking fun at the FBI in general and Hoover in particular. Hoover had instilled a vigilance regarding criticism in his subordinates; he must have been pleased to note that without any prompting from Washington, the day after the article was published Special Agent R. C. Hendon had written and placed in the file a three-page memorandum summarizing

Carter's professional career. It concluded that an informant "claimed [Jay] Franklin had an international bias with at least liberal if not radical tendencies."[39]

More recent items in Carter's file included a We, the People column from March 1941 accusing Hoover of attempting to create an American Gestapo and predicting that as a result of congressional investigations into illegal arrests and wiretapping "our No. 1 G-man may become the first American political casualty of World War 2." Carter concluded that Americans "don't want a gang of G-men to go around beating us up and destroying our liberties in the name of high-pressure patriotism."[40]

The columns alone would have been more than enough to turn Hoover against Carter. In addition, Hoover felt that Carter's work for Roosevelt was an incursion into territory that should be reserved for the FBI. If these infractions weren't enough, the improvisational, and in many cases incompetent, style in which Carter ran his operation infuriated Hoover.

Given the trust the president had placed in Carter, Hoover couldn't insult him or refuse to cooperate—at least not until he'd collected some dirt on the upstart. A memo Hoover dictated for the FBI's files immediately after his first meeting with Carter reflected his caution. It noted that Carter and Munson had visited to inform him that Munson was traveling to New York at Roosevelt's request to study the refugee situation. Hoover added that he had informed B. Edwin Sackett, the special agent in charge of the bureau's New York Office, "to be very courteous to Mr. Munson in view of his influential backing."[41] The memo stated that "J. Franklin Carter, who writes under the name of Jay Franklin, has always viewed the FBI as a fascist organization and has stated that we are opposed to liberal thought; therefore, I instructed Mr. Sackett to see that Mr. Munson received as good an impression of the Bureau and its attitude as possible."

Hoover's distaste was of little importance to Carter as long as he had Roosevelt's confidence. The president seemed to enjoy Carter's company and appreciate the boyish enthusiasm the newsman and novelist brought to serious matters. Regardless of his workload, he always found time to talk with Carter, to read and comment on his reports, and to give him oddball assignments that straight-laced military leaders and cabinet officials would have been reluctant to undertake.

Carter didn't wait for Roosevelt to assign him tasks. He sent a never-ending flow of memos to the president consisting largely of voluminous, useless, or absurd intelligence reports, harebrained schemes, and gossip, leavened by occasional nuggets of genuine insight or valuable intelligence. These often included half-baked suggestions for or criticisms of government officials. FDR usually had Tully pass Carter's reports to the head of the relevant government body with a terse note asking them to look into a matter or read one of Carter's memos and return it to the White House. These notes made it clear that although Carter had no official status he enjoyed the president's trust, a fact that led senior government officials to return his calls, meet with him, and at least pretend to collaborate with him.

While most of Carter's voluminous intelligence output was of little or no use beyond providing entertaining diversion for the president, he did produce some valuable information. The country would have been well served if FDR had acted on reports he requested from Carter in the fall of 1941 assessing the loyalty of Japanese living on the West Coast. Roosevelt was very concerned about the threat from fifth columnists, and he knew that Japanese living in California had many reasons to resent the American government. They were subject to prejudice and abuse that was in some ways worse than the treatment of blacks in the South.

Acting on orders from Carter, Munson spent three weeks on the West Coast interviewing FBI agents, military intelligence officials, and people from all walks of life—businessmen, students, fish packers, lettuce pickers, and farmers—to assess the loyalty of the Japanese community.[42]

Rather than restricting himself to the immediate task, assessing whether Japanese Americans posed a security threat, Munson felt it necessary to educate Carter and the president about the Japanese mind and soul. A sentence from a report he sent Carter on October 18, 1941, that was intended to sum up the mentality of Japanese Americans is typical of Munson's muddled approach (and his maddening run-on sentences):

> Take the Shinto religion, Buddist [sic] religion, Christian religion, ancestor worship, family worship, all tied back to sun worship of which the emperor of Japan is the living titular head on earth; add to this the Oriental mind, western business culture, innate politeness and fear; add also the fact that each individual Japanese is playing all by himself in a field the size of the Yale Bowl with his own conscience as umpire, carrying the ball with as much competitive spirit as an American, while the stands— whom he wishes to please—are filled to overflowing with his departed ancestors each of whom is vitally interested and sitting judgement on his personal gyrations; add again a number of other things of varying impor- tance, such as the fact that the Japs are the greatest joiners in the world and have associations for everything to join from "Fixing flowers prop- erly in a bowl" to "War relief for Japanese Soldiers in China."[43]

Munson's memos make it clear that the idea of putting Japanese Americans behind barbed wire was in the air. He argued that because rounding up the Japanese would be relatively easy, it was safe to leave this as a last resort. "In the first place there are not so many people of Japanese descent in the US that in an emergency they could not all be thrown into a concentration camp in 48 hours," Munson wrote. "Of course you might get a few Chinamen too because they sort of look alike. But the looks are a great aid to rounding them up and in keeping them away from sabotage or other troublesome pastimes."[44]

Such extreme measures were, Munson pointed out, unnecessary. "We do not want to throw a lot of American citizens into a concentration camp of course, and especially as the almost unanimous verdict is that in case of war they will keep quiet, very quiet. There will probably be some sabotage by paid Japanese agents and the odd fanatical Jap, but the bulk of these people will be quiet because in addition to being quite contented with the American way of life, they know they are 'in a spot.'"[45]

Despite his racism and fascination with plumbing the depths of the Japanese soul, Munson managed to produce a report that in its conclusions was remarkably prescient. He told FDR that the Japanese in California were "straining every nerve to show their loyalty to the US. The Japs here are in more danger from us than we from them."[46]

Munson's most valuable source was Kenneth Ringle, an Office of Naval Intelligence (ONI) lieutenant commander who had learned to speak Japanese during a three-year posting to Japan. When Munson met him, Ringle had spent over a year spying on the Japanese community in California. His activities included planning and leading a second-story job straight out of a Hollywood movie. One night in the spring of 1941, Ringle drove to the Japanese consulate in Los Angeles and, with police and FBI agents keeping watch outside, broke into the office. Just like in a B-movie, he had sprung a safecracker from prison to help with the caper. The ONI officer carefully removed and photographed every document in the safe, returned them to their original positions, and drove the safecracker back to prison.[47]

The burglary provided ONI and the FBI a comprehensive list of Japanese agents in California and taught American counterintelligence something critically important: the Japanese government distrusted American-born Japanese and was very unlikely to recruit them as intelligence operatives or saboteurs.

Carter presented Munson's findings to FDR in late October, telling the president that "reports from Curtis Munson still confirm the general picture of non-alarmism already reported to you."[48]

Munson's final report from California, delivered to FDR on November 7, 1941, emphasized that while the majority of Japanese were loyal, there were some Japanese intelligence operatives in California. He reported that ONI had 750 to 900 Japanese suspects under surveillance, of whom they thought 150 to 180 "can be classed as really dangerous." The threat of terrorism couldn't be discounted, he noted, as "there are still Japanese in the United States who will tie dynamite around their waist and make a human bomb of themselves . . . but today they are few."[49]

Munson discovered a vulnerability more worrying than the possibility that a handful of Japanese Americans were capable of terrorism or treason. He was "horrified to note that dams, bridges, harbors, power stations etc. are wholly unguarded everywhere."[50] This point, far more than Munson's and Carter's assessment that the vast majority of Japanese Americans were loyal, attracted FDR's attention. Roosevelt's responses to Munson's reports made no mention of his overall conclusion that the vast majority of Japanese were loyal Americans. In a November 11, 1941, "Dear Jack" letter, the president instructed Carter to discuss West Coast security with coordinator of information William Donovan and Hoover "in view of the fact that immediate arrests may be advisable."[51]

After spending several weeks in California, Munson sailed to Hawaii to continue his investigation, leveraging his status as a personal representative of the president to gain access to FBI agents, ONI officers, and other Navy personnel, who were remarkably free with information and opinions. Admiral Harold Stark issued an order granting Munson access to naval intelligence records.

The long, mostly irrelevant reports Munson sent from the Pacific failed to mention the most important conversation he had in Honolulu.

Munson had asked Navy captain Ellis Zacharias, commander of the *Salt Lake City*, a cruiser based at Pearl Harbor, and an expert on Japan, if Japanese residents of Hawaii were likely to mount an armed insurrection in case of war. "Forget about it," Zacharias replied. "Hostilities would commence by an air attack on the fleet, [and] because of the necessity of secrecy on the part of the Japanese, they would not have been able to disseminate the necessary information on which to base an uprising or extensive sabotage."[52]

Zacharias had devoted decades to studying Japanese military strategy and tactics. In 1926, while posted to Washington, he spent long evenings drinking martinis, playing poker, and trying to penetrate the mind of the Japanese naval attaché, Isoroku Yamamoto.[53] Fifteen years later, Yamamoto planned the attack on Pearl Harbor.

Based on his knowledge of Japanese military tactics—sneak attacks were integral to Japanese military doctrine—and conversations he'd had in February 1941 with the Japanese ambassador to the United States, Admiral Kichisaburo Nomura, Zacharias predicted to Munson that a Japanese attack on Pearl Harbor would be launched on a Sunday; that it would happen at a time when three Japanese diplomatic envoys were in Washington; and that the attack would come without warning from the north.

Like Munson, Admiral Husband E. Kimmel, commander-in-chief of the US Pacific Fleet, had heard and disregarded Zacharias's predictions. American planes were parked wingtip to wingtip, maximizing the damage from Japanese bombers.

On December 8, 1941, the day after the attack on Pearl Harbor unfolded precisely as Zacharias had predicted—on a Sunday, from the north, when three Japanese envoys were in Washington—Carter forwarded to FDR a rambling, seventeen-page report from Munson. Roosevelt couldn't possibly have had time to struggle through Munson's musings about the socioeconomic structure of Hawaii. Defense workers who moved to the islands from the mainland, Munson informed the president, "contain the dregs of the waterfront element" and "include many of the 'Okie' class . . . to [whom] any brown-skin is 'Nigger.'"[54] The report is valuable in retrospect, however, because it reveals how ONI's lists of suspected Japanese agents made it possible to neutralize Japanese espionage in Hawaii without resorting to mass arrests.

The Pearl Harbor attack shocked Americans, but it was secretly celebrated by the nation's closest allies. Prime Minister Winston Churchill knew the blow would bring the United States into the war, a goal British intelligence had been pursuing relentlessly for almost two years through an enormous intelligence operation that included covert operatives based in the National Press Building.

Carter and Americans working for the Brits weren't alone in realizing the potential of the Press Building as a base for espionage. As separate conflicts in Europe and Asia merged into World War II, the United

States remained nominally neutral. The Press Building and especially the Press Club came to resemble Humphrey Bogart's Casablanca. Operatives working for Japan, Great Britain, Germany, the Soviet Union (Germany's ally from August 1939 until June 1941), and American intelligence services worked and relaxed in intimate proximity, squeezing together into crowded elevators, passing each other in narrow corridors, and standing elbow-to-elbow in front of the Press Club bar.

CHAPTER SIX

BRITISH SECURITY COORDINATION

In the spring of 1940, as war raged in Europe, Britain launched a vast, covert foreign-intelligence operation in the United States, deploying legal and illegal techniques to subvert America's political institutions and manipulate its news media. British intelligence operatives, including American journalists in the National Press Building, worked to elect candidates who favored US intervention, defeat those who advocated neutrality, and silence or destroy the reputations of American isolationists they considered a menace to British security.

During the desperate year and a half between Dunkirk and Pearl Harbor, British intelligence operated from several outposts in the National Press Building. These included a front company that produced polls engineered to influence rather than assess the opinions of the public, spied on and smeared isolationist members of Congress, and organized and supported organizations of émigrés from neutral and Nazi-occupied countries to press for American intervention. The Press Building was also home to the Washington bureau of a news agency that was subsidized by, and served the interests of, British intelligence. Complementing the efforts of those on London's payroll were a number of reporters and columnists working in the Press Building who, motivated by opposition to fascism and a desire to get the United States into the war as soon as possible, volunteered to serve as clandestine operatives for British intelligence. Scores—perhaps hundreds—of American journalists who believed that fighting fascism justified unethical and, at times, illegal behavior, cooperated with British intelligence in 1940 and '41.

Reporters, including several in the Press Building, infused American newspapers and radio programs with fake news that had been generated in London, and ran pro-intervention lobbying organizations that secretly took directions from British intelligence. They did so because they knew that by shaping public opinion they might change the course of history. Franklin Roosevelt's ability to send food, fuel, and weapons across the Atlantic that were vital to Britain's survival, and ultimately to the security of the United States, hinged on his ability to persuade skeptical Americans and their elected representatives of the wisdom of assistance.

Given the stakes, Britain's intelligence services certainly weren't going to sit by and simply hope for the best. They targeted American public opinion aggressively and tenaciously. The scale and audacity of the British Secret Intelligence Service's (SIS) activities in the United States in the eighteen months prior to Pearl Harbor were without parallel in the history of relations between allied democracies.

British intelligence employed the full range of cloak-and-dagger techniques in America. In addition to recruiting and running espionage agents, covert weapons it unleashed on its closest ally included: forgeries, seductions, burglaries, electoral dirty tricks, physical surveillance, intercepting and reading letters, disrupting public meetings, and illegally bugging offices and tapping phones.[1] Practices that are usually reserved for enemies were employed because the competition for American public opinion was at least as important to the outcome of the fight against fascism as anything that happened on a battlefield. Newspapers and radio programs were the front lines in hard-fought battles to determine whether Americans would back Britain or keep to itself, antagonize or appease Japan, or even help Germany.

American communists, fascists, and isolationists protested bitterly that Britain was manipulating the US media and secretly intervening in elections as part of a campaign to pull America into the war. These accusations, dismissed by liberal politicians and newspaper columnists as paranoid ravings, were inaccurate only in that they were understated. Even the most alarmist commentators and conspiracy mongers underestimated the depth and effectiveness of British covert activity.

The isolationists were right about one thing: While pledging to keep America's sons home, Roosevelt was doing everything he could to prepare the country to intervene in the war. British prime minister Winston Churchill was eager to lend a disguised hand. The task of persuading the president to accept secret assistance from Britain fell to William Stephenson, a Canadian businessman, World War I flying ace and former bantamweight boxer who served as the head of British intelligence in the United States.

The last thing British leaders wanted to do was antagonize or undercut Roosevelt, They knew that sending spies to a friendly country could irritate even the closest ally. Stephenson decided in the spring of 1940 to test the waters. First, he asked a mutual friend, the former heavyweight world boxing champion Gene Tunney, to arrange a meeting with FBI director J. Edgar Hoover. Hoover, a master of bureaucratic knife fighting, told Stephenson that he would be pleased to cooperate with his British counterparts, but under US law any communication between an American government agency and a foreign government would have to be conducted through the State Department. This requirement could be set aside, he noted, only on the personal orders of the president. Employing the bureaucratic version of a wink and a nod, Hoover added that if Stephenson got FDR's okay, "we'll do business directly. Just myself and you. Nobody else gets in the act. Not State, not anyone." Stephenson replied that he would secure the president's endorsement.[2]

To accomplish this, Stephenson sent another athletic emissary, Ernest Cuneo, to query Roosevelt. Cuneo's career had started with stints as a professional football player for the Orange (New Jersey) Tornadoes and the Brooklyn Dodgers, and the sensibilities of the gridiron—intense personal friendships, loyalty to one's team, and ferocious rivalry with opponents—infused his subsequent careers as journalist, consigliere to politicians and pundits, and spook. In 1940 he was an advisor to Roosevelt, attorney for muckraking journalist Drew Pearson and the king of gossip Walter Winchell, and one of the most effective fixers in New Deal Washington.

Roosevelt told Cuneo that he favored "the closest possible marriage between the FBI and British Intelligence."[3] The president used the same expression in a separate conversation with the British ambassador, Lord Lothian. This gave Hoover the green light to work with Stephenson. Remarkably, FDR asked both Cuneo and Lothian to keep the State Department in the dark about the SIS's activities.[4]

Stephenson worked from a base in New York, initially as director of the British Passport Control Office, the traditional cover for the UK's SIS. When the operation became so large that it couldn't plausibly hide under the Passport Control cover, Stephenson turned to Hoover for advice. The FBI director suggested that SIS create a new entity and call it British Security Coordination (BSC). The organization's duties were as vague as its name. By mid-1941, BSC had almost a thousand employees in the United States and another two thousand in Canada, Central America, and South America, making it one of the largest foreign operations British intelligence had ever mounted.

A great deal of information about the BSC is available because Stephenson ordered his staff to write a history of its activities. The account, written in 1945, when memories were fresh, and kept secret until 1999, provides a candid picture of London's espionage and propaganda activities in America.[5]

The BSC history makes it clear that although most of the American reporters and editors who collaborated with BSC to create and disseminate propaganda were not on the British payroll, it isn't an exaggeration to characterize them as British agents. In fact, this is precisely how BSC thought about them. "The conduct of political warfare was entirely dependent on secrecy," notes the BSC history. "For that reason the press and radio men with whom BSC maintained contact were comparable with subagents and the intermediaries with agents. They were thus regarded."[6] Discussing the relationship between reporters and BSC, Edmond Taylor, an American journalist, said that British intelligence agents "connived" with "Americans like myself who were willing to go out of regular (or even legal) channels to try to bend US policy towards objectives that the British, as well as the Americans in question, considered desirable."[7]

One of Stephenson's most pressing objectives in 1940 was to convince Roosevelt to authorize the transfer of superannuated American destroyers to Britain. The destroyers were needed to augment Royal Navy ships that were protecting convoys in the North Atlantic. Sending them would have great symbolic significance, showing the British people that America was standing behind them.

The destroyer deal, and the larger issue of sending American weapons to Britain, was hostage to a conflict between two factions within the US government. One advocated supplying Britain weapons, food, and any other supplies it needed to fight Germany. The other, led by US ambassador to Great Britain Joseph Kennedy, deemed Britain a lost cause and advocated cutting off aid and husbanding resources that would be needed to meet the threat from Germany.

Most of Roosevelt's cabinet and the nation's military leadership supported Kennedy's view. They found it hard to believe that the twenty miles of salt water separating England from France would be an insurmountable barrier to German troops who had occupied most of continental Europe with shocking speed. Military leaders knew the United States was undermanned and completely unprepared to fight a modern war.

The BSC history draws a straight line from planting pro-British stories in the American media to Roosevelt's decision to send destroyers to London. The transfer happened, according to BSC, because Stephenson had "means at his disposal for influencing American public opinion in favour of aid to Britain. In fact, covert propaganda, one of the most potent weapons which BSC employed against the enemy, was harnessed directly to this task."[8]

Two of the BSC's most enthusiastic connivers, a *Chicago Daily News* reporter named Edgar Ansel Mowrer and William "Wild Bill" Donovan, a lawyer, World War I military hero, and friend to FDR, played leading roles in overcoming America's, and Roosevelt's, skepticism about the United Kingdom's ability to hold out against Germany.

The operation started with Stephenson suggesting to Donovan that he visit London on a fact-finding trip for the president. Roosevelt had known Donovan since they were classmates at Columbia Law School, and although Donovan was a Republican, the president trusted him.[9]

Donovan brought the idea to Frank Knox, secretary of the Navy, publisher of the *Chicago Daily News*, and one of the few enthusiastic supporters of Britain in the cabinet. Knox arranged for Donovan to pitch Roosevelt on Stephenson's idea of obtaining an independent assessment of Britain's prospects. Knox offered to provide cover for the trip by arranging for Mowrer, the most talented journalist on the *Daily News* staff, to accompany Donovan and by commissioning the pair to write a series of stories based on their trip. Roosevelt readily agreed.[10]

Mowrer had a thirst for adventure, a deep hatred for fascism, and a strong affinity for secret intelligence and espionage tradecraft. Fearless reporting from Berlin earned him a Pulitzer Prize in 1933; it also gave him bragging rights as the first American reporter to be thrown out of Nazi Germany. Getting expelled by dictators became a habit. Mussolini forced Mowrer to leave Rome in 1936, and Stalin booted him out of Moscow the next year. Mowrer continued reporting on Europe's descent into barbarism from Paris, fleeing in June 1940 just ahead of the German army.[11]

Explaining their mission to Mowrer, Donovan told the reporter that "at Knox's request he and I were to collect and publish information on the 'Fifth Column' activities which had so helped the Germans in Norway, Poland, Belgium, France. What were the British and Americans doing about the problem? Beyond this, however, lay [our] real assignment—finding out for President Roosevelt the thing he most needed to know: would and could the British hold out against the Germans?"[12]

"Knox knew of my intimacy with members of the Churchill government," Mowrer recalled. "As a newsman I could legitimately poke my nose into everything and ask indiscreet questions."[13]

On July 15, 1940, Donovan telephoned his wife with the news that he was leaving on a secret mission of indefinite duration to a location that he could not disclose. The next day, Stephenson triumphantly cabled Sir Stewart Menzies, head of the SIS: "Colonel William J. Donovan personally representing President, left yesterday by Clipper," the transatlantic flying boat. Donovan's dramatic exit was marred by a leak to the press. Mrs. Ruth Donovan, and anyone else who cared, learned the next day from the *New York Times* that her husband had traveled to London on an undisclosed mission.[14]

The Brits pulled out the stops for Donovan, arranging an audience with King George VI and Queen Elizabeth, dinner with Churchill, briefings by Menzies, and a tour of the code-breaking campus at Bletchley Park, the crown jewel of British intelligence, as well as meetings with George Orwell and other prominent intellectuals. Everything was choreographed to showcase the determination, grit, and ingenuity of the British people, and to create the not-entirely-accurate impression that the country was well prepared to repulse an invasion.

Mowrer was given similar, if less flashy, treatment. He was appalled by the lack of military preparations for the invasion that everyone believed was coming, but this perception was outweighed in his mind by Churchill's steely determination. During his month in England, Mowrer filed only one story. The Vichy government couldn't be trusted and the only Frenchmen the United States should support were those "fighting, or ready to fight, against Nazi Germany," he told Americans.[15] Behind the scenes, Mowrer interceded on Charles de Gaulle's behalf with Churchill, urging the prime minister to recognize the prickly general as the leader of France. Before leaving London, Mowrer and Donovan agreed on their message to Roosevelt: "Britain under Churchill would not surrender either to ruthless air raids or to an invasion."[16]

Having been persuaded that with enough American support Britain could hold off the Germans, and determined to do everything he could to increase the flow of weapons, food, and fuel across the Atlantic, Donovan boarded a camouflaged British flying boat on August 3. He arrived in

New York the following day and was greeted by a *New York Times* reporter who had clearly been briefed on the mission. The paper reported that Donovan "denied he had discussed the possibility of turning over old destroyers in this country to England and he declined to discuss the war conditions in England."[17]

Stephenson cabled London: "Donovan greatly impressed by visit and reception ... has strongly urged our case re destroyers ... is doing much to combat defeatist attitude in Washington by stating positively and convincingly that we shall win."[18]

Donovan joined Roosevelt on a driving vacation across New England, spending two days touring, picnicking, and bending the president's ear about the need to support Britain.[19]

Mowrer made his way back to the United States in less spectacular fashion. By August he was at the *Chicago Daily News* office in Washington, in the Colorado Building, a block from the National Press Building. He frequented the Press Club and spoke on NBC radio's "National Press Club Forum" broadcasts. While serving as the *Daily News* bureau chief, Mowrer devoted all of his time and talent to overt and covert attempts to hasten United States engagement in the fight against fascism.[20]

Mowrer's first byline from Washington, on August 19, 1940, was shared with Donovan. An introductory note written by Knox explained that it was the beginning of a series that was being "made public by secretary of Navy Frank Knox in connection with the national defense program." Knox wrote that it was a "most thoroughgoing survey of German 'fifth column' methods used in weakening resistance of possible enemies and undermining the morale of countries they propose to attack." To maximize their impact, Knox offered the articles free to competing papers. Hundreds, including the *New York Times* and the *Washington Post*, accepted the offer, ensuring that Americans from all walks of life read them. Anyone who didn't read the stories may have heard Donovan discuss them on the first national radio broadcast featuring a speaker other than the president.[21]

The articles painted a wildly exaggerated picture of the effectiveness and scope of Nazi subversion, claiming that Germany spent $200 million annually on foreign propaganda, a figure that was a figment of the SIS's imagination. The critical point, which Donovan and Mowrer pounded into their readers, was that Germany's success in decimating its neighbors' armies and occupying almost all of Europe save the British Isles was the result not of superior military strategy, technology or training. Instead, they attributed the victories to years of psychological warfare and legions of fifth columnists—threats they said had been recognized and neutralized in the United Kingdom, making it far less vulnerable than its continental neighbors.[22]

"No amount of genius would have accomplished what the Germans accomplished in so short a time without . . . the Germans abroad and sympathizers in the victim countries," the first article in the Donovan/Mowrer series explained.[23]

Donovan and Mowrer made fanciful claims that Hitler, who in fact had given little thought to the United States, was plotting to use German Americans as an advance force that would help turn the United States into a "Nazi Gau," or state. "It is safe to say that a very fair proportion of the non-refugee Germans who have become American since Hitler came to power did so with the secret intention of turning free and democratic America into 'their'—that is, Hitler's, America," they wrote.[24]

"It is conceivable that the United States possesses the finest Nazi-schooled Fifth Column in the world, one which, in case of war with Germany, could be our undoing,"[25] Mowrer and Donovan told their readers. It was conceivable—but there wasn't a shred of evidence behind the assertion, which turned out to be wrong.

In early September FDR informed Congress—he did not seek its approval—that the US government had agreed to exchange American destroyers for leases on British bases in the Caribbean, a move that he called "the most important action in the reinforcement of our national defense that has been taken since the Louisiana Purchase."[26]

Coming in the heat of an election campaign that hinged on the president's ability to persuade Americans that he would keep the nation out of war, the destroyers-for-bases deal, which effectively made the United States a nonbelligerent ally of Britain, was a bold step. It was particularly remarkable because more was at stake than losing an election. The legal basis for bypassing Congress was so weak that Roosevelt believed he was risking impeachment.[27]

Roosevelt had been emboldened to release the destroyers by reports that American public opinion had shifted over the summer, swinging from a strong belief that German domination of Europe, including Great Britain, was inevitable to a conviction that, with sufficient American assistance, Britain could hold on. BSC believed this shift was a decisive factor in Donovan's success in persuading Roosevelt to agree to the destroyers-for-bases deal—and that British propaganda, especially the Donovan/Mowrer articles, had been responsible for changing Americans' attitudes.

Convinced that Donovan had immense influence with Roosevelt, and that he was a completely reliable friend, the British government bolstered his standing with the president. Stephenson had been maneuvering behind the scenes for months for FDR to create a centralized intelligence service and to put Donovan in charge of it. This work culminated in a meeting held at the White House at 12:30 p.m. on June 18, 1941, between Donovan, Knox, and FDR at which Donovan was put in charge of a new organization, the Office of the Coordinator of Information, and charged with overseeing all of the US government's intelligence activities. Soon after leaving the White House, Donovan briefed Stephenson on the meeting, and the next day Stephenson sent an encrypted telegram describing the conversation to Menzies.

"Bill [Donovan] saw the President today and after long discussion wherein all points were agreed he accepted the appointment," Stephenson wrote. "He will be co-ordinator of all forms of Intelligence and will control all departments including offensive operations . . ." Donovan, who was given the rank of major general, reported directly to Roosevelt.

"Bill accuses me of having 'intrigued and driven' him into appointment," Stephenson reported. "You can imagine how relieved I am after three months of battling and jockeying for position at Washington that 'our man' is in a position of such importance to our efforts."[28]

The office of Coordinator of Information was a British idea, according to Cuneo, who was involved in its creation. "It was conceived by Stephenson as an American solution to British problems in the Western hemisphere," Cuneo wrote in an unpublished memoir. Stephenson had persuaded Donovan "in the interests of the common defense of Western civilization, to build an American intelligence agency which would assist him in carrying on his covert and clandestine operations in the Western hemisphere." The Office of the Coordinator of Information was later expanded into the Office of Strategic Services (OSS), which formed the basis for the CIA.[29]

Mowrer stayed in close touch with Donovan and conducted at least one secret overseas mission for the Coordinator of Information. In August 1941, Donovan asked him to travel to East Asia on a mission similar to their trip to London. "Knox will provide a letter identifying you as his personal representative, but you will pass as a newspaper correspondent just as you did in England," Donovan told him.[30]

Mowrer visited Singapore, Java, Thailand, Burma, and China. Everywhere he was told Japanese invasion was inevitable and imminent. The only disagreements were about the route: some were confident Tokyo's target was Siberia, while others told Mowrer war would come first to the Philippines and Southeast Asia. One American government official even predicted a Japanese sneak attack on Pearl Harbor and a simultaneous invasion of the Philippines. Like the American military, Mowrer failed to pluck this strand from the tangle of rumor and deception that contributed to America's costly intelligence failure.[31]

Mowrer wasn't the only journalist who participated in BSC's multidimensional project to persuade FDR to release destroyers or its larger campaign to influence American views about the war. British intelligence also supported the activities of an informal network called the Century Group, which played a pivotal role in the destroyers-for-bases deal.[32] Named after a private club in New York where it held many of its meetings, the Century Group consisted of about three dozen highly placed individuals who decided in the summer of 1940 to dedicate themselves to three goals: persuading the public to support "all aid short of war" to Britain, including the transfer of destroyers; publicly combating isolationists; and advocating government actions that would inevitably result in the United States' joining the war.[33]

The Century Group's Washington operations were run by Ulric Bell, an old-school, hard-drinking newspaperman, from a Press Building suite across the hall from John Franklin Carter's office. Bell, a former National Press Club president who had been among the small group of Press Club members who guaranteed the original construction loans for the Press Building, was the Washington bureau chief for the *Louisville Courier-Journal*. Little of his reporting in 1940 and 1941 made it into print, and that was fine with the paper's publisher, Barry Bingham Sr. Bingham paid Bell's salary and expenses while encouraging him to work full time for the Century Group and for other pro-intervention groups with close links to British intelligence. Years later, Bingham forged a close relationship with the CIA.[34]

Unlike most of BSC's American operatives, Bell met directly with British intelligence officers and diplomats. He believed that American and British interests were indistinguishable and that the best way to help his own country was to work on behalf of a foreign government, including by acting as an intermediary between BSC and the White House. Bell was on friendly terms with President Roosevelt.[35] He was also a close friend of FDR's press secretary, Steve Early, and of General Edwin "Pa" Watson, the president's friend and military aide, and schemed with both to nudge the president and the country closer to intervening in the war. At Bell's request, Early assigned White House typists to compile mailing lists for the Century Group based on pro-interventionist correspondence that had been sent to the White House. Bell and other leaders of the Century Group, and a larger group that it spawned, were in daily touch with Roosevelt's speech writer, Robert Sherwood.[36]

The White House was happy to have the Century Group pushing for intervention—as long as the president's fingerprints weren't evident. On one occasion, concerned that FDR might take offense at a planned article criticizing him for being timid in backing Britain, Bell brought the draft text to the White House and handed it to the president. Roosevelt, according to one of his advisors, "read it, and then—cocking his cigarette holder at a jaunty angle—turned to Bell. 'If you're going to give me hell,' he said, 'why not use some really strong language? You know, pusillanimous isn't such a bad word.'"[37]

Bell and other members of the Century Group operated as covert liaisons between the British government and the American press, providing leaks and disinformation generated by BSC to friendly reporters and columnists. The Century Group also conducted delicate, secret negotiations between the Republican presidential candidate, Wendell Willkie, and FDR. The connection to Willkie, who had put his election at risk by tacitly supporting FDR's efforts to prepare the United States for war, was to prove critical to getting the destroyers deal done.[38]

Willkie was probably unaware of the attention and resources BSC devoted to smoothing the path for him to gain the Republican nomination. The Brits wanted Roosevelt to win, but they hedged their bets by trying to ensure that if a Republican replaced him the White House wouldn't be home to an isolationist. Part of the strategy was to marginalize Republican leaders who wanted to cast the GOP as the "peace party."[39]

On June 25, the second day of the GOP's national convention, the *New York Herald* reported that a poll found that three-fifths of the delegates supported helping the allies "with everything short of war."[40] The result was a surprise given the strong isolationist streak in the Republican Party. The story reported that the poll had been "conducted by Market Analysts, Inc., an independent research organization." It didn't reveal that Market Analysts had organized and phrased its questions in a manner that was designed to make the case for intervention and to exclude the possibility of opposing increased assistance to Britain. For example, delegates were asked "If you think we are endangered, do you favor our helping the Allies with everything a) short of war; b) would you declare war now; or c) send navy or air force units to Europe." While the *Herald* positioned the results as a strong show of support for aiding Britain, in fact the majority picked the answer that was least interventionist. They were not given the option to suggest that the United States withhold assistance. Market Analysts didn't reveal the premise of the question, or that only 0.7 percent of those surveyed favored a declaration of war.[41]

In fact, contrary to the *Herald* story, Market Analysts was anything but independent. It was run for the BSC by Sanford "Sandy" Griffith, an American who had worked for British intelligence since the late 1930s. His experience included serving in the French and US armies in World War I and as a *Wall Street Journal* reporter in London. Griffith returned to New York in the late 1920s, turned his hand to selling securities, and, accused of swindling his clients, avoided jail by the skin of his teeth. He operated Market Analysts from an office in New York City that housed several other BSC operations.[42]

Griffith hired an experienced covert operator, Francis Henson, as his right-hand man. Henson had a colorful background, which included working in Europe to rescue refugees who were fleeing Nazi Germany and a job in Detroit trying to flush communists out of the United Auto Workers union.[43]

Henson worked undercover for Griffith in 1940 and 1941 from the eleventh floor of the National Press Building. Sometimes Henson said he worked for Market Analysts; on occasion he presented himself as an employee of a fictitious company called "Information, Incorporated." Letterhead advertised Information, Inc.'s ability to provide "Confidential Research for the Facts You Seek," and directed correspondence to "Mr. Francis A. Henson, Regional Director, Washington Research Division, 1196 National Press Building, Washington, D.C." The stationary conjured images of a well-appointed office. The reality was less grand. Henson rented a desk in a room with two reporters and a representative of the Bible Truth Seekers Foundation.[44]

One of Henson's many jobs for Griffith and BSC was conducting public opinion surveys, like the poll taken at the Republican National Convention that appeared to show strong support for aiding Britain. Many of these polls were aimed at influencing politicians.[45]

In a resume written in 1948, Henson recounted that his job from 1940 to 1942 "was to use the results of our polls, taken among their constituents, to convince on-the-fence Congressmen and Senators that they should favor more aid to Britain."[46] Market Analysts' polling results always supported British goals. Henson and Griffith accomplished this by asking questions like those posed at the Republican convention that were crafted to elicit the desired responses, by carefully selecting the individuals whose opinions were solicited while pretending that they had been chosen at random, and by suppressing any results that didn't come out as intended.

William Allen White, a respected voice in the Republican Party who headed a pro-intervention group called the William Allen White Committee, had commissioned the poll of delegates to the Republican convention. He wrote in a newspaper column that it had been "carefully and rather expensively made . . . by a professional group of interviewers."[47] The column, which was printed in the *Boston Globe* and other newspapers across the country, cited the poll as evidence of the delegates' opposition to Hitler, as well as their eagerness to bolster American defenses and to forge an economic alliance with Central and South American nations against Germany. White argued that the survey results demonstrated that Willkie, a former Democrat who felt that "America's first line of defense is Great Britain," best represented the Republican Party's views.[48]

It isn't clear whether BSC's assistance was decisive, but Willkie, who did not campaign in the primaries, went into the convention an underdog and—to London's delight and the astonishment of the Republican establishment—emerged as the GOP candidate.

Henson and Griffith were also deployed to the Democratic convention in July.

Newspapers stories based on their polling reported that more than 90 percent of "advance guard delegates" favored sending aid to Britain, and after the convention was underway 86 percent of an unspecified number of delegates felt that Britain's defeat would endanger America, and 45 percent believed that if Hitler conquered Britain, he would immediately attack the United States. The poll was intended to show that rank-and-file Democrats were more inclined to go to war to prevent the defeat of Great Britain than the men who wrote the party's platform, which pledged that the United States "will not participate in foreign wars, and we will not send our army, naval or air forces to fight in foreign lands outside of the Americas, except in case of attack."[49]

The White Committee declared in a press release that "a wide disparity exists between the Democratic Platform and the opinions of the individual delegates, as revealed in a very complete poll."[50]

In addition to their polling work at the Democratic convention, Henson and Griffith posed as representatives of Information, Inc., handing out business cards with Henson's Press Building address and interviewing delegates who were promoting pacifism. The interviews, which were forward to Cuneo, were intended to help BSC develop propaganda to counter pacifist arguments.[51]

Although they worked to solidify Democratic support, the BSC's operatives devoted far more attention to Republicans in the summer of 1940 as part of an all-out push to keep the destroyers-for-bases deal alive. Willkie supported FDR's foreign-policy goals, but he also wanted to win the election, so the White House couldn't assume that he would acquiesce to sending American ships to Britain without congressional approval. Even a hint that Willkie might accuse Roosevelt of overstepping his authority could have scuttled the deal. As the first president to snub George Washington's precedent of voluntarily stepping aside after two terms, Roosevelt was vulnerable to accusations that he was behaving like a dictator. He also knew that while the public was split about the merits of helping Great Britain, most Americans wanted to stay out of the war, and that Congress wouldn't agree to transferring destroyers to Britain.

Bell worked behind the scenes with other members of the Century Group to persuade Willkie to endorse the transfer, or at a minimum to adopt a neutral attitude toward it. On August 30, Bell and other members of the group gathered at the Hay-Adams House, Washington's most luxurious hotel, awaiting news from their contacts in the Republican campaign. They received two telephone calls that afternoon from Willkie's aides conveying the candidate's promise not to criticize the destroyer deal. Bell wasted no time in conveying the news to the White House. The president, assured that he wouldn't pay a devastating political price, announced the deal at a press conference four days later.[52]

BSC's championing of Willkie was exceptional. Most of its interventions were intended to destroy rather than build political careers.

CHAPTER SEVEN

FRYING FISH AND FIXING FRANKS

Engineered polls at the Republican and Democratic conventions were the opening salvos in an extraordinary campaign BSC waged in 1940 and 1941 against isolationist politicians. British intelligence intervened in American elections with an intensity and employing methods that no foreign government had ever attempted. BSC agents based in the National Press Building were central players in the drama.

Hamilton Stuyvesant Fish III, a New York Republican and leading isolationist who had represented residents of the Hudson Valley in Congress since 1920, was at the top of the British hit list. Removing a politician who threatened American support for Britain was far more important to BSC than respecting the will of his constituents.

To dig Fish's political grave, BSC created and funded the Non-Partisan Committee to Defeat Hamilton Fish. It operated from the same New York City address as Market Analysts Inc. and other fronts for British intelligence. Like the faux polling firm, the committee was run by Sandy Griffith and Francis Henson. In October 1940 Henson traveled from his Press Building office to Poughkeepsie, New York, where he set up a war room in the Campbell Hotel. In addition to pulling a thorn from the British government's side, the campaign against Fish was intended to "put the fear of God into every isolationist senator and congressman in the country," one of Henson's comrades told a potential financial contributor.[1] In a letter to Cuneo dated October 18, 1940, Henson wrote that because there was "a very good chance of . . . putting Fish on ice," he and

Griffith planned to remain in Poughkeepsie working on the campaign until election day.[2] The Democratic Party, which did not consider Fish vulnerable, put almost no resources into the race, so for the most part the campaign against a sitting member of Congress was led by British operatives.

The Non-Partisan Committee engineered a series of dirty tricks. For example, Henson and Griffith manufactured a tale about Fish renting property to German Nazis who paid him inflated rents as a covert bribe.[3] In a classic "October surprise," Drew Pearson and Robert Allen, acting in concert with Cuneo, reported the story in their Washington Merry-Go-Round column on October 21, just a few weeks before the election. They were fortunate that Fish decided against following through on threats to sue them for libel.[4]

Henson and Griffith also circulated a photo that appeared to show Fish meeting with the "American Hitler," Fritz Kuhn. The leader of the German American Bund was serving a jail sentence at the time for embezzlement. The caption asked "Voters of Dutchess, Orange and Putnam Counties is Hamilton Fish Pro-Nazi?" Contrary to the impression created by the photo, Fish had never met privately with Kuhn. The photo had been taken in 1938 at a congressional hearing.[5]

Fish was reelected by 9,000 votes, half the margin he'd had in 1938. In an after-action report to Cuneo, Griffith wrote: "Francis [Henson] probably reported to you on the Hamilton Fish fight. Our size-up of the situation was correct—that $2,000 or $3,000 additional a week or two ahead would have been sufficient to put it over. The local Democratic machine in the district was of practically no help." Griffith also sent Cuneo a four-page memo with recommendations for the best methods to beat Fish and other congressmen in the future. His pointers included avoiding all appearance of a centralized campaign, the need to make planned attacks seem spontaneous, and the importance of keeping "in the background any protests emanating from New York City, and protests from Jewish and foreign groups." Covert campaigns should take care to "tie-in attacks with current events. Study, and where necessary create, incidents which give sufficient news pegs on which to hang a story." He also recommended actions in Washington, including pinning "on the pro-Nazi and obstructionist labels" and cooperating "with the Administration and hostile colleagues to assure their ganging up on Fish whenever he obstructs."[6]

Henson and Griffith weren't the only assets BSC deployed against Fish. In spring 1940, British intelligence threw out a net that ultimately snared Fish, two dozen other isolationist members of Congress, and to the delight of the White House linked the America First Committee to Nazi Germany.

The story started when a man named Henry Hoke became curious and, as he investigated, furious about pro-Nazi propaganda that was flowing through the mail to hundreds of thousands of Americans. Hoke, publisher of *The Reporter of Direct Mail Advertising*, took an interest in the techniques that were used to target and disseminate the propaganda.[7]

In May 1940 Hoke published a story in *The Reporter* revealing that the German Library of Information sent a pro-Nazi publication, *Facts in Review*, every week to 90,000 ministers, school teachers, legislators, and publishers. Hoke detailed other German-financed propaganda activities, such as an initiative by the German Railroads Information Office to send "about 40,000 weekly mimeographed bulletins to hotel managers, travel agencies, stock brokers, bankers, and small businessmen" that were intended to "convince Americans that the Nazi system of doing business was *best*." The Postmaster General should prevent foreign governments from using the US mail to distribute propaganda, Hoke demanded.[8]

The article also reported that individuals on the German Library mailing list were "receiving reprints from the *Congressional Record*, mailed under a Congressman's frank, containing Nazi-phrased and Nazi-inspired material which followed the line of editorials appearing in *Facts in Review*." The "frank" Hoke referred to was a privilege extended to all members of Congress to send an unlimited amount of mail at no cost on envelopes that bore their printed signatures instead of postage stamps. Such envelopes were supposed to be used exclusively for communications sent by a member of Congress, such as the *Congressional Record*, an official government periodical that publishes congressional speeches and debates.[9]

Hoke's story garnered a small amount of attention in left-wing newspapers but didn't make a major splash. The waves were strong enough, however, to come to the attention of BSC, which, sensing an opportunity to disrupt a Nazi subversion operation and embarrass isolationist politicians, provided Hoke undercover investigators and funding. Before long, BSC's Griffith in New York and Henson in the National Press Building were supporting what had become a personal crusade for Hoke. Two other BSC collaborators in the National Press Building, Bell, who had become a leader of a BSC-aligned group called Fight for Freedom, and one of Fight for Freedom's members, Washington Merry-Go-Round columnist Robert S. Allen, also helped investigate and publicize what became known as the congressional franking scandal.[10]

BSC had infiltrated the German Library's staff, so it was a simple matter to arrange for the insertion of phony names at BSC-monitored addresses onto its mailing list. Soon letters containing reprints of the *Congressional Record* with speeches that would have warmed Joseph Goebbels's heart started showing up at these addresses. The letters were sent postage-free under the franks of more than two dozen members of Congress. American taxpayers were footing the bill for the dissemination of German propaganda.[11]

BSC determined that addresses on the franked envelopes were printed using an antiquated duplicating machine, and found that the Steuben Society, a Nazi organization in New York, owned one of the few working models of the machine. It obtained confidential bulletins issued by the society and learned not only that the envelopes were printed on the society's duplicating machine, but also that the group was inviting its members to come to meetings where they could pick up speeches by isolationist senators Burton Wheeler and Gerald Nye in franked envelopes to mail to their friends.[12]

BSC and Hoke had uncovered part of the story, but they had not learned how the *Congressional Record* reprints and franked envelopes ended up in the hands of the Steuben Society. They got a break when a representative of the Order of the Purple Heart wrote to Hoke complaining that his article had incorrectly accused the veteran's organization of sending propaganda to its members in franked envelopes. BSC looked into the matter and determined that the Order had been falsely accused. The investigation also uncovered a very interesting bit of news. The Order's "Commander" in Washington was a WWI veteran named George Hill who worked as a personal secretary for Representative Fish.

BSC zeroed in on Hill. It either had sources in place on Capitol Hill capable of keeping a close eye on Fish's offices or quickly recruited them. Henson was almost certainly involved in this aspect of the operation. The Brits also targeted Hill with an agent identified in British intelligence reports as "a very capable female operator."[13] She extracted information from Hill about his background, associates, and financial situation.

The sleuthing revealed that Hill had accumulated wealth far beyond the level that could be obtained as a secretary to a member of Congress. BSC figured out that Hill was running an elaborate and lucrative scam that linked unwitting members of Congress to Nazi propagandists.

Hill's enterprise was based on an intimate knowledge of Capitol Hill procedures. He knew that members of Congress routinely stood up on the floor of the House or Senate and asked for unanimous consent, which was always granted, to have written remarks inserted into the *Congressional Record*.

Hill had cultivated a group of female secretaries on Capitol Hill who, in exchange for small gifts, arranged to have their bosses insert speeches into the *Record* that Hill had supplied. Although the congressmen were listed as authors, they rarely read them. The speeches coincided with their isolationist beliefs, so they didn't recoil on the rare occasions when they did skim the text.

Acting in his capacity as Fish's secretary, Hill sent orders to the Government Printing Office for thousands of reprints of the speeches and paid for them at the official rate, which was less than a third of the cost of commercial printing. He then sold them at a hefty markup to organizations like America First and the McWilliams Anti-Semitic League. If these groups knew Hill was profiting on the arrangement, they wouldn't object because he provided the reprints in franked, unaddressed envelopes, thus saving the groups the cost of postage.[14]

Hill used his relationships with the secretaries of isolationist members of Congress, and his knowledge of their postal habits, to create a related business. Senators and representatives receive massive amounts of mail from constituents. Sorting and replying to constituent mail is still a major activity in every congressional office. In those days the common practice was to reply to as much mail as possible as soon as it arrived and to destroy the vast majority of incoming correspondence within a day or two. This was an act of self-preservation: so much mail arrived on Capitol Hill that retaining a week's worth would have created a fire hazard, and the legislative branch would have drowned in the mail accumulated in a month.

Instead of destroying them, Hill persuaded the secretaries to set aside mounds of letters from constituents who had expressed pro-isolationist sentiments. He had bags of these letters delivered to an office where eight women typed the return addresses on notecards. Hill had the cards duplicated and sold the resulting mailing lists to the same organizations that bought the speeches.[15]

BSC brought the fruits of its investigation to the attention of the FBI, but the bureau expressed little interest in pursuing a case. BSC had more luck persuading a sympathetic federal prosecutor to convene a grand jury to investigate illegal franking.[16] The grand jury sent a subpoena to one of Hill's associates requesting that he turn over copies of *Congressional Record* speeches in franked envelopes. The associate panicked and called Hill demanding that he immediately pick up twenty sacks of franked mail.

BSC operatives were watching as a truck marked "US House of Representatives" picked up the sacks and delivered them to Fish's office, not to his storehouse as Hill had instructed. The secretary who met the delivery man knew what was in the sacks, and it was her turn to panic. The deliveryman refused her adamant demands to remove all of the bags, and after a heated argument agreed to take all but eight of them to the address she provided—the Washington office of the America First committee.

A BSC operative, possibly Henson or someone working for him, called the Federal Marshal's office to report the location of the subpoenaed mail sacks. The operative also tipped off a *Washington Post* reporter who observed the Marshals' raid on America First, and then raced back to Capitol Hill where he poked around in the sacks that had been left outside Fish's office. A breathless description of the escapade made it onto the front page of the *Post* and was picked up by newspapers around the country.[17]

A secret report BSC sent to London in May 1941 noted that the delivery mix up and raid were "our opportunity to see that Hamilton Fish's office, and therefore George Hill, as Fish's Secretary, got into the newspapers." The BSC report added that "most of the stories printed in the newspapers are only partially true as we only gave them sufficient [information] to drag Hill's name before the public and the appropriate Washington authorities."[18]

Pro-intervention newspapers seized on the opportunities to run headlines linking Fish to the Nazis. A *Washington Post* story ran under the banner "8 Bags of Evidence in Nazi Probe 'Turn Up' at Rep. Fish's Bin in House Storeroom," while the leftwing *PM* plastered "Ham Fish Snatches Evidence Wanted in US Nazi Hunt." In an hour-long speech to the House, Fish asserted his ignorance of Hill's activities and denied any connection to Nazis or tolerance for anti-Semitism.[19]

Although BSC spun the news to reporters in a way that made Fish look culpable, in its internal report it acknowledged that it had painted him as an active participant in the scandal when in fact he had been an unwittingly victim. The congressman's public remarks about the affair were "ridiculous, due no doubt to the fact that Fish simply doesn't know what he is talking about and did not wish to know what had been going on right under his nose," the BSC report noted. BSC's assessment accurately predicted "that the case will develop into the biggest scandal Washington has had in many years."[20]

Tying the bow on the box, BSC revealed to the press and the Department of Justice that the speeches Hill had arranged for isolationist members of Congress to insert in the *Congressional Record* had been written by George Viereck, a well-known Nazi propagandist who had registered with the State Department as an agent of the German government. The connection to Viereck seemed to validate Roosevelt's assertions that America First, which was distributing the speeches, was a Nazi front. Stories linking the Nazi propagandist to America First tarnished the group's reputation, alienating isolationists who wanted nothing to do with Nazis.

BSC's friends in the press, including reporters in the Press Building office of the *New York Herald Tribune*, as well as Pearson and Allen, ran with the story, taking care to mention Fish, who denied all knowledge or involvement. BSC's sleuthing and the publicity led the Justice Department to indict Viereck for failing to report his Nazi ghost writing activities on foreign agent registration forms.[21]

BSC's staff took complete credit for the franking scandal. "In May 1940 we first claimed there was a 'tie-up' between the Nazi Propaganda Organization in the United States the postal 'Franking' privilege of members of Congress of the United States. Recent indictments of George Sylvester Viereck, and George Hill (secretary to Congressman Hamilton Fish) have been the direct results of our efforts to expose the 'tie-up,'" BSC boasted in a report to London.[22]

BSC continued to chase Fish. For example, in September 1941 it obtained a franked envelope from his office and stuffed it with anti-Semitic literature, including excerpts from the notorious and libelous *Protocols of the Elders of Zion*. A BSC operative wrote "Fight for Jewdom" above Fight for Freedom's address on the envelope and dropped it into a mailbox. Despite Fish's honest assertions that it was a fabrication, *PM* newspaper ran a story with photographs of the envelope and its contents.[23]

Even after America's declarations of war against Japan and Germany rendered them toothless, British intelligence didn't give isolationist politicians any peace. In October 1942, Griffith and Henson arranged another October surprise for Fish. A Washington Merry-Go-Round column falsely accused the congressman of accepting $3,100 from German propagandists in the Romanoff Caviar company. Fish managed to hang on by a fingernail, winning the election by 4,000 out of 100,000 votes cast.[24]

Two years later, after twenty-four years in Congress, Fish was defeated by a liberal Democrat. In his concession speech, the Republican said his loss "should be largely credited to Communistic and Red forces from New York City backed by a large slush fund probably exceeding $250,000." A few weeks later he claimed it had taken "most of the New Deal Administration, half of Moscow, $400,000, and Governor Dewey to defeat me." As BSC's secret history crowed: "He might—with more accuracy—have blamed BSC."[25]

Fish, one of the strongest voices against coming to Britain's assistance, was on the wrong side of history. Policies he advocated would have made America disastrously unprepared for war. On the other hand, contrary to BSC's slurs, there is no evidence that he was either an anti-Semite or a Nazi sympathizer. The fact that a foreign government led a years-long effort to trick New York voters into voting against Fish does not make him a more sympathetic figure, but it also doesn't burnish the reputation of British intelligence or the Americans who helped it. Whatever their feelings for Fish, most of his constituents, and Americans across the country, would have been outraged if they had learned that a foreign government had conspired to engineer his defeat.

Frying Fish was far from an isolated incident.

CHAPTER EIGHT
ZAPPING ZAPP

BSC recruited some of America's most prominent journalists and columnists, including several in the National Press Building, to disseminate truths, half-truths, and outright lies as part of Britain's attempts to sway American public opinion and deceive Nazi Germany. Still, the pages of American newspapers remained contested territory for much of 1941.

In spring 1941 Bill Donovan warned BSC's William Stephenson that the two German news agencies, DNB and Transocean News Service, were being far more effective than the British in setting the tone of American press coverage of the war. At the end of April 1941 Stephenson sent a coded cable to Menzies noting that over the previous fortnight there had been an "almost complete failure to prevent Axis monopoly of war news coverage" in US newspapers. "Axis news reports reach here more quickly than ours, and Transocean and DNB keep the flow and build up stories even in quiet periods." Stephenson and his allies were determined to undermine the credibility of the German news agencies, especially Transocean, and if possible to prevent them from sending news to or operating in the United States.[1]

When it was founded in 1914, Transocean News Service was a legitimate news service, a German version of Reuters or Associated Press. After Hitler took power it portrayed itself as being independent of both the German government and the Nazi party. By 1939, when it opened its US headquarters in New York and a Washington bureau in the National Press Building, Transocean was, in fact, an arm of Joseph Goebbels's Ministry of Propaganda and Public Enlightenment, which wrote much of its copy. German intelligence officers working under diplomatic cover in the Washington embassy handled Transocean's US business affairs and helped direct its efforts to influence public opinion throughout the Americas. It used journalism as a cover for espionage, and traded on its pre-Nazi reputation to persuade newspapers to print Nazi propaganda.[2]

Transocean's US operations were headed by a small man adorned with an extravagant mustache and an electric name, Manfred Zapp. Zapp lived in style in the Waldorf Astoria Hotel in Manhattan and also had a home in the Washington suburbs. A Federal Communications Commission counterintelligence team that pioneered radio-monitoring technology targeted his house in a unsuccessful effort to catch him sending clandestine radio signals to Germany.[3]

It must have irritated Zapp's Washington correspondent, Tom Davis, every morning when he had to walk past the offices of the Jewish Telegraph Agency to reach Transocean's office in suite 1092 of the National Press Building. Davis and Zapp tried to integrate into the routines of Washington correspondents, but were only grudgingly accepted by the press corps. Press Club members advised Roosevelt, who habitually made off-the-record remarks during press conferences, to be on guard when German reporters were present. US State Department officials pressured American reporters to shun job offers from Transocean, and reporters harassed stringers when their connection to the news service came to light.[4]

Zapp frequented the Press Club, where members remembered him as "an inconspicuous little man trying to make friends."[5] He didn't make many. Curiously, while he lived in luxury, Zapp was habitually late in paying his Press Club dues, a failing that anti-fascist reporters tried unsuccessfully to use as an excuse to expel him. The atmosphere in the club, where many members had traveled to Europe to report on fascist dictatorships, was cold for Germans.[6]

Zapp tried to fly under the radar, but he attracted the attention of investigators for the House Special Committee on Un-American Activities. In 1940 the committee subpoenaed Transocean's records, and its investigators raided the press service's New York and Press Building offices, seizing financial records and private correspondence. For an organization that was acting clandestinely, Transocean kept a lot of incriminating documents in its offices, including correspondence with German government officials and American citizens that hinted at illegal activities.[7]

Committee investigators found a letter sent to Zapp in November 1939 by a German intelligence officer, Ernst Schmitz, who operated under the cover of directing the German Railroads Information Office. Schmitz invited Zapp to dine with him and "a number of people of the Intelligence Service of the Rome-Berlin Axis." Zapp's handwritten note on the letter indicated that he had attended the dinner. In another letter, Zapp informed a client in Berlin that he'd found "a suitable racially pure German editor" who could send information from America.[8]

The Committee concluded that "Transocean News Service was nothing more nor less than a propaganda arm of the Nazi regime." It also noted that Zapp's activities "were not confined entirely to the United States. It was also his job to set up Transocean in South and Central America."[9]

Transocean gave its news to some South American newspapers free, and even paid some to print its stories. These included propaganda intended to arouse anti-American sentiments, like fictional accounts of US military incursions into Mexico and stories falsely blaming the American government for an airplane crash that killed the president of Paraguay.[10]

Zapp had a much harder time marketing the German perspective to American newspapers. He complained in a letter to his superiors in Berlin that "my difficulties are almost superhuman." Contrary to fearmongering about Fifth Columnists, there was little appetite in the United States for Nazism or even for news provided by an ostensibly independent German news service. Zapp wrote in despair to the German Foreign Office that while he had been successful in peddling Transocean's news in South and Central America, readers in the United States "hold the peculiar subjective notion that only they are objective and consequently they will not read news that does not sail under their own flag. They are avid for 'news' but it must come from American sources."[11]

In addition to peddling propaganda, Zapp proposed a two-track strategy for keeping the United States out of the European war: exacerbating tensions between the United States and Japan on the theory that America lacked the resources and will to fight in both the Pacific and Europe, and winning over business leaders to an appeasement policy. "The only and at the same time the strongest guarantee of American neutrality appears to be continued ruffling of American relations with Japan," Zapp wrote in a cable to Berlin. "Such a course for the present and for an indefinite period will not permit a European involvement of the United States."[12]

Transocean's tactics included covert sponsorship of the printing and distribution of forged documents. In 1940 Zapp paid Ralph Beaver Strassburger, the pro-Nazi publisher of the *Norristown Times-Herald*, a daily newspaper published in rural Pennsylvania, to print and distribute 60,000 copies of *The German White Paper*, which was billed as a dossier of State Department cables that had allegedly been discovered by the Germans in the Polish Ministry of Foreign Affairs. The forged cables allegedly documented how American diplomats in Europe deliberately provoked war with Germany.[13]

At first, the scheme seemed to be a success. Representative Hamilton Fish trumpeted the *White Paper*, claiming it constituted grounds for impeaching Roosevelt. Asked about the documents at a press conference, the president said that they should be taken "with a grain of salt," amended that to "two grains of salt," and a moment later advised reporters to "make it three grains of salt."[14] The caper backfired when the *White Paper* was revealed to be a fabrication.

British intelligence turned the episode against Fish, informing American reporters that his reelection campaign had placed full-page ads in Strassburger's *Times-Herald* and one other newspaper that was among the handful of American publications that subscribed to and printed stories provided by Transocean.[15]

A year later, on March 11, 1941, a grand jury indicted Zapp and one of his employees, Guenther Tonn, for violating the Foreign Agents Registration Act by failing to register as agents of the German government and Nazi party. Zapp posted $5,000 bail and was able to attend the annual dinner of the White House Correspondents' Association a few days later. Having received an advance copy of Roosevelt's speech, Zapp and Kurt Sell of DNB, departed before FDR, whose speech was broadcast live across the country, called the Nazis barbarians who must and would be defeated. The president shot barbs straight at Zapp and his collaborators. "From the bureaus of propaganda of the Axis powers came the confident prophecy that the conquest of our country would be 'an inside job'—a job accomplished not by overpowering invasion from without, but by disrupting confusion and disunion and moral disintegration from within. Those who believed that knew little of our history. America is not a country which can be confounded by the appeasers, the defeatists, the backstairs manufacturers of panic."[16]

Five days after Zapp's arrest, the Nazis snatched a United Press International reporter, Richard Hottelet, off a Berlin street and imprisoned him on espionage charges. Hottelet was, of course, being held hostage for the two Transocean employees. The gambit worked. Zapp and Tonn were deported and Hottelet was released and allowed to return to the United States.

Zapp left behind an unpaid debt of sixteen dollars at the Press Club.

Prompted in large part by intelligence BSC had provided the FBI and State Department, on June 16, FDR moved to evict Axis spies. German consulates and several German businesses, including Transocean, were ordered to close and repatriate their employees by July 10.

Zapp and Tonn were tried in absentia. Summing up the case, George A. McNulty, an assistant attorney general who had worked with BSC on the Viereck prosecution, argued that the "real purpose of the Transocean agency was war. Not a shooting war, but a war of propaganda, a phase of the Nazi ideal of total war."[17] Evidence presented at trial proving that Transocean was a German government operation rather than a legitimate business included documents showing the news agency earned a grand total of $3,045.46 from sales of its products in the twenty-five months it operated in New York and Washington, and received $164,652 in subsidies from Berlin during that period.[18]

Memories of Zapp's illicit promotion of fascism apparently faded. In the 1960s, he headed the German office of Hill & Knowlton, a multinational public relations firm.[19]

CHAPTER NINE

FAKE NEWS

A new line of black lettering neatly drawn on the glass door of suite 1059 of the National Press Building in the spring of 1941 spelling out "Overseas News Agency" was the first sign in Washington of one of BSC's most intriguing enterprises.

ONA had been launched in July 1940 as an adjunct to the Jewish Telegraphic Agency. JTA informed newspapers that the ONA's mission was to "gather and distribute news about minorities in Europe, supplementing news coverage of other services." It promised to "devote itself exclusively to reporting facts" and claimed that it would "indulge in no propaganda, preach no theory or philosophy."[1] The new name alerted editors that JTA was expanding its coverage beyond reporting on issues of relevance to Jews. It also facilitated work in Central and Eastern Europe at a time when the only doors a business card with the word "Jewish" on it would open were hanging on prison cells.

From the start, attacking Nazi Germany was a higher priority for ONA than hewing to the truth. Much of its copy was based on sources close to the imagination of its writers and their friends in London. For example, its second bulletin, distributed in August 1940, cited anonymous "qualified Czech" sources reporting that "Czechoslovak girls and young women have been transported from the Protectorate to German garrison towns to become white slaves." It claimed that "Nazi officials, dispatching these trainloads of prospective white slaves to the Reich, informed husbands and relatives that the women 'will be entrusted with the important work of amusing German soldiers, in order to keep up the morale of the troops.'"[2]

A few weeks before ONA opened its Washington office, the president and chairman of JTA reached an agreement with William Stephenson, the head of British Security Coordination. BSC agreed to give the ONA a monthly subsidy in return for a promise of cooperation. The commitment included giving ONA credentials to British spies around the world. British intelligence reports to London about propaganda activities in the Americas routinely mentioned securing ONA employment as cover for agents. ONA also recruited its own spies.[3]

JTA and ONA founder Jacob Landau spent the last five months of 1940 in South America, setting up bureaus in Buenos Aires and Rio and hiring correspondents in other countries. After the United States entered the war, it became clear what he had been doing when he approached a senior FBI agent, offering to help in the fight against fascism. Landau said he had established "particularly intimate contacts" with Jewish groups and leaders in South America, and noted that there were 600,000 Jews living on the continent who "are anti-Nazi and are vitally interested in the victory of the United Nations."[4]

In addition to providing information from South America, Landau told the FBI that it could use the ONA "for the gathering of information among the foreign-language groups and the various foreign politicians who have come to our country." In case the FBI didn't understand what he was offering, Landau made it plain: "It is suggested that a special division be established [at ONA] devoted to the gathering of information in which your office would be interested." He stressed the advantages of using an intermediary like ONA to obtain information from non-citizens: ONA's staff would be in a better position than the FBI to judge the informants' trustworthiness, and in case anything went wrong the bureau's involvement would be hidden.[5]

There is no record of the FBI availing itself of ONA's services.

Landau also discussed his Latin American intelligence organization with Soviet intelligence officers, though the extent of his collaboration with the KGB isn't clear from the available decrypted cables.[6]

There can be no doubt about the ONA's close relationship with British intelligence. As the BSC history notes, ONA's primary value "lay in its ability not only to channel propaganda outwards but to assure wide dissemination of material originated by BSC and intended for internal [American] consumption."[7]

In part because of the money and information—both true and false—provided by BSC, the ONA became a trusted source of news from around the world for newspapers that reached most Americans.

ONA's reporters were almost certainly unaware of the fact that their salaries were being underwritten by a foreign intelligence organization that had, according to the BSC history, "effective control" over the news agency. They probably wouldn't have been bothered. ONA staff felt an affinity for Britain's war aims and a passionate hatred for Americans who favored neutrality.[8]

The publishers and editors of scores of newspapers, ranging from the *New York Times*, the *New York Herald Tribune*, the *San Francisco Chronicle*, the *Philadelphia Inquirer*, and the *Washington Post* to tiny papers like the Circleville, Ohio, *Daily Herald*—all important sources of information in the pre-television era—had no idea that ONA was sending them stories written with a keener eye on Britain's war needs than on objective truth.

British funding helped ONA send copy in various languages, so its reports appeared in hundreds of foreign-language papers published for immigrant communities throughout the United States. Many of these papers were also distributed in Nazi-occupied and neutral countries.[9]

ONA hired Harry Hart Frank, a talented writer who used the pen name Pat Frank, to run its Washington bureau. He was already working in the JTA's National Press Building office writing a syndicated column called Frankly Speaking that had been warning of the Nazi threat for years.

Frank's first big scoop for ONA, a series of stories based on a November 1940 trip to Martinique, was typical of the news agency's best work: brave, compelling, and slanted to advancing the war aims of Great Britain. The story, which ran in newspapers across the country, began by establishing

Frank's credentials as both a Washington insider and an intrepid reporter: "The Caribbean Sea is supposed to be an American lake, according to what you hear in Washington. But after you've looped around it a while you discover there are some people in the Caribbean who don't agree with that and are preparing to argue the issue with guns, not words."[10]

Frank reported that he'd been sent to the largest island in the French West Indies, "where a group of French soldiers, sailors, and civilians are quarreling about what to do with some $240,000,000 worth of gold bullion and several million dollars' worth of bombing planes and warships."[11]

Frank depicted an island preparing for a siege, and ready to serve as a base for attacking shipping in the Caribbean. He also suggested that it was ripe for a pro-American uprising. The "250,000 inhabitants of the island are on the verge of revolution, but have no arms to rise against their rulers," Frank reported, adding that "to the people of Martinique, Roosevelt is practically a God."[12]

Frank's observations, which were at odds with the picture painted by both the US government and French officials on Martinique, and with the report Curtis Munson gave FDR in the summer of 1941, were printed in hundreds of American newspapers, and he was interviewed on national radio programs. ONA's stories about Martinique served British interests by piercing Americans' comfort zone, reinforcing the idea that if they didn't go abroad to fight the fascists, they would have to fight them much closer to home. Frank's stories also bolstered arguments against America's continuing to trade with the Vichy government. Convincing the United States to sever financial ties with the French puppet government was a high priority for Britain.

Frank returned to the theme of tropical fascism in February 1941. Papers around the country ran his stories from Puerto Rico and Haiti which painted a dire and unrealistic picture of Haiti joining the Axis and serving as a jumping off point for Nazi raids on the Panama Canal, Miami, and Puerto Rico. "There is enough Nazi activity in Haiti to create a Caribbean Sudetenland," Frank claimed.[13] Like his reporting from Martinique, the stories were intended to shake Americans' sense of comfort and drive them to take the war to Hitler before he brought it to their doorsteps.

BSC fed about twenty rumors a week to American reporters and kept close track of its success in getting them into print. The British didn't restrict themselves to stories that had the potential to inflict immediate or severe damage to the enemy, and they weren't concerned about the veracity or believability of the rumors. For example, in August 1941 the *New York Times* published ONA's report, which had been concocted in London, that the death of a 130-year-old Bedouin soothsayer was seen in the Middle East as "a sign of a coming defeat for Hitler."[14] BSC also sponsored a US tour for Louis de Wohl, a Hungarian "astro-philosopher." In press conferences and an appearance at the annual convention of the American Federation of Scientific Astrologers, de Wohl pontificated about astral signs of Hitler's doom and Roosevelt's success: "A yogi once told me a man born on the date Hitler came into power would cause his downfall. Hitler rose to power on Jan. 30, and that is Roosevelt's birth date."[15]

American newspapers and radio played an important role in conveying false information to the Axis during the two years between the Nazi/Soviet invasion of Poland and Germany's declaration of war on the United States. The Brits would feed a rumor to a London newspaper, which could be relied upon to cable its New York correspondent for confirmation. BSC then fed the New York reporter additional information. "At the same time, the London newspaper would make inquiries of an American news agency, which in turn would cable its Berlin correspondent. The rumour would thus be planted in Berlin—with the German censors, the Gestapo and the Berlin correspondent of the US news agency, who would in all likelihood discuss it with other correspondents," according to the BSC history.[16]

One of ONA's tasks was to help BSC get disinformation broadcast on WRUL, a shortwave radio station located on Long Island with a powerful signal that could be heard clearly throughout Europe. The operating rules for WRUL, which had programming in several languages, specified that it would broadcast only news that had already appeared in print. ONA published BSC-generated rumors, WRUL repeated them, and by the time other newspapers and radio stations picked them up, BSC's and ONA's fingerprints had disappeared.

These rumors weren't the result of happenstance.

The British government had a well-oiled, coordinated scheme for generating and disseminating rumors, which it called "sibs," short for *sibilare*, the Latin word for *whisper* or *hiss*. In continental Europe British sibs were distributed almost exclusively through whispering campaigns. In the United States ONA was used to place sibs in American newspapers that were unaware that the material was in any way inspired by the British government.

Many of the sibs were silly or outlandish, but British intelligence took them extraordinarily seriously. "The object of propaganda rumours is in no sense to convey the official or semi-official views of H.M.G. [His Majesty's Government] by covert means to officials in the countries concerned," a secret report circulated to British intelligence officers and diplomats noted. "It is rather to induce alarm, despondency and bewilderment among the enemies, and hope and confidence among the friends, to whose ears it comes. If a rumour appears likely to cheer our enemies for the time, it is calculated to carry with it the germs of ultimate and grave disappointment for them." Rumours, the memo stated, "are expected to induce a certain frame of mind in the general public, not necessarily to deceive the well-informed." The memo said that rumors are "the most covert of all forms of propaganda. Although the enemy may suspect that a certain rumour has been started by the British Government, they can never prove it. Even if they succeed in capturing an agent engaged in spreading whispers, there will be no written evidence against him, and should they exhort a confession from him, nothing is easier [than] for the British Government to deny the whole story."[17]

BSC didn't mince words in describing the goals of its American fake news operations. In a memo to the British Foreign Office, Sydney Morrell, one of two journalists in charge of BSC's work with the press, described his unit's remit as conducting "subversive propaganda in the United States" and "countering isolationist and appeasement propaganda which is rapidly taking on the shape of a Fascist movement, conscious or unconscious." It also sought to leverage "America's prestige and neutrality by directing ostensibly American propaganda towards the three Axis powers and enemy-occupied territories."[18]

British intelligence agencies were careful about terminology. To set out the distinction between "publicity" and "propaganda," the UK Political Warfare Executive (PWE) produced a memo titled "The Meaning, Techniques and Methods of Political Warfare." Each copy was numbered and marked "Secret," and carried on its cover page the instruction: "To be kept under lock and key." The memo defined "publicity" as "the straightforward projection of a case; it is the build-up of a picture in the mind of the audience which will win their confidence and support," and explained it was intended to persuade through "the presentation of evidence, leaving the judgment to the audience."[19]

Propaganda, PWE made clear, was publicity's evil twin. The term was used in reference to deliberate, covert activities, not run-of-the-mill publicity campaigns, its purpose being to "direct the thinking of the recipient, without his conscious collaboration, into predetermined channels. Propaganda is," PWE summed up, "the conditioning of the recipient by devious methods with an ulterior motive."[20]

An organization called the Underground Propaganda Committee (UPC) met twice a week in London to approve new sibs. The UPC sent thousands of sibs out into the world. For many, the first stop was ONA's New York and National Press Building offices.

To cite one example, at a meeting of the UPC on August 8, 1941, a decision was made to release a series of sibs that, according to the meeting minutes, were "intended to suggest that the Führer, who is alone responsible in the face of a good deal of opposition for the Russian campaign, is becoming more and more unbalanced as he realises that the vast gamble is miscarrying."[21] Summaries of the planned rumors included:

Sib SD/7: Hitler's megalomaniac paranoia is getting rapidly worse. He can't bear any contradiction or opposition. He is in constant fear of assassination. His memory is becoming confused. There is great secrecy about his movements.

Sib R/183: Sauerbruch (Hitler's doctor) visiting Switzerland told Professor Jung that Hitler isn't at the Russian front at all, but at Berchtesgaden suffering from violent epileptic fits.

Sib R/185: Hitler's paranoia has reached the point where he suffers from delusions. He has an uncontrollable fear that his mustache is growing more and more like Stalin's, and he has it shaved every morning much closer than usual.

Eight days later the *New York Post* ran an article supplied by ONA citing "circumstantial evidence for a belief that Hitler is not at the Russian front but at Berchtesgaden suffering from a severe nervous breakdown." The article went on to assert that the Führer's personal physician had traveled to Switzerland to consult with the famed psychiatrist Carl Jung to discuss "the rapid deterioration of Hitler's mental condition," which ONA reported was characterized by delusional rages in which he confused the contemporary battle for Smolensk with a World War I battle in France. "Confusion of memory and rage at any kind of opposition were stated to be symptoms of the Führer's condition, accompanied by the return of his old megalomaniac paranoia in aggravated form."[22]

Even the Soviet press helped propel this rumor on its trip around the world. TASS Washington bureau chief Laurence Todd cabled it from the National Press Building to Moscow, which published the news under a Swiss dateline. British reporters picked up the Russian story, and, completing the circuit, a United Press International reporter read it in

London and cabled it to the United States, where it is was published in numerous papers as fresh news.[23]

On July 11, 1941, the UPC approved a sib for distribution in US newspapers, where Japanese diplomats would read it, indicating that if Japan attacked Indochina, the Soviet Union would attack Japan by air. The next day the *New York Times* and other American newspapers ran an AP story that cited "reliable persons" reporting that Japan was poised to "make a move against French Indo-China soon." The story noted that "Russia has a large air force within easy range of Japan's vulnerable centers of population."[24]

The UPC approved another sib involving Hitler on July 11, this one alleging that the German leader had purged a number of mid-level Nazis whom he believed to be plotting against him. On August 18 the *Baltimore Sun* ran a story that had been provided by the *New York Herald Tribune*, one of BSC's favorite vehicles for disseminating disinformation. The headline asked "Purge of Nazi Minor Officials?" Like many UPC sibs, the story relied on anonymous sources and was built not on reporting but on paraphrasing a story from another newspaper that had itself relied on murky sources. The first sentence read like an abstract of the UPC's sib: "Reliable information from Germany leaves no doubt that there is grave disunity within the Nazi party and between the party and the army leaders with neither side daring to openly express the points in dispute, according to an article to appear in the *Daily Telegraph* and *Morning Post* tomorrow by the paper's diplomatic correspondent."[25]

The British devoted a lot of attention to persuading German soldiers that any attempt to cross the English Channel would be foolhardy. The men in charge of the sibs were thrilled when they learned that captured German pilots had expressed horror to interrogators about a new secret weapon that could set the sea on fire, incinerating any pilot who ejected or was forced down over the water. The imaginary weapon was one of the UPC's rumors.[26]

Some of the sibs were so outlandish that they must have been aimed more at bolstering morale in England, or giving the men who came up with them a laugh, than alarming the enemy. There is no evidence that any German believed rumors the UPC spread that two hundred man-eating sharks had been imported from Australia and released in the Channel, where they could devour pilots and sailors unlucky enough to find themselves in the water.[27]

BSC asked ONA in November 1941 to help dent the morale of U-boat crews. ONA released a report, allegedly based on news from Ankara, stating that the British had invented a new super-explosive and were frantically stuffing it into depth charges. American reporters followed up on the ONA story with questions to British officials, who played along with the game. Newspapers gave prominent coverage to an AP story disclosing that "the British were filling their depth charges for naval warfare with an explosive forty-seven times more powerful than TNT." Testing the credulity of their readers, the papers reported that the "new ammunition is more than ordinarily secret," and in the same story quoted British military sources providing details about its manufacture and deployment—as if the British government was in the habit of revealing military secrets to any reporter clever enough to ask the right questions.[28] To its credit, after publishing the AP story on its front page on November 2, the *New York Times* ran a small story buried on page C18 of the next day's paper suggesting that "the more imaginative rumors crediting the British with new and 'highly secret' ammunition for use against German submarines in the Battle of the Atlantic should be taken with perhaps a little more than the proverbial grain of salt."[29]

A surprising number of sibs were aimed not at the brains, or even the hearts, of targeted populations, but rather at the genitals. For example, on December 5, 1941, three sibs were approved:

"The tremendous demand for aphrodisiacs among quite young soldiers returning from Norway seems to tie up with the general fear of impotence which is spreading among German troops."[30]

"The drugs the Germans give foreign workers to supplement the poor
food supply are rendering them impotent."[31]
"The Germans are blaming the housing crisis for the decline in their
birthrate; actually the food concentrates now used are causing
widespread impotence."[32]

The practice of planting rumors in American newspapers did not
stop when the United States joined the war. Officials responsible for
British propaganda carried on a lively debate in February 1942 about the
merits of informing coordinator of information Bill Donovan about its
system for planting fake news in American newspapers, and of seeking his
prior approval for rumors connected with or disseminated in the United
States. One official, who referred to Donovan as Britain's "'underground'
friend," argued that he shouldn't be burdened with the information, presumably because he would be expected to keep it secret from his superiors. Another official characterized the suggestion that Donovan should
be given any say over fake news involving the United States as "outrageous," and he vowed to do his utmost to kill it. In the end Donovan, and
the American government, were kept out of the loop.[33]

CHAPTER TEN

BATTLING THE FRENCH AND IRISH

Long before the United States entered the war, a handful of American reporters and editors in the National Press Building privately declared war against Germany and its partners in the Vichy French government. Their actions went well beyond writing articles designed to elicit sympathy for the British people or blacken the reputations of isolationist politicians, and included pressuring the US government to seize German companies and working with BSC to neuter Vichy espionage capabilities. BSC operatives in the Press Building were also active in a less successful operation aimed at Britain's neighbor Ireland.

Preventing the Vichy government from conducting espionage, disseminating propaganda, and benefiting from commercial operations in the United States was a difficult problem for BSC. There was a good deal of sympathy in the United States for the French people, and as an officially neutral government, the Vichy regime was legally permitted to operate in the United States.

BSC was typically thorough and ruthless in its approach to the problem. First it dispatched an American agent, Betty Pack, wife of Arthur Pack, a British diplomat, to seduce Charles Brousse, the press attaché in the French embassy in Washington. After gaining his admiration and confidence, Pack, referenced in BSC files by the cover name Cynthia, "confessed" to him that she was an American intelligence agent. It was a shrewd deception because the Anglophobe Brousse would never have divulged secrets to someone he believed was a British agent.

She persuaded Brousse to provide unencrypted copies of all encrypted cables sent to and received by the embassy, as well as detailed reports of private conversations involving the ambassador, Vichy officials in France, and the German government. The cables kept Britain informed of Vichy activity in Washington and helped its cryptanalysts defeat French codes. Brousse also provided the names and addresses of undercover agents in the United States. A male BSC officer used romance to recruit a lonely embassy secretary who filled in details that Pack's lover was not privy to.[1]

The British were so curious about the activities of a Vichy agent named Jean Louis Musa that a BSC operative befriended him, proposed a business partnership, and, to facilitate the fictitious business, provided an office. BSC bugged the office, tapped its phones, and swooped in every night to copy documents, including those locked in a safe. Musa may have attracted BSC's attention because he was involved with Havas News Agency, a pro-Vichy news service that had an office in the National Press Building.

In July 1941 BSC wrote up a summary of Vichy operations in the United States that included transcripts of illegal telephone taps and copies of secret documents, and gave a copy to Roosevelt. He awarded it his highest compliment, saying he was reading it "as a bedtime story," and gave his permission to have the information made public.[2]

BSC, which had some of England's most talented journalists on its staff, spun the Vichy dossier into a series of newspaper articles. The stories were handed to a BSC contact, Ansel E. Talbert, who worked in the *New York Herald Tribune*'s National Press Building office. The first article in the series, which was reprinted in over one hundred American newspapers, was published on August 31, 1941. It accurately reported: "Operations of a clique of Vichy agents, working under direct control of Gaston Henry-Haye, French ambassador to the United States, whose activities are designed to create sentiment for the Nazi 'new order' in Europe, have come to light in Washington." The story described how the Vichy government's intelligence operation in the United States had "thwarted actual military moves of Britain and her allies," and said it aimed to create "an ever-widening network to bring Vichy's message of defeatism before isolationists, noninterventionists, and all others who will listen."[3]

The stories revealed that Vichy agents had attempted to obtain blueprints and plans of the improved Bren gun, a mainstay of the British invasion defenses, and described Musa's role in thwarting efforts to mass produce an improved version of the machine gun in the United States for export to England.[4] Remarkable details were included, such as news that an Allied effort to overthrow the Vichy garrison at Dakar, Senegal, had been derailed because de Gaulle's plans for the battle were smuggled into the United States for transmission to the Vichy in the gasoline tank of an automobile shipped from London to Hoboken aboard a Greek steamer. The gas tank also held lists of French officers and pilots who were fighting Germany as part of the Free French movement.[5]

The BSC-written articles pointed out that the US Treasury was unintentionally financing Vichy's nefarious activities by unfreezing $1 million per month of French government funds, which were supposed to be used only for diplomatic activities and to provide assistance to colonies like Martinique that had been cut off from France.

Treasury secretary Henry Morgenthau publicly praised Talbert and personally complimented the journalist for his brilliant exposé. Morgenthau was apparently unaware of the source of the articles, and Talbert didn't tell him that his biggest contribution to the series was lending his byline.

The articles had their intended effects. The Vichy embassy was indelibly marked as a tool of Nazi Germany, the State Department and FBI forced the Vichy intelligence service to curtail its activities in the United States, and American sympathy for representatives of the Vichy government evaporated. A BSC source in the French embassy reported to BSC that the ambassador had "described the whole affair as 'De Gaullist-Jewish-British-FBI intrigue.' But he never really suspected the British."[6]

At the same time as it was battling the Vichy embassy in the press,

BSC was using similar tactics to combat commercial collaboration between American and German companies. Stephenson's men worked on the project with some of the most prominent reporters of the era.

Drew Pearson and Robert S. Allen were particularly aggressive in confronting Nazis. They coordinated closely with Ernest Cuneo, BSC's liaison to American government officials and reporters. One example of this collaboration is a May 1941 Washington Merry-Go-Round report that "Justice Department sleuths" had discovered that the US subsidiary of the German pharmaceutical company Schering AG was illegally funneling millions of dollars to Nazi Germany. The story followed revelations from other reporters that the pharmaceutical company had violated antitrust laws.[7]

Pearson and Allen knew, but did not disclose, that the sleuths who discovered Schering's illegal ties to Nazi Germany had more in common with Sherlock Holmes than Elliott Ness. Schering was targeted, according to the BSC history, because it was part of a "vast and intricately organized network of companies [that] became the backbone of the German intelligence and propaganda systems in the Western Hemisphere, and its existence seriously endangered the security and the economy of both Britain and the United States. To devise a way in which to combat and if possible to liquidate it was one of the most important problems which confronted BSC in late 1940."[8]

BSC's first step was to obtain proof that the subsidiaries of German companies operating in America were sending money to their parent companies in violation of US law. The second step was to expose these connections, launch a campaign to persuade the public that American/German firms posed a threat to America, and finally to pressure the US government to take control of German and collaborationist businesses.[9]

The Brits recruited a Schering employee in New Jersey who revealed the company's secret connections to Germany. In addition, he photocopied documents demonstrating that Schering was a party to cartel agreements that violated the Sherman Anti-Trust Act. BSC contacted a friendly reporter at the International News Service who, in return for exclusive rights to the story, "agreed to follow a course of action which BSC suggested to him and promised at the same time not to reveal his source."[10] The course involved showing the documents to a Justice Department official and giving him an ultimatum: The United States must initiate legal proceedings against Schering within three weeks or contend with headlines asking "Why is the Department of Justice sleeping at such a critical time?" The reporter obeyed his instructions, as did the Justice Department.

"Startling facts indicating that Nazi Germany is waging a concerted undercover 'economic blitzkrieg' on the US through an ingenious network of 'dummy' corporations has been unearthed by the department of Justice," Americans read on April 10, 1941.[11] Pearson and Allen were among the scores of journalists who reported the story. The media firestorm prompted the Canadian government to confiscate the assets of Schering's Canadian subsidiary. The US Department of Justice first fined the US subsidiary, and later acquired its stock and supervised the firm's operations for the duration of the war.

BSC operated with impunity because Stephenson knew that he had enthusiastic, though passive, backing from the highest levels of government. Roosevelt encouraged British covert operations in the United States, even telling Stephenson, "I'm your biggest undercover agent."[12] On April 1, as Washington Merry-Go-Round was preparing to break the Schering story, Stephenson cabled Menzies with news that FDR had told Cuneo he planned to bring the United States into the war "very shortly." Menzies passed the message on to Churchill.[13]

British efforts to push America into the war were not universally admired in Washington, and as BSC became bolder in the autumn of 1941 isolationists began to detect hints of its activities.

On the morning of November 10, 1941, Burton Wheeler stood on the floor of the Senate and excoriated the US and British governments for conspiring to disseminate pro-intervention publicity through front groups that typically had the word "committee" in their name. He decried a "rising tide of propaganda" created by "committee after committee" and said that many Americans wondered "how far the Government of the United States and the British Government have acted in collaboration behind these committees."[14]

Wheeler read from the confidential minutes of a meeting that had been held a month earlier in Donova'sn office. The meeting was held, Wheeler noted with a hefty dose of sarcasm, to plot the formation of an organization dedicated to lining up Irish Americans "behind the war policies of the United States and on the side of Ireland's ancient and warm-hearted friend, the British empire." The group "is called American Irish Defense Committee," Wheeler reported. "There is very little Irish about it except the green ink in which it prints some of its literature." Wheeler didn't reveal the source of the confidential minutes.[15]

Turning up the heat on his sarcasm, Wheeler told his colleagues that the meeting had been attended by "great Irish champions and prominent Hibernians," and proceeded to list several attendees who had non-Irish names. Wheeler's colleagues were familiar with, and weary of, his conspiracy theories and attacks on Roosevelt. The few who listened to the speech paid little or no attention to his claim that the American Irish Defense Association "originated in New York, in the minds of gentlemen closely associated with the British government." Wheeler's accurate assertion that the association was not seeking dues or contributions from prospective members because "expenses will be paid by England," was reported in only one major newspaper, the isolationist, Roosevelt-hating *Chicago Daily Tribune*."[16]

The senator from Montana was shooting in the dark. If he had been well informed when he read into the *Congressional Record* the names of those in attendance at the meeting, he wouldn't have been content to note that Sanford Griffith ran the meeting and the attendees included Francis Henson; he would have identified them as paid agents of British intelligence.

In fact, Wheeler's guess was correct. BSC created the American

Irish Defense Association because existing Irish American groups were militantly anti-British. The Ancient Order of Hibernians and the American-Irish Historical Society had teamed up with isolationist, violently anti-Roosevelt organizations like America First. In the minds of BSC's leaders, this marked Americans of Irish ancestry as fair game.

Describing the origins of the American Irish Defense Association, the BSC history states: "After the usual preliminary steps had been taken in the way of collecting intelligence, BSC sponsored an Irish interventionist society in the autumn of 1941."[17] Any overt connection with the British government would have rendered the association radioactive to Irish Americans, so BSC was careful to maintain contact through "a good cut-out, a man who followed directives from the BSC office and kept BSC posted on every move it made." This was probably Henson.

BSC's effort to organize pro-British sentiment among Irish emigrants was a direct response to requests from Winston Churchill. The prime minister wanted the American government and private citizens to pressure the Irish government to allow Britain to use bases in southern and western Ireland to provide air and naval cover for Atlantic convoys.[18]

Prominent Irish Americans were recruited to lead chapters of the association in New York, Boston, Washington, and other cities. BSC funded a publicity blitz that included radio broadcasts, news releases, dinners, mass meetings, street corner meetings, and personal appearances of film stars and other Irish celebrities. Although it failed to persuade Ireland to join the war or provide naval bases for Britain, the association was effective in mobilizing Irish Americans to set aside their antipathy to Britain and to endorse American aid to the United Kingdom at a time when interventionists needed every friend they could muster.[19]

Wheeler's denunciation of the American Irish Defense Committee fell on deaf ears. The idea of a conspiracy between the Roosevelt administration and the British government to create a phony propaganda operation didn't seem credible, even to Republican senators.

A week after Wheeler's speech, BSC and the White House rushed operatives, including several based in the National Press Building, to Detroit to collaborate on an urgent project. Their mission was to defuse the threat posed by John L. Lewis, leader of the United Mine Workers of America (UMW) union, who was openly plotting to use a convention of the Congress of Industrial Organizations (CIO) to launch an insurrection against the White House's plans to prepare the nation for war.

Lewis and Roosevelt had once been close allies, but by 1940 they had parted ways. Hatred for the president had so clouded Lewis's judgment that he first aligned himself with communists and then backed Herbert Hoover—the man many Americans believed was responsible for the Depression—as the Republican presidential candidate.[20] After the GOP convention, Lewis endorsed Wendell Willkie and said that if workers did not follow his lead he would regard it as a personal repudiation and would step down as head of the CIO. Workers did not follow him and Lewis quit.

In November 1941 Lewis, desperate to regain his stature and determined to stymie Roosevelt's efforts to prepare labor and business for war, threatened to paralyze the steel industry by calling a massive coal miners' strike. At the same time, he plotted to push isolationist resolutions through the CIO national convention that could have led to widespread strikes in other industries. A *Wall Street Journal* headline captured Lewis's motives and intentions: "He Hates Roosevelt; He Hates War; He Wants a Showdown" and is "Ready to Go Through with the Coal Strike, Come Hell or High Water."[21]

The conflict was as important to Churchill as it was to Roosevelt: if Lewis prevailed, the flow of materiel across the Atlantic would stop, and with it hope for Britain's survival. BSC mobilized its forces, in close coordination with the White House, to battle Lewis. The CIO convention, the BSC history noted, "offered BSC a dramatic opportunity to attack the union's isolationist façade." There was, BSC believed, grave danger that the convention would adopt isolationist resolutions "which would have long-lasting and possibly disastrous consequences."[22]

Repeating a tactic from the previous summer, Henson conducted a poll of delegates. "The questions asked were designed to be 'educational,' a euphemism in this case for tendentious," according to the BSC history. The poll, newspapers around the country reported, showed that 98 percent of CIO delegates believed it was more important to defeat Hitler than to keep the United States out of war.[23]

Fight for Freedom, a pro-intervention group backed by BSC, launched a massive publicity campaign at the convention, handing out buttons and flyers and meeting with CIO leaders. John Franklin Carter's representative, Jim Gillan, circulated among the delegates at Detroit's Moose Temple Lodge. Gillan called Carter with frequent updates, which he had typed up and delivered to the White House. The news was good for Roosevelt. Lewis was marginalized and the isolationists were routed. The convention voted overwhelmingly for a resolution stating that "Hitler and the Nazi government . . . directly menace the security of the United States," condemning appeasement, calling for "all possible aid" to Great Britain, the Soviet Union, and China, and backing FDR's foreign policy without reservation. Lewis lost control of the CIO and, a few weeks after the convention, called off the coal strike.[24]

President Roosevelt was aware of and appreciated the role Fight for Freedom, and BSC, had played in defanging Lewis.[25]

It took decades for information about some of BSC's operations to start leaking out, and by the time a reasonably complete picture emerged few remembered how fraught the situation had been, or how bitter were the divisions in American society.

With the clarity of hindsight, some may write off the extraordinary collaboration in 1940 and 1941 between journalists in the National Press Building and a foreign intelligence agency as little more than a historical curiosity. Japan's attack on Pearl Harbor and Hitler's declaration of war vaporized notions of neutrality, rendering British intelligence's efforts to defeat America's isolationists superfluous. In reality, given the depth and strength of the opposition to FDR's efforts to aid Britain in 1940 and 1941, and the importance of the lifeline that pro-British propaganda made possible, it is clear that the efforts of Mowrer, Bell, Henson, Carter, Frank, and many others who viewed themselves as partisans in a fight to defend western civilization helped change history.

To cite one example, during the summer of 1941 the Roosevelt administration went all out to persuade Congress to amend an emergency military conscription law extending mandatory service from a year to two and a half years. The House of Representatives passed the extension on August 12 by a one-vote margin. It is easy to imagine, though impossible to prove, that the efforts of BSC's operatives in the National Press Building to bend and bully politicians away from isolationism tipped the balance in favor of the law.

BSC privately took credit for, and its operatives in the Press Building played a major role in, the destroyers-for-bases deal that provided a vital morale boost for Britain in one of its darkest hours. British influence on public opinion and shaping of the political climate were important factors in another bitterly fought pre–Pearl Harbor initiative, the lend-lease program that allowed the United States to ship massive quantities of supplies to the Allies.[26]

Without American assistance, Britain wouldn't have been able to hold Germany at bay in 1941. Roosevelt barely mustered the public support that enabled him to provide that aid. The manipulation of American opinion by British intelligence, exemplified by the covert actions of its operatives in the National Press Building, is one of the least-known and most-successful applications of covert propaganda in modern history.

CHAPTER ELEVEN

EIGHT DAYS IN DECEMBER

For a week and a day in December 1941 two separate dramas, both combining volatile mixtures of journalism and intelligence, played out in close proximity in and around the National Press Building. One involved a Japanese reporter who watched helplessly as his secret efforts to help prevent war between his country and the United States went up in flames. The other was an all-too-public and equally futile plot by two American journalists who hoped that by exposing closely guarded secrets they could stop America's slide into war with Germany. Instead of preserving peace, Chesly Manly, the Capitol Hill reporter for the *Chicago Tribune*, and Frank Waldrop, political editor for the *Washington Times-Herald*, handed Hitler's generals a roadmap to America's plans for fighting an unavoidable war.

Manly and Waldrop met for dinner at the National Press Club on the evening of December 3, 1941, to discuss the pros and cons of publishing a story they knew would define their careers—and they believed could change history. A few hours earlier Manly had been handed the biggest and potentially most damaging leak of military secrets any American reporter had ever received.[1]

By the time Manly and Waldrop finished their meal, neither had even the slightest doubt that the story should be published. The revelations would be a kick in the teeth to President Roosevelt that could, the two journalists believed, stymie his efforts to push the nation into what from their perspective was an unnecessary and unwinnable war.[2]

The next morning the *Tribune*'s headline stretched across the front page, screaming, "F.D.R.'s War Plans! Goal Is 10 Million Armed Men."[3]

The timing was especially satisfying for Manly: the *Tribune*'s world-class scoop hit the streets just in time to dim the glow of the inaugural issue of the *Chicago Sun*, a paper that had been created to diminish the influence of the isolationist, Roosevelt-hating *Tribune*.

Main Lounge, National Press Club. In 1945, the widow of Manuel de Oliviera Lima, the Brazilian ambassador to the United States, donated a painting of the Greek courtesan Phryne, adorned in nothing more than slippers and a smile, to the club. The painting became the subject of controversy after women were admitted to the club in 1971. In 1998 the Press Club's board of directors decided to remove the painting. In 2005 *Phryne* was auctioned for $80,000.

Credit: National Press Club archives

A cartoon next to Manly's story showed men in trenches with the words "Illinois," "Chicago," "Indiana" and "Ohio" written on their jackets and hats. They were standing in front of a fortress labeled "The Middle West" and were looking to the east, where the words "War Propaganda" were stenciled in the sky above the Capitol dome in Washington. The caption heralded the Midwest as "The Stronghold of Peace." The sketch illustrated the reality that even though isolationism had been infiltrated, corrupted, and discredited by anti-Semites, fascists, and racists, the movement was alive and well in the heartland.

Manly's story played on the fears of Americans who believed FDR was plotting a massive, disastrous war. "A confidential report prepared by the joint army and navy high command by direction of President Roosevelt calls for American expeditionary forces aggregating 5,000,000 men for a final land offensive against Germany and her satellites," Manly reported. "It contemplates total armed forces of 10,045,658 men."[4] The story, which had a December 3 dateline, added, "One of the few existing copies of this astonishing document, which represents decisions and commitments affecting the destinies of peoples thruout the civilized world, became available to the Tribune today." The *Washington Times-Herald* also ran the story, ensuring that military officers who would have risked their lives to prevent the information from reaching America's enemies read it as they choked down their scrambled eggs and toast.

Manly had gotten his hands on the War Department's "Rainbow Five" report—so named because it consisted of five contingency plans for war, each assigned a different color. The report revealed that America's small, ill-equipped military was completely unprepared to fight a major war. It outlined the Army and Navy's plans for building up the nation's fighting capacity and pointed out precisely where and when troops would be sent if the US military was called on to intervene in the wars that were raging in Europe and Asia.

As Manly reported, one of the plans assumed that "Germany and her European satellites cannot be defeated by the European powers now fighting against her." This, he told readers, led to the military planners' conclusion that "if our European enemies are to be defeated it will be necessary for the United States to enter the war, and to employ a part of its armed forces offensively in the eastern Atlantic and in Europe and Africa." The "report assumes that Germany, Italy, all German occupied countries cooperating with Germany, Vichy France, Japan, Manchukuo, and possibly Spain and Portugal are potential enemies. It calls for continuation of the war against this assumed combination of enemies even tho the British commonwealth and Soviet Russia should be completely defeated, and predicts that Russia will be militarily impotent by July 1, 1942."

The *Tribune* reporter cherry-picked portions of the report calculated to offend Midwestern isolationist sensibilities. For example, he plucked out a few sentences that made it seem that America's principal war aims included "prevention of the destruction of the British empire," a goal for which few American mothers were willing to sacrifice their sons. Manly also crowed that Rainbow Five proved that Charles Lindbergh, "who has been maligned as a defeatist, an appeaser, and a Nazi sympathizer by administration war propagandists and the interventionist press," was correct when he said the British and Soviets alone were not capable of defeating Germany.

Manly was right when he wrote that the document was astonishing, but its contents were not as astonishing as the *Tribune*'s decision to make them public. It was obvious at a glance that knowledge of the Rainbow Five plans would be of immense value to Hitler's Germany, Mussolini's Italy, and Tojo's Japan; it didn't take a military genius to understand that publication of the nation's most sensitive military plans would put the lives of American soldiers at risk. The *Tribune* disregarded the threat to national security because the paper's publisher, Colonel Robert McCormick, along with a large segment of public opinion, believed, as Waldrop put it, that Roosevelt was "lying us into a war with Germany and had to be stopped."[5] Manly and Waldrop felt they were fulfilling journalism's highest duty: to hold government accountable by illuminating its darkest recesses.

For isolationist politicians the Rainbow Five plan was clear proof of the president's duplicity. They immediately cited it as evidence that even as he was promising American mothers that he wouldn't send their sons to fight a foreign war, Roosevelt was privately ordering plans for just such a war. Isolationists who considered themselves patriots and who had been vilified for months as traitors and Nazi dupes were not swayed by White House press secretary Steve Early's observation that all countries engage in contingency planning and that doing so did not commit the United States to a particular course of action.[6]

A few hours after Manly's story hit the newsstands, Rep. George Holden Tinkham waved it around on the floor of the House of Representatives, shouting that the Rainbow Five plan was a "betrayal of the American republic."[7] Tinkham wasn't a know-nothing isolationist; a Republican from Massachusetts, he was known for his staunch defense of the rights of African Americans. Tinkham sought and received unanimous consent to have Manly's story printed in full in the *Congressional Record*. The report proved that "the President of the United States has assumed the position of being a dictator in this land and he is enjoying it," Kansas Republican congressman William Lambertson told his colleagues. The Rainbow Five story had landed in the middle of—and almost derailed—a ferocious debate over an $8 billion military spending bill. After a couple of hours of fulmination, however, the bill was nonetheless passed.[8]

Axis agents in the United States immediately grasped the significance of Rainbow Five. Unlike the overheard conversations, private assessments, and whispered confidences that were the raw material for most intelligence reports, the *Tribune* story, if accurate—and America's enemies didn't doubt its authenticity—was an account of the US military's actual plans for war. Within hours of its publication verbatim copies of Manly's story were cabled to Rome, Tokyo, and Berlin. Axis armies learned vital elements of America's plans, such as the number of ships that would be required to transport American soldiers to fight in Europe, how long it would take to build them, the number of airplanes American industry was expected to produce, and plans for constructing new airfields in England to serve as bases for bombing Germany.

Most crucially, German war planners, who had very little knowledge of American military strength or doctrine, learned that the United States had no intention of staying out of the war even if Britain and the Soviet Union fell. The United States was starting on a course of enlisting, training, and equipping a massive army that would by July 1943 be capable of taking on Axis forces in Europe. The information in Manly's story was far more valuable, specific, and actionable than any information Hitler's spies had learned about the United States through years of espionage.[9]

In a cable to Berlin, Hans Thomsen, the chargé d'affaires at Germany's embassy in Washington, wrote that Manly's story was "doubtlessly" based on an authentic report. Thomsen warned that the secret document confirmed that America's military and political elite believed that "Germany can be conquered neither by dollars, American bombers, nor by American subversive propaganda, [but] only by an American expeditionary force of several million men."[10] He noted that American military measures against Japan would be of a defensive character, so Japanese policymakers were "justified in concluding that America will, in the event of a two-ocean war, make its main offensive effort in the direction of Europe and Africa."

Manly's story was immediately translated and sent to Germany' top military officers. General Alfred Jodl, chief of the operations staff of Germany's Armed Forces High Command, along with Field Marshal Wilhelm Keitel and Admiral Erich Raeder, dropped everything and started at once on an analysis of the Rainbow Five plan as revealed in the article. The Nazi military planners realized that in the face of a potential invasion of the scale described in Rainbow Five, the ongoing Russian campaign was a distraction they could not afford. All of Germany's resources must urgently be diverted to fending off America. On December 6, only two days after publication of Manly's scoop, they sent the analysis and a set of recommendations to Hitler at the Eastern front.

The plan, which Hitler quickly agreed to implement, detailed steps Germany would take to immediately and dramatically change its military priorities to counter the threat from North America. Formalized as "Führer Directive Number 39," the plan was designed to take full advantage of the time it would take the United States to move its forces into Europe. It called for Germany to halt its invasion of the Soviet Union, establish a strong defensive line in Russia and redeploy one hundred divisions to occupy the entire Mediterranean coastline and Iberian Peninsula. Britain would be isolated and then crushed, and all possible routes for an American invasion hardened. The idea was to deny America any opportunity to mass soldiers and weapons within striking distance of Germany or German-occupied Europe.[11]

Thomsen's conclusion that Manly's story would have a soothing effect on Japanese leaders and strategists was correct. The knowledge that defeating Germany and Italy were America's top priorities and that it planned to devote minimal forces to the Pacific reinforced the logic behind the planned attack on Pearl Harbor and simultaneous attacks on the Philippines, Dutch East Indies, Malaya, and Singapore. Rainbow Five indicated that the United States wouldn't attack the Japanese fleet for five long years, taking advantage of its immense industrial superiority and the buffer provided by the Pacific ocean to construct an invincible Navy. Admiral Isoroku Yamamoto, commander of the Japanese Navy, believed that he could win only a short war with the United States, and that he could not prevail in the prolonged war of attrition outlined in Rainbow Five. Manly's leak reinforced Yamamoto's conviction that dealing the US Navy a rapid, humiliating and crippling defeat was Japan's best hope.[12]

As America's adversaries were analyzing the *Tribune*'s account of the Rainbow Five report, in Washington a massive effort to find Manly's source was underway. FBI director J. Edgar Hoover personally interrogated suspected leakers, including Navy secretary Frank Knox, and rumors of plots and plotters swirled around the city. At a cabinet meeting FDR wondered if *Tribune* publisher McCormick's status as a reserve officer made it possible to court-martial him. Cabinet members discussed prosecuting Manly and Waldrop for violation of the Espionage Act or bringing some kind of conspiracy charge. Publicly, however, White House officials said that Manly and the *Tribune* hadn't violated any laws.

Decades later, Manly's source was revealed to be Senator Burton Wheeler, a Montana Democrat who was among the most ardent isolationists in Congress—and one of the first to demand an investigation into the leak. It turned out that since June 1940 Wheeler had been getting secret briefings from an Army Air Corps captain who claimed the Roosevelt administration had been lying to Congress by exaggerating the readiness of the American military.[13]

On December 3 the captain, whom Wheeler never identified, brought to the senator's home a document as thick as a novel, wrapped in brown paper and labeled "Victory Program." It was the full Rainbow Five report. Wheeler asked the officer if he was afraid to deliver the most closely guarded secret in Washington to a senator. "Congress is a branch of the government," he replied. "I think it has a right to know what's really going on in the executive branch when it concerns human lives."[14]

Writing later in his memoir, Wheeler recalled that, as he scanned the document, "My blood pressure rose. I felt strongly that this was something the people as well as a senator should know about. It would awaken the public to what was in store for them if we entered the war and the fact that we probably would. The document undercut the repeated statements of Roosevelt and his followers that repeal of the neutrality acts, lend-lease, the destroyer deal, and similar measures, would keep us out of the European conflict."[15]

Wheeler also deduced that no Army captain could on his own obtain and borrow such a sensitive document. The source of the disclosure, he felt, must have been much higher in the military chain of command.

After skimming the report, Wheeler called Manly, who he knew shared his distaste for Roosevelt, at the *Tribune*'s Press Building office and invited him to come to his house. Wheeler also summoned one of his secretaries. The senator and reporter took turns that evening reading the most important sections to the secretary, who furiously scribbled their words in shorthand. The captain returned the report to its home in the War Department before its absence could be detected, and later that evening Manly and Waldrop dined together at the Press Club.

The FBI and military investigators never determined who had ordered the Rainbow Five leak. Wheeler believed that General Hap Arnold, the head of the Army Air Corps, authorized the leak because he was peeved that the plan didn't allocate sufficient resources to ramping up the production of airplanes. This theory doesn't seem plausible: the plan didn't stint on air power, and it is almost inconceivable that Arnold would commit what amounted to treason to advance his military career. It is a testament to the deviousness and inscrutability of Franklin D. Roosevelt that some historians believe he ordered the leak as part of an elaborate strategy to goad Hitler into declaring war.[16]

Manly and Waldrop quickly came to hope that a story that had seemed like the hottest scoop of their lives would be forgotten—or at least forgiven. Waldrop said that he became so disturbed by his role in making the Rainbow Plan public that "I felt like slitting my throat."[17]

The biggest leak of military secrets in American history had been overshadowed by the most devastating military intelligence failure in the nation's history. Three days after Manly's scoop hit the newsstands, Japanese bombers blasted the search for its source off the FBI's priority list.

The attack also marked the end of Masuo Kato's tenure as Washington bureau chief for Domei, Japan's official news agency.

On the morning of December 7, 1941, Kato slept late and cooked himself a breakfast of griddle cakes smothered in butter and maple syrup. Breakfast is the last meal a foreigner gives up in a new country, so Kato's fondness for pancakes and especially for butter—a food abhorred by many Japanese at the time—was a mark of his integration into American society. Still, no matter how well he assimilated, no Japanese citizen could feel comfortable in Washington in the winter of 1941. The hostility of former friends prompted Kato to work that morning from his home, an apartment on 16th Street near Dupont Circle, instead of traveling to his office in the Press Building or to the Press Club, where he often monitored the newswires and used the typewriter room as an informal office.[18]

For months American newspapers had been seething with hostility toward Japan. The press stoked anger over Japan's refusal to retreat from China and its invasion of French Indochina. The papers were full of predictions that Tokyo was planning to bomb the Panama Canal, invade the Philippines, or pivot to bite off a piece of Siberia.

Isolationist newspapers were determined to prevent war with Germany and Italy, but there were few voices calling for restraint when it came to Japan. In the popular imagination Japanese troops were short, buck-toothed runts who wouldn't be a match for American soldiers, and even top military planners in the United States and Britain believed that Japanese were incapable of flying airplanes or prevailing in combat against European or American soldiers.[19]

Months of speculation about war in the Pacific had turned the convivial atmosphere of the Press Club frosty for anyone identified with Japan. Reporters who for years had bantered with Kato turned their backs when he approached the bar. Word had circulated around the club that the talented and affable Domei editor was only pretending to be a newspaperman, that he was actually a commander in the Japanese Navy who was using journalism as a cover for spying.[20]

In fact, Kato wasn't a covert military officer, but, by American standards, nor was he an ordinary reporter. Journalism and espionage were tightly coupled in pre-war Japan. The link was so close that the Japanese government and public found it inconceivable that foreign reporters in their country were not spies. As a result, American journalists who had the misfortune to find themselves in Japan or a place under Japanese occupation during the war were treated brutally.[21]

A fluent English speaker, Kato had attended university in the United States and, starting in 1937, had served a three-year stint as Washington bureau chief of Domei. At a time when Japanese were exotic and unusual in Washington, he blended in, living at the University Club, playing golf at the Kenwood Country Club, and drinking with American reporters.[22]

Kato had returned to Japan in 1940 with no expectation of returning to Washington. He was at the dock in Yokohama on January 23, 1941, when Admiral Kichisaburo Nomura, Japan's newly chosen ambassador to Washington, and its last hope for averting war with the United States, departed in the *Kamakura Maru* ocean liner. Soon Kato followed in his wake, assigned to cover Nomura's negotiations with the US government.

Six feet tall, sporting a ready smile, an amiable manner, and a glass eye—a memento of a Chinese nationalist's assassination attempt—Nomura was the opposite of the stereotypical Japanese diplomat. He was known to be fond of America and a personal friend of President Roosevelt.

While Nomura hoped to prevent war with the United States, it wasn't clear at the time and still isn't certain whether this was really possible. Japanese politics was a byzantine swirl of intrigue and assassination. No one, including Nomura, knew if his appointment was a grand gesture on the part of a Foreign Ministry seeking to avert war or a cynical ploy intended to buy time while the imperial Army created new facts on the ground.[23]

Starting with his first meeting with Roosevelt, on February 14, Nomura's mission to Washington was extraordinary. FDR greeted the admiral like a long-lost friend and Nomura spoke frankly, declaring that he had come to try to find peace with the United States and confiding that the biggest obstacles to success were chauvinistic militarists in his own country.[24] The president suggested that Nomura enter into secret, informal discussions—the word "negotiations" was assiduously avoided—with Secretary of State Cordell Hull. Nomura was assured that he could meet with Roosevelt if the need arose and was shown a side door to the White House that he could use to avoid detection by the press.[25]

A drama worthy of a Kabuki performance played out over the coming months. Nomura and Hull had fifty or sixty secret meetings, many held in Hull's apartment, and Nomura and Roosevelt met secretly eight times in the White House. At their first meeting, Nomura and Hull vowed that they would never lie to each other. After every meeting Hull dictated a short memorandum for the State Department's files summarizing the encounter, and Nomura sent an encrypted report with his impressions to the Foreign Ministry in Tokyo. The Foreign Ministry sent Nomura a continuous stream of messages instructing him how he should conduct the negotiations.

The Kabuki aspect came into play as a result of one of the few effective intelligence operations conducted by the American government prior to World War II, the breaking of the Japanese diplomatic code. Hull and Roosevelt were reading translations of intercepts of Nomura's secret messages to Tokyo the day he sent them—and they were often able to read copies of the Foreign Ministry's messages to Nomura before he was. Hull was privy to Nomura's candid assessments of their talks, and he knew just how far his counterpart could go in making concessions to American demands. Nomura was in the dark both about America's intentions and about the intentions and plans of his compatriots.

English translations of the decrypted Japanese cables were stamped "Top Secret MAGIC," an allusion to the US Army Signal Intelligence Service chief's habit of calling his cryptanalysts "magicians." Circulation of Magic decrypts was limited to ten people: the president; the secretaries of War, Navy, and State; the chief of staff; the chief of naval operations; the chiefs of the two services' war plans divisions; and the chiefs of their intelligence organizations. The highly restricted distribution list protected the secrecy of a vital intelligence tool, but it also ensured that no one who read the cables had a deep knowledge of Japanese history or culture.[26]

Because of the Magic decrypts, Hull and Roosevelt knew Nomura's private assessments of their discussions, and because they had read his instructions they could be ready with well-considered responses to the ambassador's proposals the instant he made them. It gradually became clear to the Americans that Nomura was playing a desperate game, shading the truth or omitting details in his reports to the Foreign Ministry in an effort to avoid stirring up anti-American feelings in Tokyo. At the same time, when he thought he could get away with it, he ignored explicit instructions to deliver messages to Hull or Roosevelt that could have antagonized the American side.

Kato watched closely as Nomura attempted to outmaneuver the militarists and prevent war. Like every other Japanese enterprise operating in the United States, the news service was subject to close supervision by officials in the Japanese embassy. Kato spent as much time at the embassy as he did at the Press Building, much of it with Hidenari Terasaki, the embassy's press secretary.[27]

For a press secretary, Terasaki kept an almost comically low profile, rarely if ever communicating with American reporters, shunning the Embassy Row social scene, and managing to almost completely avoid having his name mentioned in American newspapers.[28] Despite his passion for anonymity, Terasaki was well known to American counterintelligence officers. A March 14, 1941, Magic decrypt revealed that Terasaki had been put in charge of coordinating Japanese intelligence and propaganda operations in North and South America.[29]

The day after Nomura presented his credentials to Roosevelt and the secret discussions with Hull were started, a Magic decrypt revealed priorities for Japanese intelligence operations in the United States. These included determining America's political, economic, and military strength. Tokyo also tasked its spies with identifying potential agents and collaborators by conducting "investigations of all persons or organizations which either openly or secretly oppose participation in the war," and of "anti-Semitism, communism, movements of negroes, and labor movements."[30]

If war broke out between Japan and the United States, the cable stated, "our intelligence set-up will be moved to Mexico, making that country the nerve center for our intelligence net."[31] It ordered Terasaki to "set up facilities for a US-Mexico international intelligence route." Terasaki was instructed to cooperate with the German and Italian intelligence organs in the United States.

Given his broad mandate, reclusive nature, and limited resources, Japanese reporters who spoke good English and understood American society were a valuable force-multiplier for Terasaki. They didn't have to steal secrets, or even personally favor Japanese imperialism, to be useful. Kato and most of the handful of other Japanese reporters in Washington occupied a gray area between independent journalism and espionage. At the most basic level they helped Terasaki by providing insight into the thinking of government officials, picking up gossip at the Press Club, and identifying sympathetic or vulnerable Americans who might spy for Japan.

White House and congressional credentials allowed Japanese reporters to attend press conferences and roam the halls of government buildings. Kato mingled with top Roosevelt administration officials, for example, attending Secretary of State Cordell Hull's seventieth birthday party.[32] American reporters who weren't happy about having a "Jap" in their midst kept a close eye on Kato and his colleagues.

The mood was reflected in a June 1941 column by Tom Treanor, a *Los Angeles Times* correspondent. Treanor set up the story by recalling an incident that had occurred in the State Department press room immediately after Hull had made sharp remarks about Japan at a press conference and stipulated that they were off the record. "Little Kato went to a typewriter in an adjoining office and started a story to this effect: 'Secretary Hull today in an off-the-record press conference said, etc., etc., etc.'"[33] Treanor continued: "He left the paper in the machine where all could see it and went to wash his hands." The column noted that "correspondents here think he's too smart to have done it through carelessness. It must have been some sort of diplomatic swordplay for Mr. Hull's benefit." Interviewing Kato at the Press Club, Treanor asked if anyone had told him he "should get out of Washington or that you are a spy." Kato replied, "One man told me I should get out once, but I say to him: 'That is a matter for governments to decide, not persons like you.'"

Although it did not restrict his access to press briefings, the State Department included Kato on a list of Japanese agents it provided in November 1941 to Colonel William Donovan, President Roosevelt's Coordinator of Information. The list was probably based on a secret cable sent from the Japanese consulate in New York on December 17, 1940, and decrypted by Army magicians three weeks later. Both the cable and the roster provided to Donovan included the representatives of Domei in the United States, as well as reporters for the newspapers *Asahi Shimbun* and *Yomiuri Shimbun* as possible Japanese intelligence sources.[34]

Fukuichi Fukumoto, a Japanese reporter who had been working in New York as a representative of the Osaka *Mainichi* and Tokyo *Nichi Nichi* newspapers, was also on the list. In March 1941 his employers had ordered him to return to Tokyo. In April American codebreakers learned that Terasaki had managed to have the order rescinded and to get Fukumoto posted to Washington, where he joined other reporters at the Press Building. After an American reported to the FBI that Fukumoto had offered to pay him $2,300 for drawings of an exhaust supercharger used in airplane engines, the State Department, anxious to avoid a public quarrel with Japan, quietly arranged for Fukumoto's repatriation.[35]

Japanese reporters in Washington were industrious collectors of information, but much of their work never made it into print. Domestic newspapers and radio were censored and rather than getting to read the meticulously collected reports from Japan's large contingent of international journalists, the population was subjected to relentless propaganda. Many of the cables Kato sent to Tokyo in the months prior to the Pearl Harbor attack were circulated only to a small circle of government officials that included the emperor. Aware of his elite audience, Kato tried to leverage access to leaders on both sides of the Pacific to suggest ways Tokyo could find common ground with Washington.[36]

Both sides were anxious to avoid publicity about the discussions between Nomura and Hull. Roosevelt feared that if word leaked he would be branded an appeaser, and Nomura knew that publicity prior to a peace agreement would give the militarists in Japan the opportunity to scuttle the talks. It is a mark of Kato's status as a semi-official actor that Nomura confided in him about the ongoing discussions, including Tokyo's reluctance to take steps to come to an accommodation with the United States.[37]

Kato tried to support Nomura's efforts, for example by suggesting in stories ostensibly written for publication—but in fact intended for circulation in government circles—that Japan should stop demanding that Washington cut off aid to the Chinese government because the United States would never abandon Chiang Kai-shek. He even sent a cable recommending that General Hideki Tojo be replaced with a prime minister who was less inclined to lead Japan into war with the United States. Kato, who didn't realize how brutal the *Kempeitai* military police had become since his departure, lived to tell his story because colleagues at Domei destroyed that cable before anyone in government saw it.[38]

In the last week of July 1941 developments in Washington, Tokyo, and on the ground in Southeast Asia made it impossible to continue to defer forever decisions about whether war would break out between the two nations. On July 24 Japan invaded French Indochina. In response, two days later Roosevelt froze Japanese assets in the United States, and the United States, Britain, and the government of the Dutch East Indies imposed an embargo on oil sales to Japan. FDR calculated that this would force the Japanese, who had no domestic sources of petroleum, to make concessions to the United States. If Roosevelt had a deep understanding of Japanese society, or had been advised by someone who did, he would have realized that for Japan's military leaders backing down in the face of a public threat was unthinkable.

As the cool autumn in Washington turned to a cold winter, Hull, Roosevelt, Nomura, and Kato all watched as the thin tendrils of peace the Japanese ambassador had been clutching were snatched from his fingers.

By the first week of December it was obvious to Kato and anyone else paying attention that at a minimum Japan was planning to break off diplomatic relations with the United States, and that in all probability war was just around the corner. Nomura was kept in the dark about Japan's plans, as were American policymakers who relied heavily on decrypted Japanese diplomatic cables. Although war seemed inevitable, the conventional wisdom, which Kato shared, was that it would begin with an incursion into the Dutch Indies. Japan, American leaders believed, would try to secure the oil its military needed to survive and stop short of provoking a strong American response.[39]

When Kato received a cable on December 2 ordering him back to Tokyo, he replied that he wanted to continue to work in Washington "to the end, whatever happened."[40] A few days later he learned that embassy staff were burning documents, a clear signal that a break in relations with the United States was expected.

On December 3, Roosevelt was briefed on a Magic decrypt of a cable the embassy in Washington had received ordering it to destroy all but one of its code machines. He understood its significance immediately: war was imminent. The only reason for scuttling the machines was to prevent them from falling into the hands of the enemy. Embassy staff disassembled two electromechanical code-making machines, smashed them with hammers, and dissolved the remaining bits in vats of acid. Some of this frenetic activity took place in the embassy garden, where an Office of Naval Intelligence officer observed it.[41]

At noon on December 6, Kato attended a going-away party at the Mayflower Hotel for Terasaki, who was being transferred to Rio de Janeiro. Other embassy officials had already departed for Mexico, Brazil, and Argentina.[42] Kato must have realized that Terasaki's departure was yet another sign that war was close. It was a clear signal to American intelligence analysts that Tokyo was putting in place the contingency plan for moving its intelligence operations to Mexico and South America that had been mentioned in the January cable.

That evening Kato dined with two Japanese reporters at a Chinese restaurant and shared gallows humor about how they would pass their time in an American prison after war broke out. Kato said he would write a book.[43]

In his reports Kato grasped at any sign that war could be avoided, but by the morning of December 7, there wasn't much hope to cling to. The smell of pancakes was still in the air when he handed the text of a story—his last dispatch from the United States—to a Western Union messenger at 2:00 p.m. The cable reported on the American public's reaction to the breakdown in negotiations between Washington and Tokyo and concluded that "there is still a thirty percent hope for peace."[44] Kato walked out of his apartment on 16th Street half an hour later, just missing the first radio broadcasts that would have forced him to revise his estimate.

The Domei reporter was literally dressed for a funeral—a senior Japanese officer had died in Washington a few days earlier and the service was slated for 3:00 p.m.—as he strolled down 16th Street, passed the White House, and turned right. He had almost arrived at the State Department when he hailed a taxi, oblivious to the tense drama unfolding a few blocks away in Hull's office. Japanese diplomats who, like Kato, were unaware of the Pearl Harbor attack were handing the furious secretary of state, who was all too aware of the attack, a note cutting off diplomatic relations.

As he settled into the backseat of the taxi, Kato caught the tail end of a news bulletin on the radio—something about Japanese forces bombing Manila. "God damn Japan," the driver declared, apparently unaware of the nationality of his passenger. "We'll lick hell out of those bastards now."[45]

Kato ducked out of the funeral with another Japanese reporter and headed to the Japanese embassy on Massachusetts Avenue. They were greeted by an angry crowd that had gathered on the sidewalk. The two reporters, who were well known to the embassy guards, were admitted at once.

Inside, Kato learned that the bombs hadn't fallen just on Manila and that his initial suspicion—that rogue elements of the Japanese military were to blame—was wrong. Officers in Tokyo might have imagined that they could push the Americans out of Asia with a single decisive blow, but men like Kato who had lived in the United States did not share this delusion. "There was no excitement evident in the faces of those gathered there that afternoon," Kato remembered in a memoir published after the war. "There was more of a disheartened sense of failure. Everyone spoke in hushed, expectant tones. There was no cheering or speech-making. The atmosphere was more like that of the funeral from which I had just come than that of an embassy drawing-room on the first day of war."[46]

Kato spent about an hour in the embassy. As he stepped out of a side exit he smelled smoke, looked up, and saw white puffs drifting into the clear sky. He ran inside to raise the alarm, unintentionally provoking the only laughter heard in the embassy that afternoon; embassy staff told him they were torching papers to keep them out of the hands of the Americans. There wasn't much left to get rid of: the bonfire had been burning for five days.

When Kato reached the sidewalk, he saw that the crowd had grown larger and angrier. "You," a man told him, "are the last son of a bitch we're going to let out." Kato's first instinct, like that of many other reporters, was to head to the Press Club. If he had followed through on the impulse, he would have been astonished by the scene—and the presence of a representative of Japan's news agency would have caused a stir. Hundreds of reporters had crowded into the club, seeking the company of comrades and competitors, all scrambling for information about the worst military disaster in American history. The bells on the wire service teletype machines were ringing like fire alarms, ten bells on the United Press machine, a dozen bells on the AP printer preceding one urgent bulletin after another. Seven floors below, a Japanese reporter on temporary assignment in Washington spent the evening in the United Press bureau bowing, weeping, and apologizing.[47]

Instead of heading to the Press Building, Kato sought sanctuary in the home of an acquaintance who worked for the State Department. When he returned home, two FBI agents were waiting in the lobby. They told him to stay in his apartment. A short time later Thomas Qualters, a Secret Service agent who served as FDR's personal bodyguard, knocked on Kato's door.

He had been sent by the president, not to make an arrest but rather to confiscate Kato's White House Correspondents Association card.[48]

The next morning, Kato and other Japanese citizens were interned at a makeshift detention center near Philadelphia. Germans and Italians joined them after Hitler declared war on the United States.

In his December 11 speech to the Reichstag announcing the declaration of war, Hitler blamed the United States and claimed that Germany was defending itself against American aggression. "With no attempt at an official denial there has now been revealed in America President Roosevelt's plan by which, at the latest in 1943, Germany and Italy were to be attacked in Europe by military means," Hitler said.[49] He was referring to Manly's story about the Rainbow Five report.

The Wehrmacht was already laying plans to implement Führer Directive Number 39, the strategic pivot from trying to conquer the Soviet Union to focusing on defeating America's Rainbow Five plans. The directive might have worked; in any case, its implementation would have immensely complicated America's invasion of Europe and changed the course of the war in the East, altering the fate of millions of people.

The directive was never put into effect because Hitler, enraged by reverses on the eastern front, ripped it up on December 16, took personal command of the army, and ordered an irrational and disastrous continuation of the Russian campaign. Just as the German army's path into the Soviet Union had been smoothed by Stalin's insistence that warnings from his intelligence services of impending invasion were provocations, Germany's best shot at avoiding defeat was scuttled by a dictator's decision to reject recommendations based on an accurate assessment of his adversary's capabilities and strategy.

A similar failure led America to stumble into a war with Japan as a result of a devastating attack that could have been avoided or thwarted. The Pearl Harbor disaster was not the result of a lack of intelligence, but rather of the lack of a coordinated system for synthesizing and analyzing all of the nation's intelligence.

It was obvious in November and December 1941 that war with Japan was both inevitable and imminent. The American government had several separate streams of intelligence suggesting the Japanese were planning a surprise attack on Pearl Harbor. These weren't detected because they were embedded in a blizzard of intelligence reports, and there was no mechanism in place to sift through these reports or even to systematically analyze them. The Army and Navy didn't share intelligence with each other. Rather than solving the problem Roosevelt dithered and put up with it. As his relationship with John Franklin Carter demonstrated, FDR also believed that methods that had served George Washington and Thomas Jefferson—sending friends and acquaintances abroad to spy on foreign powers and having the president personally evaluate their reports—were sufficient to cope with the risks posed by a much more complex world.

CHAPTER TWELVE
CARTER GOES TO WAR

It took the Pearl Harbor debacle, a sucker punch that cost 2,400 American lives and destroyed much of the Pacific fleet, to convince Franklin Roosevelt he needed to sort out the nation's intelligence mess. To prevent another sneak attack, and to support the war the attack had launched, America would have to emulate its enemies and allies by creating secret services capable of seeing, hearing, comprehending, and influencing events around the globe. The need was obvious. The disaster in Hawaii sparked a frenzied competition among the leaders of government agencies to fill it—and in the process vastly expand their power and prestige. They all knew that decisions about divvying up responsibilities and creating new intelligence capabilities would be made personally by the president.

John Franklin Carter, the newspaper columnist operating a secret, unofficial intelligence unit from a nondescript office in the National Press Building, was in the scrum as ambitious rivals seeking an oversized piece of the intelligence pie jostled for the president's attention. He was competing with FBI director J. Edgar Hoover; FDR's coordinator of information, William Donovan; State Department officials; and the heads of Army and Navy intelligence. Compared to its rivals, Carter's unit was infinitesimal. Based on its capabilities and his experience, he shouldn't have been a serious contender in turf battles with men who had spent decades in law enforcement, diplomacy, and the military. The journalist and amateur spymaster was in the mix because he had an asset they lacked: a close relationship with and easy access to Roosevelt.

While others wrote formal memorandums to the president through official channels and begged for coveted time on his calendar, Carter sent him chatty notes and lingered behind in the Oval Office after White House press conferences for informal meetings. He was in constant touch with Grace Tully, officially one of Roosevelt's private secretaries but in practice an influential, trusted member of the president's inner circle. Tully was the only person other than FDR who was fully aware of Carter's activities; she occasionally responded to his requests without consulting the president.

Hoover summed up his feelings about Carter in a handwritten note scrawled at the bottom of an internal FBI memo: "We know Carter well & most unfavorably. He is a crack-pot, a persistent busy-body, bitten with the Sherlock Holmes bug & plagued with a super-exaggerated ego."[1]

The FBI director barely disguised his contempt, but Donovan, who shared Carter's love of idiosyncratic schemes and sought to exploit the journalist's access to the White House, maintained cordial relations. "Yesterday afternoon," Carter wrote in a January 9 memo to Roosevelt, Donovan's aide "David Bruce showed me the master-plan he has developed for organization of a general world-wide secret intelligence service for the United States." Carter damned the plan with faint praise, writing that it was a good "model for a central-office organization of intelligence," but was "very hazy on actual operations." He added that the plan was based on British and German methods that weren't suitable for the United States. Replicating the hazy thinking he criticized in Donovan's plan, Carter wrote that European intelligence methods were "the result of experience, plus development, plus national character" and therefore weren't applicable to the United States.[2]

Summarizing his own approach to intelligence, Carter suggested that "we should strive to develop something much simpler, more happy-go-lucky and casual, and utilize ignorance in the place of secrecy as a method." By ignorance, he meant a decentralized intelligence system composed of teams that operated independently and without knowledge of each other's existence. Of course, Carter also knew just the man to lead such an organization. "I am very ambitious to be allowed to try to do something along these lines on a modest and experimental scale and would like to tell you my concrete plan of operations the next time you can spare a couple of minutes after a press conference," he wrote to the president.[3]

A week later, Roosevelt signed a secret directive that, to Hoover's delight, assigned to the FBI authority for intelligence and counterintelligence throughout the Americas, from the Arctic to Tierra del Fuego. Hoover immediately telephoned the heads of intelligence at the State Department, Army, and Navy to inform them of the arrangement, making a point of reading a note the president had handwritten on the order: "I think that the Canadian and South American Fields should not be in the Coordinator of Information Field, nor in that of the J. Franklin Carter Organization." Office of Naval Intelligence (ONI) director Rear Admiral Theodore Wilkinson told Hoover he was pained that FDR had acknowledged Carter's organization in writing, even in a secret directive. Hoover consoled Wilkinson, observing that FDR's note meant that "Carter would only operate in the United States."[4]

In reality, Carter was not restrained by geographic or bureaucratic boundaries. Reporting only to the president, he dispatched agents to roam around Mexico and the Caribbean, travel to Moscow, and collect intelligence from and about every continent except Antarctica. The topics of Carter's inquiries were as wide-ranging as Roosevelt's curiosity, touching on military and geopolitical issues, political intelligence about Democrats and Republicans, the loyalty and competence of government officials, wacky inventions, screwball conspiracy theories, labor issues, military and civilian morale, domestic and foreign propaganda, the latest gossip from New York's "Café Society," and countless other topics.

Carter's activities during the first full month of the war, January 1942, exemplify his activities over the coming years. He and his team were frenetically busy, but most of what they stirred up was dust. FDR seems to have kept the game going because Carter uncovered a few flecks of gold, and because he provided a welcome diversion.

On New Year's Day, Vannevar Bush, the government's top scientist, rebuffed Carter's request for information about an experimental internal combustion engine. Writing under letterhead with his National Press Building address, Carter had informed Bush that he was inquiring about the invention on FDR's instructions. The skeptical scientist requested "a copy of your direction from the President," which Carter was unable to provide as Roosevelt refused all his requests for credentials or official documentation of his status.[5]

The next day Tully called Carter conveying a request from FDR to discuss his proposals about enlisting organized labor to fight Axis sabotage with secretary of labor Frances Perkins. There is no record of the secretary's response to Carter's offer to serve as a "personal, unofficial, informal point of liaison for various efforts of organized labor to contribute intelligence as well as strength and skill to the conduct of the war."[6] Carter's offers of unconventional assistance often left cabinet officials nonplussed.

On January 3, Carter forwarded a useless report to Roosevelt on an interview one of his agents had conducted with an American lawyer who had been posted to Tokyo. He sent scores of similar reports over the coming months.[7]

A few days later, the president was treated to the first of a series of fantastic, and fantastically stupid, reports that Carter's number two, Henry Field, claimed had been produced "under conditions of extraordinary secrecy from a man who is believed to have accurate and swift means of communication with Moscow." The reports spun a tale that would have seemed ridiculous even in one of Carter's novels. An American military genius working for Stalin was directing the operations of the "Siberian Army," an entity that, Field's report claimed, was poised to attack Japan within days using 8,300 planes that had been hidden in underground hangars. The imaginary American was, Field claimed, a member of Stalin's Strategy Board, "which is composed of 3 Americans, 1 German (brother of the man who arrested Hitler in Munich Putsch), 1 British General (hated by Chamberlain), and a Frenchman named Collet (brother of General

Collet in Syrian campaign)." The report presented an elaborate back story for the hero, including graduating from MIT and leading victorious Soviet military campaigns from Finland to Rostov.[8] Subsequent reports claimed the USSR had spent $6 billion building a series of underground forts from Leningrad to Odessa that were stuffed with troops waiting for orders to emerge and vanquish the Wehrmacht. The reports were filed in FDR's personal safe and were shared with Army intelligence.[9]

On January 9, Roosevelt dictated a note to Tully requesting that Carter inform Army and Navy intelligence of his concerns about Nazi infiltration of the United Service Organizations (USO), the voluntary organization formed to entertain American troops. The same day, another note communicated the president's tentative approvals of Carter's plan to send a *Saturday Evening Post* reporter to Mexico City to report on Axis activities, and his proposal to investigate wealthy refugees in New York.[10]

As Tully was banging out these notes, Carter was dictating a cover letter for his first valuable report of the month. It was an accurate and chilling account of the Soviet government's abysmal treatment of Polish soldiers and civilians who had been arrested when the USSR occupied half of their country. Tens of thousands were suffering in Russian prisons and labor camps.[11]

Also on January 9, Carter sent FDR his critique of Donovan's plans and his own proposal to establish a worldwide intelligence unit. The package he dropped off with Tully included a request, which the president ignored, that Vice President Henry Wallace sign identification cards for Carter's agents who were operating overseas.

Roosevelt and his closest advisors were certain that Hitler had sprinkled secret agents throughout the United States who were busy collecting intelligence and waiting for orders to begin sabotage operations. Carter fed the paranoia, for example with a January 12, 1942, report from one of his agents, the retired businessman Curtis Munson, expressing confidence that "there is a wealthy and entrenched fifth column in this country" that was waiting for a "green light by their superiors." Ironically given his passionate defense of the civil rights of Japanese Americans, Munson advocated following Lincoln's Civil War precedent by suspending the right of *habeas corpus* and imprisoning thousands of German Americans or, alternatively, rounding them up and sending them to South Dakota to plow fields. FDR instructed Carter to "talk this over with the Attorney General and possibly the Immigration Commissioner and Mr. Hoover."[12]

The German fifth columnists were no more real than Stalin's Strategy Board or the Nazi spies Carter imagined were hiding in Bob Hope's USO entourage.

Carter had assigned to another of his agents, a journalist named William Irwin, the task of investigating Japanese intelligence activities along the US-Mexico border. Irwin drove for thousands of miles through Mexico and Texas compiling lists of Japanese doctors, dentists, and ice-cream-shop proprietors. Based on rumors and intuition, he labeled many of them "key men" in a massive, and largely imaginary, intelligence operation directed from Tokyo. On January 16, Carter forwarded scores of pages of Irwin's notes to FDR, the FBI, the State Department, and military intelligence organizations.[13]

Additional topics of Carter's reports to Roosevelt in January covered: infighting between American intelligence organizations, such as attacks on Donovan by the FBI, Army and Navy intelligence, and the State Department; "sedition among the South Boston Irish"; efforts to manufacture the Sea Otter, a crackpot idea for a ship powered by automobile engines that had caught FDR's imagination; notes on interviews with American businessmen who had been stationed in Asia; a scheme to recruit members of de Gaulle's Free French intelligence operation in Mexico as American operatives; intelligence on proposed Japanese bombing targets; a report on Argentinian domestic politics based on an interview with the Buenos Aires representative of the Otis Elevator Co.; and plans to send Field on an intelligence-gathering mission to Trinidad.

Along with this flurry of covert activity, Carter attended press conferences at the White House and produced newspaper columns.

With the help of a staff that grew to twenty-five, Carter maintained this frenzied pace for three and a half years. Hoover, Donovan, generals and admirals, senior State Department officials, and nearly every member of the cabinet came to dread the notes Tully sent from Roosevelt forwarding one of Carter's memos with a request for comment or action. Nine times out of ten they were time-sucking nonsense: a suggestion forwarded to General Hap Arnold that the Army Air Forces consider bombing Japanese volcanoes to set off earthquakes; a report asserting with great confidence that the labor leader John L. Lewis was conspiring with French intelligence to mount a coup and depose Roosevelt; or fantasies about Ukrainian terrorists hell-bent on assassinating the president.[14]

Some of Carter's intelligence, however, was helpful. He passed on a tip in July 1942 from Gerald Haxton, Somerset Maugham's secretary, who noted that it was possible to pick up a telephone in New York and put a call through to Switzerland. Given the ease of communicating between Germany and Switzerland, this posed an obvious security risk, most immediately from German submarines to ships departing from Atlantic ports. As a direct consequence of Carter's information, Roosevelt ordered restrictions on communications with neutral countries that undoubtedly reduced the flow of intelligence to Germany.

Along with piles of garbage, Carter's agents provided Roosevelt with information that was accurate and even profound.

Of the thousands of reports Carter sent Roosevelt, the most alarming and probably the most significant was a 130-page dossier titled "Reports on Poland and Lithuania." Compiled by the Polish underground, it was the most detailed report to date to reach the White House about the Holocaust. The dossier, which Roosevelt and undersecretary of state Sumner Welles received on December 30, 1942, reinforced and expanded on information the administration had received from other sources.[15]

The report included the first news to reach Washington about the Belzec concentration camp in southeastern Poland: "Inside and outside the fence Ukrainian sentries are posted. Executions are carried out in the following manner: a train carrying Jews arrives at the station and is moved up to the wire fence where the guards are changed. Now the train is brought to the unloading place by German personnel. The men are taken into barracks on the left, where they have to take their clothes off, ostensibly for a bath."[16] It went on to describe how men and women were herded into a building and killed, their bodies buried in a ditch that had been dug by "Jews who, after they have finished the job, are executed."

The dossier revealed the existence of mobile extermination trucks in which poison gas was used to murder Jews, described the Auschwitz concentration camp, liquidation of the Warsaw ghetto, and atrocities in Lithuania. An appendix containing photographs of corpses stacked like firewood and other horrors made it difficult even for anti-Semites in the State Department to doubt the authenticity of the information.

Carter's team also continued in early 1942 to collect intelligence on the threats posed by—and, even more, to—Japanese, both citizens of the United States and of Japan, living on the West Coast and in Hawaii.

"We are drifting into a treatment of the Japanese corresponding to Hitler's treatment of the Jews," Munson warned in a note to Tully.[17] It was late February 1942, and Munson, Carter's agent on the West Coast, was despondent. Rather than protect the Japanese as Munson advised, the government was standing by as anti-Japanese hysteria threatened to boil over into an American version of Kristallnacht.

Carter had been sending reports to Roosevelt for months—before and after the Pearl Harbor attack—reiterating his conviction that 98 percent of Japanese on the West Coast and in Hawaii were loyal to America. There is "no substantial danger of Fifth Column activities by Japanese," Carter informed FDR on December 16, 1941.[18]

In January 1942, Carter gave Roosevelt Munson's recommendations for handling the "West coast Japanese problem." These included the president or vice president issuing a statement reassuring loyal citizens of Japanese descent that their rights would be protected, giving reliable second-generation Japanese Americans responsibility for ensuring the good behavior of all Japanese American residents, and creating a process to clear Japanese Americans for work in defense plants.

Despite Hoover's determination to sideline Carter and his organization, the amateur spy kept tabs on the bureau's energetic efforts to round up suspected Japanese spies operating in California and Hawaii. Working from lists prepared in advance by the Office of Naval Intelligence, the FBI quickly neutralized the real threats of sabotage and espionage.

Carter was also receiving from and sending to the White House reports from sources in local law enforcement and British intelligence, as well as private citizens, describing how unscrupulous individuals were terrorizing Japanese Americans into giving up their homes, farms, and businesses. In California, the Hearst newspapers were fomenting racial hatred, politicians were calling for mass evacuations, and there was an ever-present threat of vigilante violence.

In addition to Roosevelt, Carter's reports about West Coast Japanese were circulated to Hoover, the secretaries of War, State, and Labor, and Army officers who were responsible for defending the Pacific Coast. By the time Munson wrote to Tully in February, it was clear that the battle for a morally defensible policy was lost. Plans were already being drawn up for internment. To Carter's credit, he continued to stand up for the rights of Japanese Americans even after tens of thousands were sent to desolate concentration camps.[19]

Carter's most spectacular operation was even more controversial than his advocacy for Japanese Americans. It centered on his and Roosevelt's fondness for the prominent Nazi, Ernst "Putzi" Hanfstaengl, whom Carter had met in 1932 at FDR's suggestion, and their decision to bring him to the United States.

Hanfstaengl had taken a wildly improbable path to America. One of Hitler's earliest supporters, by the time the Nazis came to power he had fallen out of favor with the party leadership, so it came as a surprise when Hermann Göring summoned him to Berlin in February 1937. Göring, second only to Hitler in the Nazi hierarchy, told Hanfstaengl that the

Führer had personally ordered him to travel to Salamanca, Spain, on a secret mission.

The journey began eight days after Hanfstaengl's fiftieth birthday, on February 10, 1937. After take-off, he was horrified when the pilot said that rather than landing in a part of Spain controlled by the pro-German nationalists, his orders were to eject Hanfstaengl over Republican-held territory. Terrified that he wouldn't survive his first parachute landing or that he'd be killed by anti-fascist forces, Hanfstaengl wasted no time when the plane developed engine trouble and landed near Leipzig. He fled, first to Switzerland and later to Britain, defying Göring's orders to return home.

At the start of the war the British government interned Hanfstaengl as an enemy alien. In a bid to escape confinement, he expressed an interest in aiding the fight against Hitler. Asked if he was willing to help destroy Germany, he replied that he wanted to overthrow Hitler, not destroy his country. The Brits decided correctly that Hanfstaengl was still a Nazi, locked him up, and in September 1940 shipped him along with hundreds of Nazis to an internment camp in Ontario, Canada.[20]

In February 1942 Carter, seeking information about a friend of Eleanor Roosevelt's whom he erroneously believed was a Nazi spy, asked the FBI to track down Hanfstaengl and obtain permission from British intelligence to conduct an interview.[21] When Carter met with Hanfstaengl in March 1942, their conversation was supposed to be about the counterintelligence investigation. Instead, Carter quickly turned it into a recruitment pitch. Hanfstaengl was in a tight spot, squeezed between Canadian guards who treated him with all the consideration they believed a despicable Nazi deserved and German inmates for whom he was a traitor. Half starved, suffering from untreated dental maladies, and fearing violence from fellow prisoners, Hanfstaengl viewed Carter's offer as a lifeline.

Soon after he returned to Washington, Carter met with Roosevelt and Welles and proposed that they spring Hanfstaengl and bring him to

Washington. When they asked what Putzi could possibly contribute to the war effort, Carter replied, "He actually knows all these people in the Nazi government. He might be able to tell you what makes them tick."[22]

Hanfstaengl's potential value as an analyst didn't come close to justifying the political risks associated with bringing him to the United States. The American public would have been outraged if word leaked out that Roosevelt or his administration was collaborating with a leading Nazi. The presence of Hitler's confidant in Washington could also cause troubles in Moscow by exacerbating Stalin's fears that the United States and Britain were plotting to negotiate a separate peace with Hitler that would free the Germans to defeat and occupy the Soviet Union.

Roosevelt seemed to have something in mind other than importing an analyst or propagandist when he agreed to Carter's plan. The Germans were at the apogee of their power. It was hard to envision how the United States could defeat a military machine that had occupied most of Europe and appeared to be on the verge of victory in Russia. Roosevelt apparently hoped Hanfstaengl could help devise or implement a strategy that would inspire the German military to depose Hitler and negotiate peace with the Allies. That's certainly how Carter and Hanfstaengl interpreted Roosevelt's invitation.[23]

Giving Carter the green light to bring Hanfstaengl to Washington, Roosevelt said, "You can tell him that there's no reason on God's earth why the Germans shouldn't again become the kind of nation they were under Bismarck. Not militaristic. They were productive; they were peaceful; they were a great part of Europe. And that's the kind of Germany I would like to see. If he would like to work on that basis, fine."[24]

The British government fought to keep Hanfstaengl in Canada but gave in when Roosevelt raised the issue with Churchill. The Brits insisted that Hanfstaengl remain under guard and that his presence in the United States be kept strictly secret. Sir Gerald Campbell, British Consul General to the United States, wrote to Carter in May 1942 noting that the "British authorities view the proposal to make use of Hanfstaengl with considerable misgiving." He added, "I think we can all agree about the danger of confusing anybody's mind at this time into the belief that there are good and bad ex-Nazis."[25]

In fact, Carter had long believed in good and bad Nazis, and he put Hanfstaengl in the former camp. His idea to bring Hanfstaengl to Washington, and apparently FDR's consent for the plan, were animated by this belief.

These notions weren't a secret. In a May 1941 newspaper column, Carter had suggested that the flight to Scotland of Rudolph Hess, the third most powerful man in Germany, was a sign that the conflict between warring Nazi factions was coming to a climax. He wrote that one faction wished to "stabilize German victories, leaving Germany the supreme power on the continent, but foregoing political empire," while the other "propose to follow the world-revolution to world supremacy at any cost to German manpower and German ideas." He informed his readers that "from the start of the Hitler revolution it has been obvious that there was a group of sincere, able and patriotic Germans who worked whole-heartedly for a greater Germany and a German mission which would create a Germany and a German people free to work out their destinies and to socialize and to rationalize the life of Europe."[26]

It was, of course, incredible for anyone to make such statements at a time when German troops were enjoying their opportunity to "socialize" in Paris, Jews all over the continent were experiencing the Nazi efforts to "rationalize the life of Europe," and innocent civilians were experiencing Luftwaffe pilots' attempts to "work out their destinies" by bombing British cities.

In the column, which was printed in the *Boston Globe* and newspapers across the country, Carter counted Hess and several other leading Nazis as likely members of the enlightened Nazi group: "Putzi Hanfstaengl, long since exiled, also belonged to this group, as perhaps did Dr. Goebbels himself. Theirs was a European concept which, however brutal and inconvenient, was not necessarily incompatible with a world-order or Christian civilization."

According to Hanfstaengl, when discussing terms for the transfer, Carter had attributed the restrictions to the machinations of small-minded men— and Jews. "There was quite some opposition to your being brought to Washington from some small unimportant men—some were jealous, some were Jews, some incompetent and stupid and afraid of competition," Carter said, Hanfstaengl recorded in his diary a few hours after the conversation.[27]

Roosevelt was anxious to avoid publicity. While in the United States, Hanfstaengl was referred to as "Dr. Sedgwick" after his mother's maiden name, or simply as "Dr. S.," and the enterprise was referred to as the S Project.

The S Project began in a dramatic fashion.

On the afternoon of June 30, 1942, Hanfstaengl, the most senior Nazi to set foot on American soil during World War II, shook hands with the commanding general at Fort Belvoir where he was to be interned and strode across a conference room, stopping in front of a large world map. "There is only one place for you to start the invasion of Europe, General, and that is here," he boomed, thumping a long, bony finger on Casablanca. "Here is the weakest spot."[28]

Hanfstaengl, believing he had merely stated the obvious, wasn't prepared for the response to his pronouncement. The general stormed out of the room, ordered a tripling of the guard outside the bungalow where the German prisoner was being held and had him confined to the building during daylight hours. As Hanfstaengl learned later, Casablanca was one of the primary targets for the most closely guarded secret in the American military, Operation Torch, the Anglo American invasion of North Africa that was launched in December 1942. Roosevelt had to intervene personally to persuade the Army that their prisoner had made an educated guess and that he wasn't a Nazi spy.[29]

Carter's enthusiasm for working with Putzi was tempered by one concern. The British government had spread the rumor that Hanfstaengl was homosexual. While Carter was happy to associate with a racist anti-Semitic Nazi, he was wary of homosexuals. He consulted Claire Boothe Luce, who suggested leaving the German alone with Gerald Haxton,

Maugham's German-speaking secretary and lover, to see what transpired. When Hanfstaengl told Carter "I wish you'd get rid of this man. One of the things I couldn't stand about Hitler was all the fairies he had around him," Carter decided he had passed the test.[30]

Hanfstaengl quickly wore out his welcome at Fort Belvoir after terrorizing African American soldiers. Souring on Hitler did nothing to sweeten his racism. He was moved to Bush Hall, a crumbling estate in Alexandria, Virginia, that Carter rented from two of Field's aged relatives. The scene quickly degenerated into a cross between the television comedies *Hogan's Heroes* and *Fawlty Towers*. The madcap scene, which Carter found amusing only in retrospect, featured the moody and petulant Hanfstaengl, drunken rebellious servants, balky plumbing, and a leaky roof. FDR, who remembered his German acquaintance's performances at the Harvard Club, ordered that a Steinway piano be placed in the house. Field, who despised Hanfstaengl and secretly kept the British government informed of his activities, ensured that it was never tuned. It was appropriate that the piano, like the whole S Project, was off-key as Hanfstaengl filled Bush Hall with the sounds of Bach, Beethoven, and Wagner, music that he'd once used to arouse Hitler. Carter and Field visited often, occasionally bringing intelligence officers who sought advice from "Dr. S." Adding to the farcical nature of the adventure, for a time, Hanfstaengl was "guarded" by his son Egon, an American citizen who had enlisted in the US Army.[31]

When Egon shipped out for service in the Pacific, he left his .38 caliber revolver with his father. One day a Pentagon official happened to see it sitting on a table at Bush Hall and was appalled at the idea that a Nazi prisoner had access to a weapon. Carter took possession of the gun and later issued it to a recent college graduate named Alexander Sturm, whom he had recruited into his operation. The day Sturm reported for work Carter gave him the .38 in a left-handed holster—Sturm was right-handed—along with a temporary National Press Club membership card, a check for twenty dollars, and vague instructions about his duties as guard and assistant to "Dr. S."[32]

Hanfstaengl listened to German radio broadcasts on a shortwave receiver that had been installed at Bush Hall by technicians from the Federal Communications Commission and wrote memos suggesting counterpropaganda, lacing his recommendations with information that he believed would get under the skin of Hitler and his inner circle. Roosevelt took an active interest in Hanfstaengl's work, reading his reports and occasionally sending questions through Carter. FDR solicited Hanfstaengl's ideas about how "word could effectively be brought to reach the German people with the assurance that we do not propose a general massacre of Germans and that in future a peaceful German people can protect and improve their living standards." In response, Hanfstaengl suggested a broadcast to German soldiers by General Eisenhower or Marshall. The idea, which was never put into practice, was to plant the seeds for the German military to mount a coup against Hitler.[33]

In his reports, Hanfstaengl often urged the United States to drop its demand for Germany's unconditional surrender. For example, in an analysis of one of Hitler's speeches he wrote that "it is alone the 'unconditional surrender' clause which is in effect acting as a welcome corset in favor of the reeling Hitler regime, holding together what otherwise would burst asunder. That Hitler's days could be very substantially shortened by modifying the intransigence of this clause can be doubted by no one."[34]

Hanfstaengl wrote a psychological profile of Hitler, spicing it up with salacious tidbits and speculation about the Führer's sex life. Hitler had an erotic fascination with whips, and he had probably been infected with a venereal disease by a Jewish prostitute in Vienna in 1909, his former supporter and friend wrote. "Real and complete sexual fulfillment" was impossible for Hitler, and sexual frustration led him to "into brooding isolation, and artificially dramatized public life." Hanfstaengl commented somewhat cryptically on "rumors" that "Hitler's sexual life, such as it is, demands a unique performance on the part of the women, the exact nature of which is a state secret." The Führer's combination of artistic sentiments and cruelty made him a hybrid of a romantic poet and a gangster, according to Hanfstaengl. "He is a compound, say, of Lord Byron and Al Capone."[35]

When she heard about the Hitler profile, Tully knew Roosevelt would be interested. She arranged for a copy to be bound and delivered to the White House. As predicted, Roosevelt loved it, reading it in bed and advising Harry Hopkins and other White House officials to study it carefully for insights into Hitler.[36]

Hanfstaengl also wrote profiles of four hundred "key Nazis" that were turned over to Army intelligence.

In December 1942, journalists at *Cosmopolitan* magazine learned of Hanfstaengl's presence in the United States—almost certainly from British intelligence—and the broad outlines of his activities. *Cosmopolitan's* editor told Carter he planned to give the story to the virulently anti-Roosevelt Hearst newspapers. Carter convinced the editor to hold off until February 1. The State Department and White House agreed to Carter's plan to get in front of the story by issuing a press release on January 28. Carter contacted the columnist Dorothy Thompson; the foreign editor of the *New York Herald Tribune*; Henry Luce, the publisher of *Life*, *Time*, and *Fortune* magazines; and several other journalists, persuading them all to spin the story in a way that was favorable to FDR.[37]

Incredibly, Carter himself broke the news in an article distributed by the North American Newspaper Alliance. Writing as if he had only recently learned the bare outlines of the story, Carter told his readers that the "government is making public one of the best-kept secrets of its psychological warfare against Hitler and the Nazis, the fact that Dr. Ernst Sedgwick (Putzi) Hanfstaengl has been giving our government the lowdown on Hitlerism for several months." He added that "details of the transfer from Canadian to American jurisdiction are still shrouded in official secrecy." The story ran in newspapers around the country, including on the front page of the *New York Times*.[38]

While the *Times* didn't reveal Carter's role in the affair, other newspapers mentioned that he was involved in the operation. Carter lied to his colleagues, minimizing his role. If his fellow reporters knew anything about the other covert services Carter was providing the White House, or the existence of his intelligence unit, they kept the information to themselves.

The storm blew over quickly, but the publicity prompted an immediate and vociferous demand from the British government to return the prisoner.[39]

Carter had done just about everything he could think of to persuade Roosevelt to keep the S Project alive. On the morning of February 17, 1943, he stopped at St. Matthew's Cathedral on his way to the White House and said a prayer for Putzi, paused on the way out to drop a dollar bill into the Poor Box, and realized after it was too late to retrieve it that by mistake he'd deposited a five. It was, Carter confided to his diary, money well spent. When he arrived at the White House, Roosevelt said he would defy the British and hold onto Hanfstaengl. Carter drove out to Bush Hall with Field. "Much jubilation, rum punch and congrats," Carter recorded in his diary.[40]

Hanfstaengl's reports became increasingly unhinged from reality, featuring predictions that Germany would invade Spain, Nazi armies would occupy Sweden, and many other events that never transpired. Roosevelt rejected Hanfstaengl's requests for a personal meeting and ignored his fantasy of sitting down with both the president and Churchill to plan the post-war order.

In the summer of 1944, the British turned up the heat, threatening to leak information about the administration's treatment of Hanfstaengl to Roosevelt's Republican challenger. The threat of newspaper stories about the White House pampering a Nazi in a mansion with servants were the last straw. Any sentiment FDR may have felt toward Putzi was no match for the risk of losing an election. In any case, the president had dropped all thoughts of anything other than complete military victory over Germany, so the Nazi insider's views on strategies for provoking an uprising against Hitler were no longer of interest.

On June 28, 1944, Tully noted in a memo for the official files that

"The President directed me to notify Dr. Henry Field that he did not feel it was worthwhile to continue the Dr. S. project and therefore it will be terminated as of July 1."[41] Tully repeated the message to Carter on July 7, prompting him to write a memo to FDR praising Hanfstaengl, saying his life would be in danger in England, and arguing that returning him would serve as a deterrent against any German in the future taking risks on behalf of the American government.[42]

Roosevelt was unmoved. The British and Canadian governments squabbled over which country should take him, delaying Hanfstaengl's departure. In the end, Roosevelt said, "Hell, just put him on a plane and fly him over to England and turn him over. That's it."[43] And on September 24, 1944, that's exactly what was done.

Tully's file note on the termination of the S Project included one bit of welcome news for Field and Carter. Roosevelt had approved continuation of the "M Project," a secret study of options for post-war migration (hence "M") of the millions Europeans expected to be displaced by the war. FDR found time on the afternoon of July 30, 1942, in the midst of a schedule packed with meetings with Soviet ambassador Maxim Litvinov, Secretary of State Cordell Hull, and General Arnold, to dictate a memo greenlighting the M Project:

> I love your memorandum of July thirtieth in regard to the multi-adjectived anthropologist. I think you are completely right. I know that you and Henry Field can carry out this project unofficially, exploratorially, ethnologically, racially, admixturally, miscegenationally, confidentially and, above all, budgetarily.
>
> Any person connected herewith whose name appears in the public print will suffer guillotinally.[44]

Roosevelt was expressing satisfaction with Carter's report on his visit with Aleš Hrdlička, curator of physical anthropology at the Smithsonian Museum of Natural History. Roosevelt had carried on a lively correspondence with Hrdlička for over a decade and had absorbed the scientist's theories about racial mixtures and eugenics. Roosevelt, the scion of two families that considered themselves American aristocrats, was especially attracted to Hrdlička's notions of human racial "stock."

A prominent public intellectual who had dominated American physical anthropology for decades, Hrdlička was convinced of the superiority of the white race and obsessed with racial identity. Shortly after the Pearl Harbor attack he'd written to Roosevelt expressing the view that the "less developed skulls" of Japanese were proof that they were innately warlike and had a lower level of evolutionary development than other races. The president wrote back asking whether the "Japanese problem" could be solved through mass interbreeding.[45]

Roosevelt had asked Carter to recruit Hrdlička to head up a secret international committee of anthropologists that would study the "ethnological problems anticipated in post-war population movements." Carter's report on the meeting, which prompted Roosevelt's effusive memo, called Hrdlička a "stubborn, erudite, arrogant, charming, authoritarian, friendly, difficult, delightful old gentleman."[46]

Outlining the president's charge for the committee, Carter told Hrdlička it was expected to "formulate agreed opinions as to problems arising out of racial admixtures and to consider the scientific principles involved in the process of miscegenation as contrasted with the opposing policies of so-called 'racialism.'" The instructions were consistent with views Roosevelt had expressed for decades.[47]

In 1925, while undergoing therapy for polio at Warm Springs, Georgia, FDR wrote a series of columns for the *Macon Telegraph*, including one that touched on his ideas about immigration. He praised elements of Canada's immigration policy, especially its regulations "to prevent large groups of foreign born from congregating in any one locality." He added, "If, twenty-five years ago, the United States had adopted a policy of this kind we would not have the huge foreign sections which exist in so many of our cities." The future president remarked that "no sensible American wants this country to be made a dumping ground for foreigners of any nation, but it is equally true that there are a great many foreigners who, if they came here, would make exceedingly desirable citizens. It becomes, therefore, in the first place, a question of selection." Roosevelt informed his readers that "a little new European blood of the right sort does a lot of good in every community."

While the column doesn't define "the right sort," it provides two examples of good emigrants, those from Southern Germany and Northern Italy. Roosevelt also expressed the opinion that "for a good many years to come European immigration should remain greatly restricted," and that "foreigners" who had congregated in large American cities should be encouraged to disperse into the heartland.[48] FDR apparently held onto these opinions when he moved into the White House. They may explain why he declined to intervene in the 1930s to lift or exploit loopholes in immigration caps that prevented Jews from escaping Nazi oppression, as well as his enthusiasm for the M Project.

Roosevelt's goals for the committee were consistent with the views he had expressed in 1925. He wanted it to identify "the vacant places of the earth suitable for post-war settlement" and the "type of people who could live in those places." Initial work was to focus on South America and Central Africa. Roosevelt wanted the committee to explore questions such as the probable outcomes from mixing people from various parts of Europe with the South American "base stock."[49]

FDR asked the committee to consider some specific questions, such as: "Is the South Italian stock—say, Sicilian—as good as the North Italian stock—say, Milanese—if given equal economic and social opportunity? Thus, in a given case, where 10,000 Italians were to be offer[ed] settlement facilities, what proportion of the 10,000 should be Northern Italians and what Southern Italian?"[50]

Roosevelt "also pointed out," Carter informed Hrdlička, "that while most South American countries would be glad to admit Jewish immigration, it was on the condition that the Jewish group were not localized in the cities, they want no 'Jewish colonies,' 'Italian colonies,' etc."

Keeping with this theme, the president also tasked the committee with determining how to "resettle the Jews on the land and keep them there."[51]

Hrdlička ultimately refused to participate in the M Project because Roosevelt wouldn't give him absolute control. Isaiah Bowman, president of Johns Hopkins University, was promoted from his role as a member of the committee to the head of the project. Roosevelt knew Bowman well and so was presumably aware of his anti-Semitic views.[52] Bowman understood what Roosevelt was trying to achieve through the M Project. Years earlier, in November 1938, he had undertaken research for FDR about the prospects for European settlement in South America. Requesting the research, Roosevelt wrote to Bowman: "Frankly, what I am rather looking for is the possibility of uninhabited or sparsely inhabited good agricultural lands to which Jewish colonies might be sent." Roosevelt added that "such colonies need not be large but, in all probability, should be large enough for mutual cooperation and assistance—say fifty to one hundred thousand people in a given area."[53]

The M Project expanded far beyond Roosevelt's original charge, producing tens of thousands of pages of reports, maps, and charts analyzing the suitability of locations around the globe for settlement by Europeans who were expected to be displaced by the war, analyzing the characteristics of myriad racial and ethnic groups, and theorizing about optimal proportions in which to combine them in their new homelands.

While settlement contingencies for a wide range of peoples were studied, when Roosevelt described the M Project to Churchill during a lunch at the White House in May 1943, he focused on one particular group. FDR described it as study about "the problem of working out the best way to settle the Jewish question," Vice President Henry Wallace, who attended the meeting, recorded in his diary. The solution that the president endorsed, "essentially is to spread the Jews thin all over the world," rather than allow them to congregate anywhere in large numbers.[54]

Very few people outside the team that produced the reports were allowed to see them and they had no discernable impact on policy decisions. In retrospect, the M Project's principal accomplishment was to shed light on FDR's thinking about race and immigration, and to illuminate the hubris of 1940s social scientists who believed they could and should decide the fate of millions without consulting either those who would be resettled or the people who would host them.

When Roosevelt died on April 12, 1945, his personal files contained over three thousand pages of correspondence with Carter, profiles of hundreds of Nazis that Hanfstaengl had compiled, plus the massive outpouring from the M Project. Carter wrote to Truman explaining his work for FDR, offering to continue his unit's covert activities, and urging the new president to fund completion of the M Project.

Truman was deeply skeptical about the need for espionage or secret intelligence, and he had been informed by the State Department that the $10,000 per month that was being spent on the M Project was a waste of money. He terminated Carter's operations and cut off funding for the migration studies.

Following the termination of his career as a secret agent, Carter continued to write newspaper and magazine articles and books, including one that included a brief description of his wartime work for Roosevelt.[55]

Carter resumed his relationship with the White House in the fall of 1948, when he was recruited as a speechwriter for a campaign that most observers had written off as quixotic. He traveled on Truman's "whistle-stop" tour and wrote or contributed to most of the major speeches Truman gave in the final months of the campaign.[56] As always, Carter didn't feel any need to inform his readers that along with writing about the news, he was working behind the scenes to make it.

Perhaps because he was on the right side of history, Carter has never been publicly criticized for his decisions to use journalism as a cover for spying or for deceiving his readers and colleagues by feigning objectivity about events in which he was secretly participating.

On November 28, 1967, at age seventy, Carter suffered a heart attack and died in his chair, behind a desk in his office in the National Press Building.[57]

CHAPTER THIRTEEN

TASS:
THE AGENCY OF
SOVIET SPIES

Working from the offices of TASS, the Telegraph Agency of the Soviet Union, in New York and one floor above John Franklin Carter in the National Press Building, Vladimir Sergeyevich Pravdin did exactly what Carter only imagined he had accomplished. From the fall of 1941 to the summer of 1945, the Soviet intelligence officer used journalism as a cover for an effective espionage operation. Pravdin pulled it off because he was everything Carter wasn't: disciplined, tough, and above all ruthless. The contrasts between Carter and Pravdin exemplify the differences between professional spies who pretend to be journalists and journalists who moonlight as spies.

Although the irony of a Soviet newsman's being named Pravdin, which means "man of truth" in Russian, must have occurred to American reporters and editors, given his serious demeanor it is unlikely that anyone joked with him about it. Pravdin wore the name like the suits he purchased on London's Regent Street. The name was comfortable because, like everything about his well-tailored persona, it was a lie.

Pravdin's real name was Roland Abbiate. He was born in England, the son of a French cellist from Monaco. When Abbiate was six, the family moved to the tsar's glittering capital, St. Petersburg, where his father joined the faculty of the conservatory. Abbiate left Russia in 1920 as a sixteen-year-old, living in Monte Carlo and Marseilles before arriving in New York in 1926. According to a Russian biography, he was a waiter at the Astoria Hotel on Times Square from 1926 to 1928.[1] He actually did spend a few months working in New York hotels in 1926, but for most of his stay in New York Abbiate was an involuntary guest of the US government. He was arrested in April 1926 for impersonating an immigration officer and, after serving a two-year prison term, was deported to England.[2]

Men like Abbiate who were comfortable sliding between cultures and languages—he spoke English, French, and Russian flawlessly—were valuable to Moscow. Abbiate's sister had been recruited into the OGPU, Stalin's intelligence service, and he followed her into the service in 1931.[3]

Always impeccably dressed and occasionally armed, fond of a good drink, capable of seducing women and of calmly extricating himself from mortal peril, Pravdin was a real-life James Bond, minus the wink and witty repartee. A short autobiography he submitted in 1944 to Moscow Center, as the intelligence service's personnel referred to its headquarters, reads like the resume of a character from a spy story.[4]

"February 1935: was sent to Norway to determine the precise whereabouts of the Old Man; completed assignment in one month." The Old Man was Trotsky; locating him was the first step in a planned assassination.

"August 1936: Accompanied a ship carrying military equipment from Finland to Bilbao. In the English Channel, prevented transfer of the ship to Franco's naval forces by threatening the ship's captain with immediate execution." At the time, the Basque region was surrounded by Franco's forces and the port of Bilbao was a critical entry point for military supplies headed to the Republican government opposing Franco. Losing the ship would have been a blow to the Republicans, and a disaster for Abbiate, who would certainly have been imprisoned and would likely have been executed.

"February 1937: Was sent to the countryside with an assignment to liquidate Old Man; after failing to carry out the assignment, was recalled in May to fulfill another one." The "countryside" was Soviet intelligence's cover name for Mexico. Abbiate was one of many Soviet agents who attempted to penetrate Trotsky's inner circle. Three years later, one of them succeeded and plunged an ice pick into the Old Man's head.

"July 1937: On my own, tracked down and liquidated Raymond." Raymond was the cover name for Ignace Reiss, a Soviet intelligence officer who, disgusted by the execution of old Bolsheviks in the purges, had sent Stalin a letter returning his Order of the Red Banner medal, resigning from the NKVD, as OGPU had been renamed, and announcing his allegiance to Trotsky. Immediately after sending the letter, Reiss went into hiding from the assassins he knew Stalin would certainly send. The task of silencing his comrade fell to Abbiate. To set the trap, Abbiate seduced Reiss's one-time lover, Gertrude Schildbach, convincing the much-older woman that he had fallen madly in love with her and wanted to marry her. Acting on Abbiate's orders, Schildbach gave Reiss a box of strychnine-laced chocolates, but, fearing that Reiss's wife or child would be killed, she immediately snatched it back. Abbiate quickly improvised another plan, instructing Schildbach to lure Reiss to an isolated road in Switzerland where he "liquidated" the defector with a Soviet PPD-34 submachine gun. Reiss died with a lock of Schildbach's gray hair in his clenched fist.[5]

The execution of Reiss had been conducted sloppily. In addition to recovering the poisoned chocolates, Swiss police found a blood-stained coat at the crime scene with a receipt from an upscale London tailor in the pocket made out to "R. Abbiate." Abbiate and Schildbach eluded the police and made their way to Moscow. Her squeamishness over possibly poisoning an innocent woman and child was not appreciated in the Lubyanka. Instead of being rewarded with the romantic bliss Abbiate had promised, Schildbach was arrested and sent to a Siberian prison camp, while he was rewarded with a promotion.[6]

Lookout notices for Abbiate had been posted to borders from Dover to Singapore, but as he'd never used it before, "Pravdin" was not among the five aliases listed on the bulletins.[7]

Traveling on a Soviet diplomatic passport and with credentials identifying him as an editor at TASS, the man known for the rest of his life as Vladimir Pravdin arrived in New York in September 1941. He quickly came to the FBI's attention. For the next four and a half years, the bureau was on the lookout for Abbiate and was also keeping an eye on Pravdin; it had no idea that they were the same person.[8]

British intelligence was also in the dark. At a time when Pravdin was known to members of British Security Coordination in New York, a British counterintelligence officer wrote a memo noting that Abbiate and another Soviet agent "seem to have disappeared from human ken since they were involved in the murder of Reiss in 1937."[9] The memo suggested removing Abbiate from a "post-war black list," of individuals who were to be excluded from Britain when normal travel resumed. The recipient of this memo, a senior British intelligence officer named Kim Philby, must have been pleased. A longtime Soviet agent, Philby relished evidence of his British colleagues' cluelessness. Philby approved the proposal to strike Abbiate from the list.

Returning to Manhattan, the city where he'd been arrested fifteen years earlier, marked a complete reversal of fortune for Pravdin. Now he was dining with the editor of the *New York Times* and the chiefs of the Associated Press and United Press wire services in hotel restaurants like those where he'd once waited tables.

In January 1944, Pravdin was promoted to head of TASS operations in the United States and co-leader of the NKVD's US operations. He shared intelligence responsibilities with a twenty-nine-year-old officer who had little experience and, according to whingeing memos Pravdin sent to Moscow Center, very limited abilities. In April 1945 his rival was shipped off to San Francisco, and Pravdin was officially put in charge of Soviet intelligence in New York and Washington.

Pravdin traveled often to Washington, transforming the TASS bureau in the Press Building from a news-gathering organization that did some spying on the side into an intelligence operation that used journalism as a cover for espionage. The TASS men worked under stern photos of Lenin and Stalin in a single room on the top floor of the Press Building, certain the FBI was taping their phone and bugging the office. It isn't surprising that they didn't spend much time behind their desks, preferring to soak up whiskey and gossip at the Press Club bar, hang around the State Department press room, and attend White House briefings and congressional hearings.

The longtime TASS Washington bureau chief, Laurence Todd, was one of the most popular reporters in Washington. There is no evidence he was a Soviet intelligence agent, but he must have been aware of his colleagues' covert activities. Before joining TASS, Todd worked at a news service that was a front for Soviet espionage, and for decades at TASS Todd worked elbow-to-elbow with Soviet intelligence officers. His circle of close friends encompassed more than a dozen Americans who spied for Stalin, including several who were alarmingly indiscreet. Only an idiot would have been unaware that his colleagues and friends were stealing political and military secrets from the US government, and Todd wasn't an idiot. In November 1936 he was one of two Press Club members who correctly predicted the exact number of electoral votes Roosevelt would receive, and five years later he was the only member of the State Department press corps to pass an exam given to prospective Foreign Service officers.[10]

Todd and the other American journalists who reported to the TASS office in the National Press Building during World War II were on friendly terms with an impressive range of Washington insiders: reporters, editors, and publishers; diplomats; government officials; labor union and Democratic Party operatives; and, naturally, individuals who were openly or secretly members of the Communist Party of the United States.

Under Pravdin's leadership, the TASS bureau operated on two parallel tracks. In addition to cultivating sources who spoke with him and other TASS employees openly, treating them as legitimate reporters, Pravdin managed and recruited a roster of spies. He used the Press Building as a base for handling agents with positions in the White House, the Treasury and Justice Departments, as well as at the British embassy.

The Americans who spied for Stalin in Washington during Pravdin's tenure were motivated by a deep, almost religious faith in communism. From Pearl Harbor to the Japanese surrender they justified their actions by convincing themselves that while it was illegal, stealing secrets for an ally was honorable, even patriotic. This argument is contradicted by some uncomfortable facts: many had spied for the USSR during the time when Stalin and Hitler were allied, and those who were given the opportunity continued to spy after the war, when they believed violent conflict between the United States and the Soviet Union was inevitable.

In addition to using employment at TASS as a cover, Soviet intelligence prioritized the recruitment of American journalists. In 1941, twenty-two of the NKVD's American agents were journalists. The only occupation to surpass journalism was engineering, with forty-nine agents stealing so much sensitive military technology that the Soviets worried they would run out of the 35mm film that was used to make copies.[11]

Few reporters have regular access to classified information, but many associate with individuals who generate and are privy to the nation's most closely guarded secrets. In addition to picking up information and insights from sources and providing expert commentary on politics, journalists are well-positioned to identify individuals who might be willing to betray their country.

Pravdin had talent-spotting in mind in the spring of 1944 when he transferred Samuel Krafsur, an American working in the TASS New York bureau, to the news agency's Washington office and recruited him as an NKVD agent. Krafsur had already risked his life for communism by volunteering as a member of the Abraham Lincoln Brigade, a battalion of American communists, and being wounded in the Spanish Civil War. In a memo to Moscow Center, Pravdin wrote that Krafsur was "absolutely devoted to the USSR" and had provided a list of more than twenty potential recruits. Krafsur's "extensive connections will give opportunities for obtaining valuable information and also of studying individual subjects for signing on" as agents, Pravdin noted.[12]

Even more than their role as talent-spotters, journalists were valued as agents and sources because Moscow Center believed they had sensitive inside information that never made it into print. This was mostly wishful thinking. Then, as now, journalists generally published everything they knew—and occasionally things they didn't know.

One exception to this rule Walter Lippmann, the most influential journalist in America. Lippmann aimed to influence, not just report on events, so he spent more time working behind the scenes shaping events than reporting on them. He was a confidant of presidents, prime ministers, senators, generals, and, above all, the elite that made and executed American foreign policy.

Recognizing Lippmann's stature, the NKVD had recruited his personal secretary, Mary Price, as an agent in 1941.[13] For two years she rifled his files, eavesdropped on his conversations, and scanned his correspondence, passing on everything of interest to the NKVD. By 1943 Price was burned out. Over the objections of Soviet intelligence officers, she resigned from undercover operations and started to work openly for organizations affiliated with the Communist Party of the United States of America.[14]

The NKVD did not, however, lose access to Lippmann. To the service's surprise, Pravdin developed a close working relationship with the doyen of American journalism, whom the Soviets referred to by the cover name "Imperialist." Pravdin's cover name was "Sergey," a nod to his patronymic.

A March 31, 1944, memo from the NKVD's New York station to Moscow Center described Pravdin's unlikely success in cultivating Lippmann:

> Contrary to all expectations, the person with whom "Sergey" succeeded in achieving the biggest results in the task of establishing a good relationship was with "Imperialist." The primary reason for this is the fact that "Imperialist" himself obviously was seeking to have connections with responsible representatives of our circles in the [United States]. He views the acquaintance with "Sergey" precisely in this light, and naturally he is attempting to use the acquaintance with him to determine our viewpoint on various issues of international politics. He

is doing this, of course, very subtly, with the utmost tact. It should be recognized that, by attempting to draw "Sergey" into making candid comments, "Imperialist" is sharing his own information with him.[15]

They met so regularly that in reports to Moscow Pravdin referred to his "usual talks" with Lippmann. Lippmann, a man who couldn't list humility among his virtues, must have thought he was in control of the situation. He was, after all, the most famous journalist in the English-speaking world, while as far as Lippmann knew Pravdin was merely the director of a second-rate news agency's US operations. In fact, Pravdin, a trained and hardened intelligence operative, had the upper hand. A man who could induce Schildbach to conspire to murder the only man who had loved her wouldn't find it difficult to seduce an American journalist into telling him more than he should.

Reports the two men filed in confidence after one of their long, chatty meetings in May 1944 illuminates their relationship. After the lunch, Lippmann called Joseph Grew, a senior State Department official, to pass on information he'd acquired from Pravdin. Lippmann told Grew that the USSR had territorial ambitions in Port Arthur, in Manchuria. Pravdin had also confided that the Soviet Union was concerned about how the United States would perceive its support for communists in China. Grew, who had been US ambassador to Japan at the time of the Pearl Harbor attack, sent a report on Lippmann's account of Pravdin's unsurprising comments to the secretary of state.[16]

Pravdin's report to Moscow about the same lunch suggests that he got much more from the conversation. Lippmann had told him that the US military leadership was confident of the success of the coming invasion of Europe, and that officials in Washington had assured Eisenhower that sufficient trained reserves were available to ensure reinforcement of the invading forces. Lippmann described Anglo American relations, reporting to his Soviet acquaintance that Undersecretary of State Edward Stettinius had told him that Churchill initially opposed the Americans' invasion plans but had come around to supporting them. Lippmann passed along Washington's views on Soviet-Polish relations, advising that Moscow give up its claims to Lvov; described confidential conversations he'd had with US ambassador to the USSR W. Averell Harriman about the Soviet Union's entry into the war with Japan; and reported that the United States expected to seize the Philippines, Formosa, and Singapore by the end of the year.[17]

In December 1944 Lippmann told Pravdin about private conversations he'd had in Europe with General Dwight Eisenhower about American military plans. The US Army, Lippmann said, was planning a "breakthrough onto the left bank of the Rhine in the middle of January" and assuming it would coincide with a Soviet offensive in Poland heading toward Krakow.[18]

While signing up Lippmann as a witting Soviet agent was out of the question, recruiting or, more accurately, re-recruiting the journalist I. F. Stone, the Washington editor of the *Nation* magazine, was very much on the NKVD's agenda. The two men were, by temperament and political affinity, polar opposites.

Lippmann was conservative and elitist, an assimilated Jew who so thoroughly embodied the establishment that he advocated limiting the number of Jews admitted to Harvard. He was worshipped at the Press Club, while Stone was merely tolerated there—and only until 1943. That's when he invited an African American attorney to a club luncheon. Management refused to serve them; it might not be able to bar a black man from sitting in the ballroom, but the Press Club certainly wasn't going to feed him. Unable to persuade more than nine club members to protest against its adherence to Washington's Jim Crow traditions, Stone resigned from the Press Club and denounced it in the pages of the *Nation*.[19]

In September 1944 Pravdin and Krafsur tried several times to approach Stone to propose that he resume spying for the Soviet Union, but each time he brushed them off. Pravdin finally met privately with Stone in October and made the pitch. According to Pravdin's account of the conversation,

Stone said he'd like to help out, and that he had been avoiding the Soviets only because their approaches weren't sufficiently discreet. Stone indicated that he wasn't averse to the NKVD's topping off the salary he earned from the *Nation*. His circumstances, however, had changed since he had worked for Soviet intelligence in the 1930s. Now he was a family man with three children and a substantial income. Pravdin requested resources from Moscow to facilitate the "establishment of business contact" with Stone.[20]

Based on the information that has leaked from the KGB's files, it isn't clear whether Stone was put back on the NKVD payroll, but it is certain that he stayed in touch with Pravdin after the Soviet intelligence officer indicated he was an intelligence officer seeking secret information. Washington's loudest whistleblower, a man who made a career ferreting out malfeasance and hypocrisy, felt no need to inform his readers that the Soviet Union was trying to recruit him and other journalists as spies.[21]

While Stone didn't have access to secrets, the most important agent Pravdin recruited, Judith Coplon, routinely handled classified information that was of great importance to Soviet intelligence. A twenty-seven-year-old Barnard College graduate who worked for the Department of Justice, Coplon was brought to the NKVD's attention in 1943 by another Barnard alumna, Flora Wovschin. Wovschin was working at the Office of War Information and living with Yuri Okov, an employee of the Soviet consulate who happened to be an officer of the GRU, Soviet military intelligence. A memo in the NKVD files noted that when Wovschin became pregnant, Okov paid half the cost of an abortion, and that she frequently visited the Soviet consulate.[22]

Coplon gave confidential information from her job at the Department of Justice's economic intelligence unit to Wovschin, who told her that the secrets would be passed on to the Communist Party of the United States. Coplon was delighted and excited to be helping the cause. Unaware that Wovschin, following instructions from her Soviet friends, had broken off contact with the Communist Party, Coplon was anxious to deepen her commitment by joining the party.

The US government had a strict ban on employing Communist Party members. Although many civil servants hid their party membership, the NKVD was worried that the Justice Department would find out if Coplon joined. Not only would she be fired, but the resulting investigation could ensnare Wovschin and others. Writing to Moscow Center in February 1944, an NKVD officer in New York warned that if Coplon wasn't recruited soon and instructed in tradecraft, "it is not out of the question that she will feel so weighed down by being cut off from the local progressive movement that she will decide to officially join the local fellowcountryman organization and then she will be lost to us."[23] "Fellowcountrymen" was a cover name for the Communist Party.

The NKVD's requests to Moscow became more insistent. In July 1944 an officer in New York warned that Coplon "is talking more and more often about her desire to establish direct contact with the fellowcountrymen. It is urgent that she be recruited" and instructed to avoid contact with the party.[24]

To head off the threat and recruit her as an agent, Pravdin met Coplon on January 4, 1945. He was impressed. "There is no question about the sincerity of her desire to work with us," Pravdin reported. "In the process of the conversation [Coplon] stressed how much she appreciates the trust placed in her and that, knowing whom she is working for, from now on she will redouble her efforts."[25]

Her position gave Coplon access to information that was interesting to Soviet intelligence but not compelling. Pravdin's confidence in her, however, was soon rewarded. The Justice Department shifted Coplon to a department that reviewed foreign agent registration documents, a job that required access to classified FBI counterintelligence files. At first she worked on cases involving France, but she was quickly transferred to the department's top priority, the Soviet Union. The Justice Department even paid for her to take Russian classes.

Pravdin warned Coplon to avoid removing documents from the office until she was completely trusted. She ignored the admonition, bringing a cache of documents to Pravdin soon after their first meeting. Don't worry, she told him: no one was watching her or her co-workers, sensitive files were strewn around the office where anyone could look at them, and employees were not searched when they exited the building.[26]

Because it was far easier to prove that spies had failed to register as foreign agents than to catch them red-handed committing espionage, investigating and prosecuting violations of the Foreign Agents Registration Act was a common counterintelligence tool. As part of her job, Coplon received—and passed to the NKVD—information about FBI spy-catching methods and details of its investigations of suspected Soviet spies. The NKVD warned its agents to break-off contact with several individuals after Coplon revealed they were under investigation. Her information prevented the FBI from identifying numerous Soviet spies.

Even with the benefit of Coplon's access to information about FBI investigations of Soviet espionage, Pravdin found the task of maintaining operational security immensely challenging and nerve-wracking. He inherited sprawling networks of spies populated almost entirely by Americans who were secret members of the Communist Party. Pravdin's predecessors had given these agents freedom to operate in ways that violated the most basic precepts of Soviet intelligence doctrine and common sense. For example, in March 1945 Moscow Center reacted with alarm to its officers' failure to control Wovschin, who was known by the cover name "Zora." Instructions were sent to "immediately and in detail enlighten our liaison about the serious mistakes he has committed in the work with 'ZORA.' As an ultimatum warn ZORA that if she does not carry out our instructions and if she undertakes steps without our consent, we shall immediately terminate all relations with her. Forbid ZORA to recruit all her acquaintances one after the other." The memo cited security risks posed by Wovschin's activities as an illustration of not only the NKVD's failure to adequately control and educate its agents, "but also the lack of understanding by our operational workers of the most elementary rules in our work."[27]

Loose lips and sloppy tradecraft made it inevitable that eventually one of the many agents operating in Washington would be discovered. Agents from different networks socialized and discussed their espionage activities with each other and kept incriminating materials in their homes. Because they knew each other's identities, if a single spy were compromised or defected, the FBI could quickly learn about the activities of scores of spies. Pravdin was horrified to learn that some of his agents were so undisciplined that they attempted to recruit friends and relatives, revealing their connections with Soviet intelligence to individuals who had not been cleared by Moscow.[28]

Just as troubling for Pravdin, many of the agents working for Soviet intelligence in Washington were emotionally unstable. The NKVD's messages to Moscow Center were filled with accounts of personal and professional jealousies, bickering, adulterous affairs, even a ménage à trois. The entire edifice was resting on a house of cards that could be toppled by the slightest wind.[29]

After one particularly frustrating meeting with an agent in Washington, Pravdin wrote a bitter memo to Moscow Center complaining that American communists "are always ready to promise the moon in words, but never carry out our assignments if they require effort and time."[30]

This was an exaggeration. Although they lacked the discipline and work ethic that Pravdin expected, the agents he was responsible for in Washington and throughout the country produced a continuous, valuable stream of high-level intelligence. During Pravdin's tenure as codirector or head of NKVD operations in the United States, the service's spies obtained technical data that accelerated the Soviet Union's acquisition of atomic weapons and jumpstarted its development of radar, jet aircraft, and a host of other modern military technologies. On the political side, Stalin was briefed about secret deliberations in the White House, Pentagon, American intelligence services, and State Department. He knew about Roosevelt's conversations and conflicts with Churchill, American and British plans for winning the war and for dealing with their vanquished enemies, and their attitudes toward the Soviet Union.

In addition to recruiting agents and supervising the work of NKVD officers who ran clandestine networks, Pravdin debriefed valuable agents who had been serving the Soviet cause for many years. He met in the summer of 1944 with one of the NKVD's top sources, an Englishman named Donald Maclean. The son of a former cabinet member and a graduate of Cambridge, Maclean was the embodiment of the British establishment. At Cambridge he had been recruited into the USSR's most devastatingly effective spy ring along with Kim Philby and four others. The Cambridge spy ring penetrated the highest echelons of British government and society.[31]

When Pravdin met with Maclean, he had been posted to Washington as first secretary in the British embassy. This position gave him—and the NKVD—access to high-level diplomatic intelligence, especially about the Anglo American relationship, a topic of importance as Stalin schemed to peel back the strong bond between Roosevelt and Churchill. Maclean's work facilitating cooperation on atomic weapons between the United States and the UK also provided access to information of great value to the USSR.[32]

Pravdin debriefed some of Soviet intelligence's most productive American spies. For example, he traveled in May 1945 to San Francisco, ostensibly to report for TASS on a conference where the treaty creating the United Nations was being negotiated, but actually to meet with an NKVD agent, Harry Dexter White, assistant secretary of the Treasury.[33] White, a senior advisor to the US delegation, told Pravdin that President Truman and Secretary of State Stettinius "want to achieve the success of the conference at any price." If pushed, he revealed, they would be willing to give the Soviet Union a veto over UN actions. This and other inside information White provided to Pravdin put the USSR at an advantage in negotiations with the American and British governments.[34]

Pravdin received a rare rebuke from Moscow Center in May 1945. His decision to hire William Dodd Jr., to work as a reporter for TASS at its Press Building bureau without seeking approval from Moscow had been a mistake.[35] Dodd was the son of the former US ambassador to Nazi Germany. His work for TASS had been reported in newspapers, attracting unwanted attention to the news agency. He had been identified as a potential recruit by I. F. Stone in 1936 and recruited as an espionage agent in 1938 by his sister, Margaret Dodd.[36]

The NKVD secretly gave Dodd $1,000 in 1938 (equal to about $17,000 in 2017) to finance his unsuccessful effort to unseat a conservative Democratic member of Congress in Virginia. Moscow Center was so enthused by the notion that it could subsidize a congressional candidate that it sent a message to NKVD officers in New York asking for a budget estimate for a comprehensive program aimed at electing a slate of pro-Soviet politicians. The Soviet officer assigned the task threw up his hands, complaining that it was impossible to know how much it would cost to fund campaigns and pay off journalists; doing it right might require $1 million a year for each politician.[37]

In December 1939, Dodd, who had been assigned the cover name "President," asked Moscow to help him purchase the *Blue Ridge Herald* newspaper to support his plan to run for Congress again. "The direction of the newspaper will depend entirely on us," an NKVD officer in New York reported. "We will work out every detail of the newspaper's agenda with 'President.'" The Soviets planned to mask their involvement by ensuring that the paper hewed to a moderate editorial line. "It should not be too left-wing, and it should not be pro-Soviet—nor, it goes without saying, should it be anti-Soviet." The goal was a "moderately liberal local newspaper with a direct connection to liberal Washington journalists."[38] Moscow Center allocated $3,500 for the purchase, $1,500 short of the amount Dodd needed. He neither purchased the paper nor ran in the 1940 primary.[39]

Dodd kept in touch with Soviet intelligence, providing interesting bits of information but nothing of great value. In 1943, while working in a midlevel job at the Federal Communications Commission, he was called before a House committee that was investigating communist subversion. In a muddled performance at a public hearing, he disavowed all connection with or sympathy for communism but also admitted that he'd written several pro-communist magazine articles. Moscow Center wrote a scathing review of his performance, telling its officers in New York that Dodd had "conducted himself in a foolish and sometimes disgraceful manner."[40] Congress forced the FCC to fire Dodd.

Dodd's decision to take a job at TASS in 1945 amounted to a public advertisement that he was indeed a communist. Moscow Center, irritated by his bungling congressional testimony and seeking to avoid unwanted attention to its espionage activities, instructed Pravdin to fire Dodd.

While Pravdin and his comrades had achieved incredible access to American secrets, information from Coplon and other sources made Soviet spymasters uneasy. Hints of danger had been filtering into the Lubyanka for some time. In the spring of 1944, the NKVD learned from one of its agents, Lauchlin Currie, a senior assistant to Roosevelt, that American codebreakers were on the verge of decrypting high-level Soviet cables.[41]

In February 1945, Wovschin set off alarms in Moscow Center when she revealed that American counterintelligence knew some of the cover names the Soviets used in their encrypted communications, such as Bank (State Department), House (Moscow Center), and Club (Department of Justice). The NKVD changed its cover names and continued to try to impose discipline on its unruly volunteer spies.

Pravdin's biggest security headache was Elizabeth Bentley. Bentley, whose Russian cover name was *umnitsa* or "clever girl," had been the courier, assistant, and lover of Jacob Golos, the most important Soviet spy handler in the United States in the 1930s and early 1940s. Golos ("voice") was an alias. His real name was Jacob Reizen. Starting in the early 1930s, Golos forged tight links between Soviet intelligence and the Communist Party of the United States, operating for years with loose direction from Moscow. His romantic relationship with Bentley, whom he met after recruiting her as an agent, was among Golos's many violations of tradecraft rules.

The FBI had missed an opportunity to catch Bentley. When Pravdin first arrived in New York, the bureau took an interest in his wife, Olga Pravdina, tailing her for several months before deciding she was nothing more than an overweight housewife. If the G-men who followed her to grocery stores and movie theaters, describing her as "quite heavy set" and recording that she "has big feet and wears flat heeled shoes," had been more persistent about tracking her activities and less fixated on her appearance, they might have discovered that in April 1942 Pravdina started meeting with Bentley.[42]

Following Golos's death in November 1943, Moscow Center told Pravdin to split up the agent networks that she handled and bring them under the control of trained, disciplined handlers. Bentley bitterly resisted demands to turn over agents to professionals who had been sent from Moscow, and quickly came to despise and fear the rough-edged Russian NKVD officers who insisted on cutting her off from the tasks that made her life meaningful. Fortified by several dry martinis, in September 1945 Bentley told an NKVD officer exactly what she thought of him and his colleagues, referring to them as "gangsters." She threatened to reveal all that she knew to the FBI. After sobering up, Bentley realized she'd made a serious, possibly fatal mistake. She knew of at least one American woman who had been "liquidated" by Soviet intelligence and feared similar retribution.[43]

The NKVD did consider killing her but decided that less extreme measures—giving her a few thousand dollars, finding her a job and perhaps a husband—would suffice. These tactics might have worked, but the combination of a romantic encounter with a man who falsely claimed to be an FBI agent and a dispute over money with the Communist Party pushed Bentley over the edge. Convinced that the FBI was poised to swoop in any minute and that the Soviets would kill her if she didn't reconcile with the NKVD, Bentley decided it was time to choose sides.

Bentley later said that God had spoken to her, but it seems more likely that she analyzed her options and decided that a jail cell was more attractive than a coffin. In long sessions over fourteen days between November 9 and 29, she gave the FBI a detailed and fairly accurate picture of Soviet espionage networks in Washington and New York, prevaricating only to spare some agents whom she considered friends. On the 30th, she signed a 105-page statement that identified many of the Soviet Union's most valuable American agents and included leads that could allow the FBI to identify more.

Bentley's information was compelling, but she had no documentary evidence; in a courtroom it would be the word of a woman who could easily be depicted as hysterical or unhinged against sworn denials by men who had sterling reputations.

To gather evidence to support prosecutions, the FBI decided to turn Bentley into a double agent. Making statements in the privacy of the FBI's Manhattan offices was one thing, but meeting face-to-face with the men and women she was betraying was a far more daunting and unpleasant task. It was, however, an offer Bentley could not refuse. Having confessed to committing espionage during wartime, a crime punishable by death, Bentley felt she had to do whatever the FBI asked.

The plan might have worked if the FBI had implemented it properly. Ironically, it was disrupted by a mistake made by none other than J. Edgar Hoover. Recognizing the importance of Bentley's information, the FBI director had imposed restrictions on communicating about her identity, which were intended to prevent leaks. He even ordered the bureau to refer to her by a male cover name, "Gregory." Contrary to his own strict instructions, Hoover discussed the case with someone who did not have an absolute "need to know," William Stephenson, the head of British Security Coordination. By November 20, roughly in the middle of her first round of FBI debriefings, news of Bentley's defection traveled from Stephenson to Philby, the NKVD's agent in British intelligence. Philby immediately conveyed the news to Moscow.

On Thanksgiving Day, eight days before Bentley signed her statement, and before the FBI deployed her as a double agent, Pravdin received an encrypted message from Moscow Center: Bentley "has betrayed us."[44] The Soviets knew that Bentley's information would allow the FBI to capitalize on the shortcuts and mistakes they had made in the United States over the previous decade. Scores of agents were at risk of detection and arrest. The espionage edifice Pravdin had been desperately trying to fortify had collapsed, but the tip-off that originated with Hoover allowed Pravdin and his comrades to protect their agents from being crushed in the rubble.

Pravdin was instructed to "take the appropriate precautionary measures," such as establishing passwords and methods of contact for the future, then break-off contact with all American agents.[45]

Bentley had identified Pravdina as a Soviet intelligence officer, prompting the FBI to assign a team of G-men to resume its surveillance. It was too late. Pravdin had already warned Bentley's contacts that she had switched sides, and he and his wife had ceased communicating with American agents. Because the Soviets acted quickly, Bentley's information, which could have put scores of Soviet spies in prison, resulted in only one successful prosecution, of a government economist named William Remington.

While complete disaster had been averted, the era of virtually unfettered access to American secrets was over. Soviet intelligence had many successes over the coming decades, but it never came close to achieving the depth of penetration of the US government, military, and industry that it had during World War II.

Pravdin, Pravdina, and their daughter sailed from New York on the *Kirov* on March 11, 1946.[46] Blamed for the collapse of the Soviet Union's American networks, and under suspicion as a foreigner, Pravdin was fired the next year. He committed suicide in Moscow in 1970.[47]

Moscow Center had been warning its officers in the United States since 1941 that the FBI was bugging their offices and tapping their phones. The alarm had turned out to be premature, but by the time Pravdin departed the FBI was doing this and more. The bureau tapped the TASS office phone lines in the basement of the Press Building and photographed envelopes before the mail was delivered. It recruited a building maintenance worker who collected the TASS office's trash every evening and handed it over to agents in the FBI's Washington Field Office who had the unenviable job of sorting through the cigarette butts, chewing gum, and paper scraps for clues.[48] Before TASS moved its desks and photos of Lenin and Stalin to larger offices on the ninth floor in 1947, the FBI obtained a key to its new suite and a copy of the floor plan, and made sure that their surveillance of the news agency's mail and trash was not interrupted.[49]

In early 1948 the NKVD gradually and carefully began reactivating agents who hadn't been compromised by Bentley. Just as it looked like the situation had stabilized, however, another typhoon struck.

An American NKVD agent who was working as a linguist for a US Army codebreaking operation, William Weisband, told his Russian handler in February 1948 that the Americans were making great progress in decoding and decrypting the Soviet Union's most sensitive communications. Weisband had literally peered over the shoulder of American codebreakers as they read portions of cables sent during the war between Moscow Center and the NKVD's New York station. Separately, in 1949, Philby, who had been posted to Washington as liaison between British foreign intelligence and the FBI, learned the details of the decryption program, which came to be known by the cover name "Venona."

The NKVD's use of cover names meant that decrypting cables was only the first step toward identifying Soviet agents. In December 1948, the FBI made the first of what ended up being hundreds of identifications. The bureau didn't have to go far to find the spy. It was Coplon.

The FBI put Coplon under surveillance and fed her documents that were certain to be of great interest in the Lubyanka. Coplon took the bait, bringing the secret counterintelligence files to New York. She was arrested moments after passing them to a Soviet diplomat in March 1949. To Hoover's immense frustration, although there was no doubt of her guilt, Coplon walked away from two trials after convictions for espionage and conspiracy were overturned on legal technicalities. Even more troubling to Hoover, the FBI had been forced to acknowledge that it had illegally tapped Coplon's phone.

Coplon ended up running two Mexican restaurants in New York that during the Cold War attracted both FBI agents and KGB officers hoping to catch a glimpse of the spy who got away. She married her defense attorney and never spoke in public or with her family about her involvement with Soviet espionage.[50]

Stories about Bentley's revelations, the Coplon prosecutions, and other spy cases heralded the beginning of the Cold War and sparked a search for communist infiltrators.

Moscow Center decided it needed to get a firmer grip on its Press Building outpost. Todd was demoted to senior correspondent in 1949 when a Russian NKVD officer, Mikhail Fedorov, replaced him as bureau chief. The Army's Venona decryptions had rendered Krafsur useless as an agent so the NKVD had TASS fire him. Todd was unceremoniously put out to pasture two years later.

The Washington press corps tolerated but did not hide their distaste for the Soviets who stepped into the positions once held by Todd and Krafsur. The two congenial Americans had been replaced by sour foreigners who religiously attended White House and State Department press conferences but never asked questions, and who took great umbrage at suggestions that they were propagandists or spies.

Washington reporters' already dim view of their TASS colleagues darkened considerably in April 1951, when William Oatis, an Associated Press reporter, was arrested in Prague. Czechoslovakia resisted American demands to release Oatis, tortured him into confessing to espionage, and put him on trial. Actually, Oatis was "tried" several times, undergoing four or five dress rehearsals with real judges and prosecutors and an audience of carefully chosen government officials. Oatis didn't know until it was over if a given performance was a real trial or a rehearsal. The procedure ensured that when journalists and government officials came to watch the actual trial, Oatis and witnesses recited the lines they'd been fed. It also minimized the chances that they would ad lib or slip in anything unexpected. Oatis was convicted on July 4, 1951, and sentenced to ten years' imprisonment.[51]

Calls for reciprocation and revenge rang out from the barstools in the Press Club Tap Room to the halls of Congress. Politicians demanded that Soviet bloc journalists be expelled from the United States, or at least that their government-issued press credentials and privileges be revoked. To increase the pressure on Czechoslovakia, the FBI raided the TASS offices in New York and the Press Building, asserting the government's right to inspect business records to confirm that the news agency was complying with the Foreign Agents Registration Act.[52]

The Press Club denounced the Czech government and demanded that it release Oatis. The statement wasn't sufficient for some of its members, who agitated for throwing the TASS men out. Resistance to erecting an Iron Curtain around the club came from an unlikely source: *New York Daily News* reporter Frank Holeman, chairman of the club's Board of Governors. Holeman, a pal of Vice President Richard Nixon's, had no sympathy for communism. A young man with a quick wit and an abiding confidence in the value of fair play, he did, however, believe in the inalienable right of reporters to swap lies over the rims of alcoholic beverages.

It was certainly difficult to argue that allowing Soviets to enjoy the benefits of Press Club membership presented a national security risk. Nothing discussed in its bar stayed secret long. In those days, as Holeman remembered decades later, the club was a colorful mix of "people who could recite Beowulf and people who knew exactly which horse was running at the fifth race at Hialeah and what his chances were." It was open twenty-four hours a day, seven days a week, with a bar that was supposed to close at 2:00 a.m. but sometimes stayed open much later. Most nights three or four men could be found snoring in the library's overstuffed chairs, and at least one remittance man made the club his home, rarely venturing beyond its front door.[53]

National Press Club members at rest. In the 1950s and 1960s, Press Club members often used its comfortable chairs to recuperate after an evening at its bar.
    Credit: National Press Club archives

Holeman won the battle to ensure that TASS employees and Soviet embassy staff retained the right to wander through the blue cigar haze of the Press Club's cardroom, hear from heads of state at its formal luncheons, and enjoy the opportunity to buy a drink on Sundays, when every other bar in town was closed. To show his appreciation, the press attaché invited Holeman to a lunch at the Soviet embassy. Over vodka, caviar, and *blinis*, Holeman was introduced to Georgi Nikitovich Bolshakov, a GRU officer who had replaced Fedorov as TASS bureau chief.[54]

Bolshakov had spent a decade in military intelligence before being posted to Washington, but he wasn't stamped from the standard Soviet intelligence officer mold. Armed with self-deprecating humor and an irrepressible smile, he was the first Soviet journalist-spy in Washington since Vladimir Romm left in 1936 possessing the self-confidence to socialize with American reporters. Bolshakov owed his position to his friendship with Khrushchev's son-in-law, Aleksei Adzhubei, and had served as a personal assistant to Soviet marshal Georgi Zhukov. He had the easy manner of a man comfortable around power.

Though they were an unlikely couple, Holeman, who hid his hardscrabble roots behind a patrician persona and a bow tie, developed a tight bond with Bolshakov. The American newsman told Nixon about his comrade, and the vice president, eager for insight into Soviet politics and personalities, encouraged the friendship. For four years, Holeman peppered Bolshakov with questions about the Soviet Union, including some Nixon had suggested, and passed on the gist of the Russian's answers to a politician who had built his career on hardline anti-communism. Bolshakov, his superiors, and Khrushchev knew that his comments were being passed to the vice president.

Like other intelligence officers posted to the TASS office, Bolshakov had to perform his cover job and live on a TASS salary. This was intended to maintain the fiction that they were reporters, give them legitimate reasons to contact potential recruits, and make it somewhat more difficult for the FBI to distinguish between the "clean" TASS employees who worked exclusively as journalists and professional intelligence officers. Bolshakov wrote stories chronicling the history of American race riots and other sordid sides of life in the United States.

Just before Bolshakov's scheduled return to Moscow in 1955, he introduced Holeman to another GRU officer, Yuri Gvozdev, who was posing as a cultural officer in the embassy. Holeman's role expanded from friend and drinking companion to secret intermediary. He conveyed messages from Gvozdev, which he believed came from Khrushchev or those close to the premier, to Nixon, and Nixon used Holeman to send messages back to the Soviet leadership. Both sides felt they benefited from an informal exchange of views, unencumbered by the need to clear their messages with bureaucrats or to formulate them in the bone-dry language of diplomacy. The *Daily News* essentially gave Holeman a year-long sabbatical when he was elected president of the Press Club in 1956, so he had plenty of time to cement his relationships with Soviet intelligence operatives and with Nixon.

During crises, the messages Holeman communicated between the Soviet and American governments were urgent and specific. For example, in February 1958 Gvozdev asked Holeman how the United States would respond if Moscow's ally, Syria, moved troops into Lebanon. Holeman conveyed Nixon's response: "Stop at the Lebanon border or you'll be in real trouble." That summer, after Eisenhower sent troops to defend Lebanon, it was Gvozdev's turn to warn the United States to back off. The Soviets would interpret the movement of US or British troops toward Iraq as a provocation, he said. If it felt threatened, the Soviet Union would attack the United States, not its allies in Europe or the Middle East, Gvozdev told Holeman.[55]

Holeman also passed on a message that was intended to avoid an armed confrontation in the heart of Europe. In November 1958 Khrushchev issued a public ultimatum: the United States, Britain, and France had six months to withdraw their forces from Berlin. The implication was that if they failed to do so, the Soviets would impose a blockade. West Berlin's population had grown too large for a repeat of the 1948 airlift. The use of force to get food to the city could quickly spin out of control. In Washington and Moscow, it seemed that if there was going to be a third world war, Berlin is where it would start.

Holeman carried a message to Nixon from Khrushchev: contrary to the bellicose ultimatum, the Soviet Premier had no intention of starting a war over Berlin.[56] Back channels like the Gvozdev-Holeman connection allowed leaders of the superpowers to gain understanding of each other's intentions at a time when a false move by either side could have triggered World War III. As soon as the Berlin situation calmed, Gvozdev enlisted Holeman to facilitate a visit by Nixon to the Soviet Union. The negotiations were successful and the vice president made the trip in July 1959, famously debating Khrushchev at an exhibit about American daily life in Moscow's Sokolniki Park.[57]

Frank Holeman, *New York Daily News* reporter and intermediary between Soviet military intelligence officers and senior US government officials.

Source: National Press Club archives

The *New York Daily* news reporter told Nixon's secretary, Rose Mary Woods, that the Soviets didn't believe that he was simply a reporter. He joked with her that she should call him "Frank Holeman, boy spy." While Holeman didn't work for either American or Soviet intelligence, he was trusted by both the White House and the Kremlin. The temptation for Holeman, a tabloid reporter who had dedicated his life to breaking news, to reveal the secrets he'd learned must have been tremendous. Yet throughout the Cold War, during the countless hours he spent telling stories at the Press Club bar, and in articles he wrote for the *Daily News*, Holeman never even hinted at his role as a covert communications link between the United States and Soviet leadership.[58]

By the end of the Eisenhower administration Holeman had conveyed messages that helped defuse some of the most dangerous confrontations of the Cold War.

He was, however, just getting started. After the election of John F. Kennedy, Holeman's life became far more interesting.

CHAPTER FOURTEEN
BACK CHANNELS

Frank Holeman earned his stripes as a "boy spy" during the Cuban missile crisis. As the drama in the Caribbean uncoiled over the last two weeks of October 1962, President John Kennedy and his top advisors called on him and other reporters in the National Press Building to serve as back channels to communicate secretly with Soviet intelligence services and, through them, to the Kremlin. In parallel with these semi-official interactions, Soviet intelligence officers based in the Press Building desperately tried to gather intelligence from American journalists. The muddled messages that emerged included a shard of a conversation that flew off a Press Club barstool into the hands of a KGB officer and landed in the Kremlin at a critical moment, helping persuade Nikita Khrushchev to pull the world back from the brink of catastrophe.

Like many crises, this one started with admonitions to remain calm and assertions that everything was under control.

On the evening of Monday, October 15, Edwin Martin, the secretary of state for Inter-American Affairs, stood at a podium in the Press Club and assured reporters that Soviet military activity in Cuba was of little concern to the United States government. "As the President has said, this military buildup is basically defensive in character and would not add more than a few hours to the time required to invade Cuba successfully if that should become necessary," he said.[1]

A waiter who had been hovering a few feet from the podium handed Martin a note as soon as he finished the speech: "Call the White House. Ask for your signal. Telephone number NA 8-1414."[2] Martin finished his dinner, left the club and stopped at a telephone booth. Martin's call was transferred to Roger Hilsman, head of intelligence at the State Department. Hilsman's terse comment was as clear to Martin as it would have been incomprehensible to anyone listening in: "The pictures that were taken Sunday show those things. Start thinking. We will be seeing the President in the morning."[3]

Martin knew that Hilsman was referring to pictures that had been taken by a U-2 reconnaissance plane over Cuba, and that "those things" must be Soviet nuclear missiles. He also knew that it meant that United States and the Soviet Union were on the brink of a nuclear conflict that could kill hundreds of millions and leave much of the planet a smoldering ruin that would be uninhabitable for centuries.

The story of the roles journalists and spies played in creating and defusing the crisis started six months earlier, at 4:00 p.m. on May 9, 1961, when Holeman placed a call from his Press Building office to the Soviet embassy. He had been calling the embassy since noon asking for Georgi Bolshakov. Bolshakov, a colonel in the GRU who Holeman had befriended when he was running the TASS bureau, had returned to Washington in the fall of 1959, this time based in the embassy as press attaché, and had resumed his friendship with the *New York Daily News* reporter.[4] When Holeman finally reached him, the Russian explained that he'd been at a print shop proofreading galleys of an issue of the slick propaganda magazine *USSR*. Holeman invited Bolshakov to lunch, picked him up in a taxi, and, together, they drove to a restaurant in Georgetown.[5]

Though their friendship was real, there was more to Holeman's meetings with Bolshakov than camaraderie. At a time when Americans were digging fallout shelters and Soviet civilians were conducting civil defense exercises in anticipation of nuclear attacks, the reporter and the intelligence officer felt they were making the world a safer place. The exchange of information and views they facilitated could, they believed, reduce the chances that misunderstandings between their governments would trigger a war.

Following Nixon's loss in the 1960 election, Holeman found a way to continue serving as a carrier pigeon between the Soviet and US governments. Although he was known in Washington as a Nixon supporter, in those days it wasn't uncommon to have personal relationships across party lines. Holeman told Edwin Guthman, his best contact in the new administration, how his friendship with Bolshakov had evolved into a covert link between the White House and the Kremlin. Guthman, a Pulitzer-winning journalist, was serving as press secretary to Attorney General Robert Kennedy.

The Kennedys were convinced that tensions between the United States and the Soviet Union were caused by poor communication between the two governments and that, on the US side, the CIA and State Department were largely to blame. Seizing the opportunity to connect directly with the Soviet leadership, Robert Kennedy told Guthman to urge Holeman to continue meeting with Bolshakov. Holeman, in turn, made it clear to Bolshakov that he was briefing Guthman about their conversations and that Guthman was passing along the information to the president's brother.[6]

About forty minutes into their late lunch on May 9, at 5:20, Bolshakov caught Holeman checking his watch and asked if it was time for him to leave. "No," Holeman replied, "it is time for you. Bobby Kennedy is expecting you at 6."[7]

The Russian couldn't hide a look of alarm. "Georgi, are you afraid?" Holeman asked.

It wasn't the first time the idea of meeting the president's brother had come up. Holeman had suggested it in April, but Bolshakov was forced to decline after his superior had strictly forbidden him from accepting the invitation. The GRU, like most intelligence services, was both risk-averse and afflicted with jealousies and office politics. If Bolshakov, a relatively inexperienced officer who had achieved a prestigious posting to Washington on the strength of his social connections and language skills, screwed up a connection with Robert Kennedy, the chief of the GRU's Washington station would pay dearly for approving the meeting. And if he pulled it off, he would outshine higher ranking GRU officers who had little to show for their months or years in Washington.[8]

Given his previous order to avoid meeting RFK, Bolshakov had to think fast. Even if Bolshakov had time to drive to the embassy, his boss wouldn't be there. It was Victory Day, the anniversary of the defeat of Nazi Germany, the holiest day in the Soviet calendar, and embassy staff were out celebrating.

Bolshakov decided to go for it. "No, I'm not afraid, but I'm not prepared for the meeting," he told Holeman.

"You are always prepared, Georgi," the American replied.[9]

Holeman hailed a taxi and they drove down Pennsylvania Avenue, past the White House and the National Press Building, to the Department of Justice. "We walked slowly so we would reach the side entrance exactly at 6," Bolshakov recalled. "Robert Kennedy was standing in a white shirt with a suit jacket hanging over his shoulder at the entrance and speaking with two co-workers. Frank Holeman saluted to him by raising his hand and walked back."[10]

The two men walked to the Mall and sat on the grass. Suddenly the heavens opened, and a bromance was born. "The lightning will kill us and the newspapers will write that a Russian agent killed the president's brother," Kennedy said. "Let's go!" Kennedy and Bolshakov walked, then ran, back to the Justice Department through a torrential downpour, flying past security guards and into the attorney general's private elevator. In his office they peeled off their shirts and spent hours sitting in their undershirts talking.

Kennedy drove Bolshakov home after 10:00 p.m. The GRU officer was so excited he didn't sleep that night. With Moscow's approval, Bolshakov stayed in close touch with Kennedy, meeting forty or fifty times over the next fifteen months. The number of meetings isn't certain because many of the meetings weren't recorded on Kennedy's official calendar. Nor did he take notes about the conversations, speaking freely and off the cuff about the president's desire for peace with the Soviet Union and the pressure he faced from hawks in the military and "reactionaries" in Congress.

Holeman stayed in the picture, helping the Kennedys keep their back channel secret. To prevent the gossip and leaks that would result from repeated calls from the Soviet embassy to the attorney general's office, Bolshakov asked Holeman to make the arrangements. The reporter would call Guthman and say, "My guy wants to see your guy." Holeman often picked Bolshakov up in a taxi and tried to give the FBI and whoever else might be following the Russian diplomat the slip. Kennedy and Bolshakov sometimes met at a donut shop next to the Mayflower Hotel.[11]

While Bolshakov bantered with RFK, he never forgot who he was working for. Everything he said about Soviet policy and politics had been carefully crafted by men in Moscow. If Kennedy asked for responses to any topics that Bolshakov hadn't been briefed about, he stalled until he'd had time to check with his superiors.

In the run-up to the June 1961 summit in Vienna, Bolshakov read Robert Kennedy personal messages that Khrushchev had written to John Kennedy and conveyed messages from the president to the premier. Despite the intensive covert preparations, the summit was a disaster for John Kennedy. Khrushchev bullied the young president, berating him for the Bay of Pigs invasion, and threatening him in an effort to scare the United States into abandoning West Berlin. When they parted, relations between the two countries were worse than before the summit.

The Kennedys didn't blame Bolshakov for the failure in Vienna. Instead, they came to trust him even more. In the autumn of 1961, when Bolshakov was accompanying a Soviet delegation to the White House, President Kennedy walked over, took hold of the Russian's elbow, and steered him into an empty room. "I am grateful to you for the favors that you did before Vienna, they were very timely for me as well as for Premier Khrushchev," Kennedy told him. "I think in the future, if there are no objections from your side, we will continue communicating with Premier Khrushchev through you."[12]

In addition to meeting with Robert Kennedy, Bolshakov delivered messages from Khrushchev to John Kennedy through other members of the president's inner circle. He played up the covert nature of the communications, sometimes concealing messages in newspapers and removing them with a flourish.[13]

Bolshakov charmed his American contacts, making them feel as if they were playing a game together. He'd call Pierre Salinger, the White House press secretary, say he needed to discuss "a matter of urgency," and arrange a clandestine rendezvous. Once, on a dark street corner in downtown Washington, Bolshakov furtively slipped an envelope into Salinger's pocket, clapped a hand on his shoulder, and said "Every man has his Russian, and I'm yours." Salinger almost burst out laughing.[14] Though they'd been warned by the FBI that Bolshakov was an intelligence officer, the Kennedys and their inner circle viewed him almost as a member of their team rather than the representative of a hostile intelligence service.[15]

The FBI and the CIA had detailed information about the true affiliations of Soviet intelligence officers in the embassy and working undercover for press organizations, the United Nations, and trading companies. American intelligence knew Bolshakov worked for the GRU, and suspected that equipment in his apartment, which had a clear view of the Pentagon, was intercepting military communications.

The information Bolshakov and other intelligence officers sent to Moscow didn't prevent the GRU, and the Kremlin officials it reported to, from viewing the United States through a cracked kaleidoscope. Soviet military intelligence produced phantasmagorical reports in 1961, and again in 1962, asserting with complete confidence that the Pentagon was on the verge of ordering nuclear first strikes against the USSR.[16]

Although these reports were wildly inaccurate, there was a strong sense in Washington that the world was on a precipice and that an accidental or careless move could send it tumbling into nuclear oblivion.

Minimizing this threat was on Robert Kennedy's mind when he called Bolshakov at home on the morning of the last day of August 1962, asking him to come as soon as possible to the Justice Department. Kennedy knew that his friend was flying home the next day for a vacation—the two had discussed the possibility of RFK's joining him for a pleasure trip through Siberia. As soon as Bolshakov arrived, the attorney general told him that the president was expecting him. "He knows that you are going to Moscow and wants you to give a message to Premier Khrushchev as soon as you arrive," Robert Kennedy said.[17]

At the White House, President Kennedy told Bolshakov that the US ambassador in Moscow, Llewelyn Thompson, "has informed me that Khrushchev is concerned about our planes flying around Soviet ships that are heading to Cuba. Tell him that today I ordered a stop to the fly-overs." Kennedy, Thompson—and Bolshakov—had no idea why the Soviet leader had expressed concern about American close surveillance of ships traveling halfway around the world to the Caribbean. Whether Kennedy actually ordered a halt to the flyovers, and whether the military complied, are among the many unknowns surrounding what came to be known as the "Cuban Missile Crisis."[18]

About ten days later, Bolshakov was at Khrushchev's summer home in Pitsunda, on the Black Sea. The Soviet leader wanted to hear his impressions of the Kennedys. Khrushchev's sharpest questions were about Cuba. Would Kennedy invade the Communist-ruled island? Bolshakov predicted that he would, citing "pressure from reactionary forces, the military and extreme right who are striving for revenge for the CIA's failure at the Bay of Pigs and only waiting for a convenient moment to destroy the Republic of Cuba."[19]

Cuba was also on Kennedy's mind. On September 13, he stepped up to a podium in the State Department press room. "There has been a great deal of talk on the situation in Cuba in recent days both in the Communist camp and in our own, and I would like to take this opportunity to set the matter in perspective," he told the assembled reporters, along with the American people, who were watching a live television broadcast of his remarks. Kennedy probably had the reassurances he'd received through Bolshakov in mind when he said that although the Soviets had stepped up military assistance to their Caribbean ally, "these new shipments do not constitute a serious threat to any other part of this hemisphere" because the Soviets were sending only defensive weapons. If Cuba became "an offensive military base of significant capacity for the Soviet Union," Kennedy said, the United States would invade to remove the threat.[20]

John Kennedy wasn't as confident about Soviet intentions as he had told the American people. While Bolshakov was in the Soviet Union, Kennedy ordered intense surveillance of Cuba by U-2 spy planes, a move that he knew the Soviets would consider a provocation.

At 8:45 on the morning of October 16, National Security Advisor McGeorge Bundy told President Kennedy that a U-2 had brought home "hard photographic evidence" of medium-range ballistic missiles capable of carrying nuclear warheads in Cuba. The missiles had been unloaded and Soviet personnel were working to make them ready. There was a short time to intervene before they were operational.

The moment they learned the Soviets were shipping nuclear missiles to Cuba, John and Robert Kennedy realized that they'd been played, that trusting Bolshakov had been a blunder. They had been lulled into believing he was a friend, both to them personally and to the United States. In fact, whatever feelings Bolshakov may have had for the Kennedys, he was playing a part, and the script had been written in Moscow. His words and demeanor were calibrated to validate John Kennedy's instinct that the narrow-minded cynicism of cold warriors was to blame for poor relations with the USSR. Rejecting the views of advisors who warned that Khrushchev was irredeemably duplicitous, the Kennedys were happy to go around the professionals, and instead to lean on Bolshakov, and on amateurs, especially journalists, to establish lines of communication with the Soviet leadership.

Tellingly, in his memoir of the crisis, Robert Kennedy juxtaposes the messages Bolshakov and others had conveyed from Khrushchev claiming arms shipments to Cuba were defensive with his receipt of news that the Soviets had placed nuclear missiles on the island: "Now, as the representatives of the CIA explained the U-2 photographs that morning, Tuesday, October 16, we realized that it had all been one gigantic fabric of lies. The Russians were putting missiles in Cuba, and they had been shipping them there and beginning construction of the sites at the same time those various private and public assurances were being forwarded by Chairman Khrushchev to President Kennedy."[21] Robert Kennedy added that "the dominant feeling was one of shocked incredulity. We had been deceived by Khrushchev, but we had also fooled ourselves."

Infuriated by the deception, and determined to prevent the Soviets from making nuclear missiles ninety miles from Florida operational, the Kennedys' first impulse was to bomb and invade Cuba. Fortunately, given the stakes, rather than act immediately the president ordered an urgent review of his options.

As the president and his hand-picked team worked long hours to formulate a strategy for dealing with the missiles and the military prepared for a variety of contingencies, reporters started to pick up hints and rumors that a major crisis was brewing. President Kennedy and senior administration officials reached out to trusted reporters at the *New York Times* and *Washington Post* to persuade them to keep a lid on the story until the White House was ready to make it public. Some reporters didn't have to be persuaded. Charles Bartlett, the Washington correspondent for the *Chattanooga Times* and a columnist for the *Chicago Daily News*, dined with President Kennedy three times during the crisis, discussing the situation in detail with him as events unfolded, but didn't breathe a word about it to his editors or readers. Bartlett was one of President Kennedy's closest friends. In May 1951, convinced that Kennedy's political career would stall unless he got married, Bartlett had played cupid, introducing JFK to his future wife, Jacqueline Bouvier. Bartlett was at Kennedy's side during the presidential election, as a friend rather than journalist, and in case anyone didn't know about their relationship, *Life* magazine ran photos in December 1960 of Bartlett cradling the president-elect's newborn son, John Kennedy Jr.[22]

Unlike Bartlett and other White House favorites, the *New York Herald Tribune*'s scrappy Pentagon reporter, Warren Rogers, was not an insider. No one thought to pledge him to silence.

Throughout 1961 and 1962, Rogers had been chasing stories around the globe, from Germany to Vietnam. To atone for his absences, on the night of October 21 he took his family to dinner at Billy Martin's Carriage House in Georgetown. As soon as they sat down, Rogers looked across the room and spotted familiar faces: experts on Soviet and Caribbean affairs from the State Department and the Pentagon huddled around a table. Rogers walked over, saying, "Hi, guys. What are you all doing working on a Sunday?" They turned green and muttered incomprehensively. Rogers walked back to his wife, who saw the look on her husband's face and said, "I guess we're going home."[23]

Rogers drove by the State Department and saw lights on at the Soviet desk. At home he worked the phones, and then called a story into the *Herald Tribune*. His story, which ran on the front pages of the *Tribune* and the *Boston Globe* on Monday morning, reported:

> Top American diplomatic and military officials held extraordinary conferences behind a wall of secrecy as large-scale air-sea and ground movements were reported under way.
> It seemed to have something to do with Cuba or Berlin or both.[24]

Rogers wrote that "it was dangerous to speculate" in the absence of any official guidance, but he did so anyway. His first guess was on the money: "Perhaps the Kennedy administration had found out that Cuba has acquired offensive military capability."

That evening President Kennedy addressed the nation: "This Government, as promised, has maintained the closest surveillance of the Soviet military buildup on the island of Cuba. Within the past week, unmistakable evidence has established the fact that a series of offensive missile sites is now in preparation on that imprisoned island. The purpose of these bases can be none other than to provide a nuclear strike capability against the Western Hemisphere."[25]

Kennedy mentioned the numerous public and private assurances the Soviet leadership had given him that only defensive weapons would be installed in Cuba. Then he outlined a measured response. Rather than invade, the United States. would start by imposing a "strict quarantine on all offensive military equipment under shipment to Cuba."[26] He made it clear that success was not guaranteed. "The path we have chosen for the present is full of hazards, as all paths are—but it is the one most consistent with our character and courage as a nation and our commitments around the world."

The entire world seemed to hold its breath for the next five days. Across the country, and especially in Washington, many went to bed believing they might not live to see another sunrise. White House officials and journalists bought camping gear, loaded cans of food into station wagons, and made plans for their families to flee the city on a moment's notice. They either imagined it was possible to outrun Armageddon or believed it was better to die trying than be incinerated in their homes.

President Kennedy and his advisors tugged on every string they could find, looking for one that would untie the diplomatic knot in time to avoid war. That included overcoming their rage at Bolshakov's betrayal and continuing to use him as a channel to communicate with Khrushchev.

Bolshakov had a series of meetings with reporters on October 23 that in retrospect fell somewhere between critically important and irrelevant. In the morning, Holeman called the embassy and said he needed to speak with Bolshakov. This time the call was official: out of work because of a New York newspaper strike, Holeman had taken a temporary job working for Guthman, RFK's press secretary. At their meeting, Holeman, who said he was conveying a message from the attorney general, suggested a swap: the United States. would remove its missiles from Turkey and Italy in exchange for the Soviets' doing the same in Cuba. As Bolshakov wrote in a report to Moscow, Kennedy had instructed Holeman to say that "the conditions of such a trade can be discussed only in a time of quiet and not when there is the threat of war." Bolshakov repeated the now discredited Soviet claim that its military operations in Cuba were purely defensive. He also told Holeman that Soviet ships would disregard the US blockade.[27]

A few hours later, Bartlett called Bolshakov and invited him to lunch at the Hay Adams hotel. Acting on Robert Kennedy's instructions, Bartlett told Bolshakov that the president, who was aware of their meeting, compared the Soviet deception to the Japanese sneak attack on Pearl Harbor. Kennedy didn't want to invade Cuba, Bartlett said, and hoped the Soviet Union would agree to have the missiles removed through an agreement mediated and verified by the United Nations.[28]

Bolshakov, who was not authorized to negotiate on behalf of the Soviet Union, had little to say to Bartlett. In an effort to get a more energetic response, Robert Kennedy pressed Bartlett to call Bolshakov to the Press Building for a second meeting a few hours later.

When the Russian entered Bartlett's office, the first thing he saw was easels with large aerial photos of Cuban missile sites. Robert Kennedy had instructed Bartlett to confront him with the pictures, which had not been publicly released and were stamped "secret." Bartlett let the Russian peruse the photos and asked how, faced with such evidence, he could deny that Soviet missile bases were under construction in Cuba. Bolshakov replied that he'd never seen photos of missile bases; the clearings could be baseball fields for all he knew.[29]

According to Bolshakov's report to Moscow, Bartlett, like Holeman earlier in the day, suggested that a withdrawal of Soviet missiles from Cuba could be linked to a reciprocal withdrawal of US missiles from Turkey.[30]

The next day, October 24, Pentagon officials told Rogers about contingency plans for an invasion of Cuba. He was one of eight reporters given the opportunity to accompany the troops. That evening, Rogers and his bureau chief, Robert Donovan, discussed their reporting on the crisis over beers in the Press Club Tap Room. Rogers asked Donovan for a

$400 advance to cover expenses to travel to Florida, where he would join the Marines if Kennedy ordered an invasion.

As they spoke, they barely noticed Johnny Prokoff, the Press Club's popular bartender, standing nearby. Prokoff, a Russian from Lithuania, had escaped desperate poverty by stowing away on a freighter. For a decade he worked as a cabin boy, dodging police on the wharves of hundreds of ports before he finally scurried off a ship in Mexico, snuck across the border into the United States and managed to obtain citizenship. Prokoff had a keen interest in the work and lives of the newsmen whose days often started at his bar with a "breakfast of champions"—a double Virginia Gentleman bourbon on the rocks. Thirsty hacks were piled four-deep in front of the bar by four in the afternoon, and most nights a few had to be ushered out the door, or onto a soft chair in the library, at 2:00 a.m. closing time. For a generation of reporters, Prokoff's shouted greeting, "Have a drink and be somebody," conjured up fuzzy memories of inebriated cheer.[31]

At about 1:00 a.m. Anatoly Gorsky, a KGB officer who worked undercover as a TASS reporter, walked into the Tap Room and ordered a drink. Prokoff, speaking softly so the other patrons didn't hear, told the Russian about the conversation he'd overheard between Rogers and Donovan. Prokoff hated communism, but he had a personal bond with Gorsky: both were avid and talented chess players.

Like everyone else at the Press Club, Prokoff must have assumed that Gorsky was an intelligence officer. It isn't known whether his disclosure was motivated by friendship, by a desire to affect history, or by a wish to taunt Gorsky. There is no evidence to support another possibility, that Prokoff was a KGB informant. In any case, Gorsky made a hasty exit and sprinted to the embassy with the first confirmation that Kennedy was planning an invasion.[32]

Either Prokoff had misheard, or Gorsky mixed things up during his late-night dash to the embassy. When he got there, Gorsky told Alexander Feklisov, the KGB *rezident*, or chief of station, that it was Donovan who was traveling to Florida "to cover the operation to capture Cuba." Gorsky said the invasion was slated to start by the 26th. Feklisov had no sources in the Kennedy administration, so he grabbed hold of this bit of bar talk and ran with it.[33]

Plaque that hangs in the National Press Club's Reliable Source bar commemorating Johnny Prokoff. A beloved National Press Club bartender, Prokoff inadvertently helped resolve the Cuban Missile Crisis by informing a KGB officer of American contingency plans to invade Cuba.
Credit: National Press Club archives

Trying to verify Prokoff's tip, Feklisov assigned one of his officers, a young embassy official, to stake out the parking lot behind the Willard Hotel, where Rogers usually parked. When Rogers got out of his car, the KGB officer asked him what he thought about the situation in Cuba. Years later, Rogers recalled that he replied that it was "extremely grim." The official also asked whether "Kennedy means what he says," to which

Rogers replied, "You're damn right he does." Back at the embassy, the KGB officer told Feklisov that Rogers had predicted that the United States would invade Cuba within two days.[34]

Rogers hadn't been in his office long when he received a call from the Soviet embassy asking if he would have lunch with an official whom he barely knew. Hoping it would yield a story, Rogers agreed. Instead of learning anything, he spent most of the lunch expressing his opinions about how Kennedy would resolve the crisis in Cuba. He said the military was planning a massive invasion, and that Kennedy was holding the soldiers back for a few days to build up the justification for action. The KGB might have believed that Rogers was in touch with the White House or had some other inside source of information. In fact, he was speaking only for himself and did not inform anyone in the US government about his conversations with embassy staff.[35]

News of Rogers's Tap Room conversation and his discussions the following day with embassy officials landed on Khrushchev's desk along with a GRU report that US forces had been placed on alert for nuclear war. These reports played into the Soviet leader's decision to respect the American blockade and to announce his decision to remove offensive weapons from Cuba.[36]

Bolshakov, Holeman, Bartlett, and Rogers weren't the only journalists in the Press Building who played a high-profile role in the Cuban missile crisis.

John Scali, a reporter for ABC television, received a telephone call from Feklisov on October 26, 1962, inviting him to meet for lunch at the Occidental Restaurant, across the street from the Press Building. Feklisov, who used the cover name "Fomin" during his postings to the United States, had first contacted Scali in 1961 to suggest that they meet occasionally for informal, off-the-record conversations. The Russian was well-acquainted with the United States. He'd worked in New York during World War II and developed a friendship with the American spy Julius Rosenberg. Unlike in the 1940s, and in contrast to the separate operations the GRU ran in Washington, Feklisov and the KGB had no ability in 1961 or 1962 to obtain valuable secret information in Washington. He was reduced to begging for table scraps over lunch with reporters who had no intention of helping the Soviet Union.[37]

Scali had notified the FBI about Feklisov's proposal. The bureau told him that Feklisov was the KGB *resident* in Washington and persuaded Scali to meet with him as often as possible and report on their conversations.[38]

According to Scali, at the Occidental Feklisov "seemed tired, haggard and alarmed in contrast to the usual calm, low-key appearance that he presented."[39] The two men were both so addled that they didn't notice until the meal was over that the Russian was eating Scali's crab cakes and Scali had consumed Feklisov's pork chop. Everything else about their interactions over the next two days was similarly muddled.

Scali went straight from the lunch to Foggy Bottom, where he gave the State Department's intelligence chief Hilsman verbal and written accounts of the conversation. According to Scali's version, Feklisov had asked if the United States would be willing to go along with a deal under which the Cuban missile "bases would be dismantled under United Nations supervision and Castro would pledge not to accept offensive weapons of any kind, ever, in return for a US pledge not to invade Cuba." Scali told Hilsman that Feklisov, anxious to receive a reply as soon as possible, had written his home telephone number on a piece of paper and handed it to him before they parted.[40]

Hilsman, the Kennedys, and other members of the team working to resolve the crisis were convinced that Feklisov was acting as a back channel from Khrushchev, and they immediately started working on a response.

Secretary of State Dean Rusk composed a response to the offer he believed Feklisov had made, ran it by the White House, and gave it to Scali. "I have reason to believe that the United States government sees real possibilities in this and supposes that the representatives of the USSR and the United States in New York can work out this matter with [UN secretary-general] U Thant and with each other. My definite impression is that time is very urgent and time is very short."[41]

Scali met Feklisov at the Statler-Hilton's coffee shop, around the corner from the embassy. After Scali recited the message, which he said "came from the highest sources in the United States government," they hurried to the cashier. Feklisov dropped a five-dollar bill on the counter for his thirty-cent coffee and rushed out without waiting for change—highly unusual behavior for a Soviet official. In the KGB's offices on the top floor of the embassy, Feklisov wrote a report that he believed could avert nuclear war.[42]

Feklisov's account of the conversation at the Occidental was similar to Scali's with one critical difference: he wrote that *Scali* had proposed the deal. According to Feklisov's cable, and comments he made decades later, he had been fishing for information when he met Scali, not conveying messages from Khrushchev.[43]

Even in an emergency, the embassy operated according to protocol. Feklisov could send cables to Moscow Center, but Ambassador Anatoly Fyodorovich Dobrynin had to sign-off on any cables for Khrushchev or other members of the Presidium. Dobrynin pondered Feklisov's report for two hours and then refused to send it. The ambassador, who was holding his own secret talks with Robert Kennedy, had a dim view of the intelligence services bypassing the Foreign Ministry. He'd already told Kennedy to ignore Bolshakov and he wasn't going to let a KGB officer hijack negotiations with the White House.[44]

Meanwhile, the Kennedys and other top American government officials were certain that Feklisov was acting under direct instructions from Khrushchev and that the Kremlin had picked Scali as an intermediary to communicate with the White House. They were angered and confused when the Soviet leader sent messages that made no reference to the deal that Scali had described or to their carefully crafted responses.

Feklisov eventually sent his cable to the KGB, where it took half a day for it to be decoded and move up the chain of command to the Kremlin.

By that time the die had been cast. Khrushchev had already decided to back down; there is no reason to believe that he ever saw Feklisov's memo. Although they thought they were on center stage, the drama between Feklisov and Scali was a sideshow, a dangerous distraction.[45]

Despite the confusion, a deal was struck. Khrushchev swallowed his pride and withdrew the missiles in exchange for Kennedy's pledge not to invade Cuba. Both sides kept secret Kennedy's promise to remove American missiles from Turkey.

After the dust had settled, the Kennedys realized that while Bolshakov had deceived them, he hadn't lied. When Bolshakov said the USSR had no intention to send offensive weapons to Cuba, it was because that's what Khrushchev had told him, and he had believed it.

The Kennedys and other American officials continued to believe incorrectly that Scali had played a decisive role in resolving the crisis. The ABC newsman kept silent about the affair until Hilsman revealed it in a book and magazine article in 1964. Journalists, with Scali's encouragement, built up the tale until it seemed that a humble journalist had saved the world from nuclear destruction.

In his memoir, Kennedy's press secretary Salinger wrote that the "nation and the world owe John Scali a great debt of gratitude. He chose to put aside his tools as a newsman in favor of the greater national interest at a crucial time in history." Salinger added that while Scali was "the meanest man who ever sat down at a poker table," his role in "averting nuclear catastrophe was of enormous importance."[46]

Scali dined out on the story of his secret diplomacy with "Mr. X," as Feklisov was called in early versions of the tale, for the rest of his life. It sent his career on a trajectory that ended with an appointment by President Richard Nixon as US ambassador to the United Nations.

In 1994, the Occidental Restaurant installed a plaque on the wall next to the table where the reporter and spy lunched. "At this table during the tense moments of the Cuban missile crisis a Russian offer to withdraw missiles from Cuba was passed by the mysterious Russian 'Mr. X' to ABC-TV correspondent John Scali. On the basis of this meeting the threat of a possible nuclear war was avoided."[47]

Across the street at the National Press Club, a plaque behind the bar commemorates Prokoff. In contrast to the apocryphal history etched into brass at the Occidental, the club memorializes him as a friend to journalists, and for his salutation "Have a drink and be somebody!" It doesn't mention the part Prokoff unwittingly played in avoiding a nuclear war.

A room at the National Press Club is dedicated to Holeman, who devoted eighteen years to representing the tire industry after retiring from journalism in 1969. Few members or visitors have any inkling of his secret life as a "boy spy."

Rogers didn't learn about the role his conversation in the Press Club's Tap Room had on history until 1997, when Feklisov's cables were described in a book by an American and a Russian historian.[48]

CHAPTER FIFTEEN

CONTINENTAL PRESS

The management of Continental Press Service never told anyone which continent the name referred to, and they were a little hazy about the services they provided. If anyone had thought hard about what was going on in its twelfth-floor National Press Building Office, the operation would have seemed suspicious. The credentials and decades of experience of the journalists who ran it, however, were solid, and for over a decade Continental Press flew under the radar, unmolested and unquestioned.

While the reporters who worked at Continental Press pretended to be independent journalists, they were in fact employed by the CIA. Their jobs were to produce propaganda, provide cover for spies and facilitate illegal domestic espionage. The news service was a cog in a vast machine the CIA had created to weaponize information and to deputize reporters as undercover partisans in America's undeclared global war against communism.

The activities of Continental Press Service, a CIA "proprietary" or front company, exemplified the cozy relationships many American reporters had with the agency during the Cold War. They also provide a glimpse of the CIA's massive overseas media operations and show how it sometimes became enmeshed in domestic politics.

The CIA's role in creating and running Continental Press surfaced in the fallout from the foiled Watergate burglary. It was disclosed by E. Howard Hunt, a man who had dedicated his life to protecting secrets. The retired CIA agent had been sentenced in 1973 to a provisional thirty-five-year prison term for planning the Watergate break-in and for refusing to cooperate with the Justice Department's investigation of the crime. When Judge John J. Sirica sentenced Hunt, he promised to reduce the punishment if Hunt broke his silence.

Traumatized by prison and grieving the death of his wife—she was killed in a plane crash with $10,000 in $100 bills in her bag, money intended to purchase legal assistance for and the silence of Watergate burglars—Hunt decided to talk. On the morning of December 18, 1973, he was driven by armed guards from the federal penitentiary in Allenwood, Pennsylvania to Capitol Hill for a private meeting with Senator Howard Baker Jr. and staff members of a Senate committee that was investigating the CIA's role in the Watergate burglary. Hunt told them that his role in Watergate hadn't been an aberration. Years earlier, when he was a senior CIA officer, he had been ordered to spy on a presidential election campaign. The operation, Hunt reported, involved a front company located in the National Press Building called Continental Press.[1]

Hunt didn't tell the investigators much about Continental Press, and the CIA still refuses to divulge anything about the operation. Enough information is available, however, from public documents and passing references in declassified documents to assemble an outline of its history and activities.

The story starts with Fred Zusy, a jovial reporter who joined the Associated Press in 1941, covered the war in Europe, and remained overseas, serving as AP's bureau chief in Cairo in 1951 and then holding the same position in its Istanbul and Rome bureaus. With his resume and contacts, Zusy could have landed a job at a major newspaper. Instead, when he quit the AP in 1959, Zusy moved to Washington and started Continental Press, a small news service that provided stories to obscure newspapers that none of his peers would ever read.

After his death in 2010, Zusy's wife explained why his career had taken such an unusual turn. "He was," she said, "in the clandestine service of the CIA after he left the AP."[2] This was accurate but almost certainly incomplete. Zusy's relationship with the agency had probably begun long before 1959. The CIA wouldn't have trusted Zusy with a sensitive operation unless it had already developed a deep trust in him. That kind of confidence is accrued over time and earned by acquitting oneself well in difficult circumstances. Certainly his reporting from the Middle East in the early 1950s, especially about the nationalization of oil companies and efforts by communists to overthrow the Shah of Iran, would have been of great interest to the CIA.

The Press Building was the logical place to locate Continental Press. At the time, it was peppered with small news shops. Lone reporters who eked out a living from freelance assignments rented tiny offices where they slept on sofas under piles of old newspapers. In slightly larger offices entrepreneurial journalists dreamed of expanding trade publications or specialized newsletters into media empires. There was a sense of camaraderie and a roguish approach to ethics among Press Building tenants in those days. It was common for reporters to write and file stories for a colleague who was incapacitated by a night of hard drinking, and nobody batted an eye at the Press Club when they overheard a reporter dictating a story from the *Washington Star* into a phone to an editor halfway around the country as if he'd written it himself.[3]

Zusy presented Continental Press as the Washington bureau for foreign publications that couldn't afford to send a correspondent to the United States. Zusy's clients consisted of newspapers like the *Globe Press* of Istanbul, Tehran's *El Akhbar & Akhbar El-yom*, the *Dawn*, headquartered in Karachi, and the *Ashanti Pioneer* of Kumasi, Ghana. Zusy never explained how clients like this provided enough income to put food on his table, cover office rent, salary for a secretary, and after a few years support several other reporters. These were not the kinds of publications that were in the habit of paying generously for stories. In fact, they weren't in the habit of paying at all, as freelancers who have worked for newspapers in developing countries have learned through bitter experience.

The newspapers Continental Press serviced were, however, precisely the kinds of publications the CIA—and the KGB—favored as vectors for disseminating propaganda. Both intelligence services purchased, subsidized, and infiltrated hundreds of newspapers in developing countries and in Europe, coopting them as combatants in the global struggle between the superpowers. Stories planted in obscure publications were often picked up by newspapers with national or regional reach. For the CIA, the fact that they were unlikely to be read in the United States or cited by American news organizations was a benefit, as the agency tried to minimize the chance of "blowback," as it called operations that ended up harming the United States. The agency was worried that false information it planted abroad could influence and distort American policy, or that the American public would be infuriated if it learned that its news was being contaminated by the CIA.

A second reporter, Russell Brines, joined Continental Press in 1961 as executive editor after resigning as editor of the Copley News Service, a wire service that was owned by the Copley newspaper chain. Like Zusy, Brines had been a foreign correspondent for AP. The wire service sent him to Tokyo in 1939 and transferred him to Manila in November 1941. A few weeks later, after the Pearl Harbor attack, Brines, his wife, and his daughter were interned by the Japanese. They were released in a prisoner swap after nineteen months. Brines wrote a book, *Until They Eat Stones*, about the brutal treatment he, and especially military prisoners, received at the hands of the Japanese.[4]

Brines started working for Copley in the 1950s, serving as the first editor and manager of Copley News Service. The company's owner, James S. Copley, had in 1947 offered the services of its reporters to President Eisenhower "as the eyes and ears . . . for our intelligence services" to fight communism.[5] He was one of a cohort of news executives CIA director Allen Dulles turned to when he wanted stories planted in American newspapers. At one point twenty-three Copley employees were working for the CIA. The Copley News Service was particularly useful to the agency in Latin America. It is almost certain that Brines had, like Zusy, been working for the CIA for some time before he joined Continental Press.[6]

A year after Brines joined Continental Press, the CIA gave Hunt responsibility for the operation. Hunt considered the assignment a punishment. He'd been deeply involved in the CIA's disastrous attempt to depose Fidel Castro by landing a ragtag group of Cuban exiles at the Bay of Pigs in April 1961. Like many agency officers associated with the fiasco, Hunt was put in a kind of purgatory, assigned a desk job that lacked the excitement or career-advancement potential of foreign clandestine operations.

Hunt supervised all CIA domestic propaganda activities from 1962 to 1964. His duties included working with the US Information Agency to coordinate CIA foreign and domestic propaganda. He ran operations that had cryptonyms like WUHUSTLER, WUBONBON, and WUPUNDIT.[7]

WUBONBON included the CIA's work with book publishers, such as Eugene Fodor, publisher of the Fodor's travel books. It is likely that Hunt used Continental Press to launder the transfer of funds from the CIA to Fodor's.

Fodor, a Hungarian who grew up in Czechoslovakia, wrote his first travel book in 1936. He joined the US Army in 1942, was recruited into the Office of Strategic Services (OSS), and, after the war, worked for the CIA in Vienna and Budapest. In 1949 he founded Fodor's Modern Guides, Inc., and began producing travel books. Starting in the 1950s he hired CIA officers as writers. He was more than willing to provide cover for clandestine activities, but he insisted the CIA only send him talented writers who were willing to do their cover jobs.

Fodor's connection to the CIA, and the CIA's connection to Continental Press, were unknown outside the agency until Hunt revealed them to Senate investigators in 1973. His testimony was leaked to the *New York Times*, which, to the consternation of Hunt, Fodor, and the CIA, in 1975 revealed Fodor's covert activities, as well as the existence of Continental Press.[8]

As part of WUBONBON, Hunt also managed the CIA's covert

relationship with another former intelligence operative turned publisher, Frederick Praeger. Praeger fled to the United States from Austria in 1938, joined the US Army in 1941, and served in Army intelligence during the war. He started Frederick A. Praeger, Inc., an academic publishing company, in 1950. While the majority of Praeger's activities had no association with the US government, the CIA provided subsidies to and other assistance for several of the company's books. The most famous CIA-Praeger collaboration was *The New Class: An Analysis of the Communist System* by Milovan Djilas, a top official in Yugoslavia's Communist Party who became the most famous dissident in the Soviet bloc. Praeger took on the book, and accepted covert payments from the CIA, after several other western publishers declined to publish it. Praeger also published CIA-subsidized books promoting the US government's perspective on foreign-policy controversies such as the war in Vietnam and the 1965 US military occupation of the Dominican Republic.[9]

Hunt imagined himself a swashbuckling secret agent and hated working as a propagandist. Even so, his supervisors couldn't have been more pleased by the way he handled the assignment. "In the WUHUS-TLER project," the cover name for Continental Press, Hunt "vindicated his faith in a moribund clandestine asset by demonstrating, after about a year and a half under his personal direction, that is it is one of the most effective activities of its kind," according to a glowing annual performance review he received in 1964.[10]

Over a six-week period in the late summer of 1964, Hunt deployed Continental Press staff to undertake a new type of project: infiltrating the presidential campaign of Barry Goldwater on behalf of President Lyndon Johnson.

There is some dispute about whose idea this was. In 1975, then CIA director William Colby told the House Select Committee on Intelligence that spying on Goldwater had been the brainchild of Tracy Barnes, head of the CIA's Domestic Operations Division. According to Colby's version of events, Barnes proposed it to Chester L. Cooper, a CIA officer working in the Johnson White House on temporary assignment to the National Security Council.

A memo Colby provided to Congress stated that in 1973 Cooper told a member of the CIA Office of Inspector General that in 1964 Barnes had asked him "if he would like to have copies of [Goldwater's] speeches and would it be useful to have them before he (Cooper) read them in the newspapers."[11] Cooper said he would. The memo concluded, "There is no question that Mr. Cooper was serving the White House in the political campaign while on the CIA payroll and that he was assisted, in part, by a member of the Agency's Domestic Operations Division." The CIA didn't say why Barnes offered to spy on Goldwater. He may have been seeking to enhance the agency's stature at a time when President Johnson had a strained relationship with its director.

In blaming Barnes and saying that he hadn't informed anyone more senior about the operation, Colby created a convenient dead end: by the time the agency pinned responsibility on Barnes, he had been dead for several years.[12]

In a memoir published in 2007, Hunt claimed the idea to spy on Goldwater originated in the White House. President Lyndon Johnson had, Hunt claimed, "become obsessed with obtaining his competitor's plans." Having come to office through tragedy, and deeply resenting suggestions that he wasn't up to the job, Johnson yearned for a blow-out victory. Hunt reported that he had arranged for some of his "outside assets"—possibly a reference to Continental Press or employees of another CIA proprietary company—to infiltrate the Goldwater headquarters. "My subordinates volunteered inside, collected advance copies of position papers and other material, and handed them over to CIA personnel" who provided the documents to Cooper, according to Hunt.[13]

Hunt's assets included a secretary on Goldwater's campaign staff, who provided advance copies of speeches and press releases. A CIA employee who worked from the Continental Press offices picked up the material and delivered it to Cooper.

Whoever came up with the idea, Johnson was aware of the spying and wasn't squeamish about using it. He did so in a blunt fashion that must have made CIA officers cringe. Goldwater campaign staff noticed that the Johnson campaign had the unnerving habit of responding to points in their candidate's speeches before he had delivered them. Johnson didn't seem to notice or care that his actions made clear to Goldwater that he was being spied on.[14]

One of the most glaring incidents took place on September 9, 1964, after Cooper had received an advance copy of a speech Goldwater was slated to deliver that evening in Seattle. The Republican planned to announce formation of a Task Force on Peace and Freedom headed by Richard Nixon that would advise the campaign on foreign affairs. The idea was to calm fears that Goldwater had insufficient foreign-policy experience and that he would pursue a radical international agenda.[15]

Johnson swung into action and called a "flash" press conference. While Goldwater was on an airplane on the way to Seattle, LBJ announced the formation of a "panel of distinguished citizens who will consult with the President in the coming months on major international problems facing the United States."[16] Johnson's ploy worked perfectly: news of his advisory panel was widely reported, including on the front page of the *New York Times*, while Goldwater's task force received little attention.[17]

The disparity caught the attention of the journalist Arthur Krock, who in a nationally syndicated column suggested that Goldwater had "forfeited a chance to name his 'task force' first, and then represent the President's as another instance of 'me too.'" Krock noted that when Johnson called the press conference, reporters in Washington had already received a copy of Goldwater's remarks but had agreed to delay reporting on it until shortly before the speech was delivered. The column didn't even hint at the possibility that LBJ had also gotten an advance peek at the speech. Instead, Krock remarked on the "incomparable" staging: "The President of the United States in the classic décor of his oval office at the White House; his helplessly scooped opponent in the modernistic carnival setting of the Coliseum that was built for the Seattle World's Fair."[18]

Krock presented the situation as a triumph for Johnson and an example of the natural advantages a sitting president had in an election campaign. "Among advantages a president in a campaign to succeed himself has over his opponent is command of the channels of publicity," he told his readers.

The truth is that by breaking a media embargo, the CIA had made it possible for Johnson to dominate the news cycle that day.

Hunt told Senate staff, and wrote in his memoir, that he'd been disturbed by the order to spy on the Goldwater campaign. This wasn't because he had any hesitation about conducting what was obviously an illegal operation. Rather, it was because Hunt was one of the few Goldwater supporters in the CIA. "However, as distasteful as I thought it was, I performed the duty, accepting White House orders without question," Hunt recalled.[19]

In October 1964 Hunt took a medical leave, blaming a stomach ulcer on the CIA's "failure to assign me to an appropriate post abroad following my participation in [the Bay of Pigs operation] and the passive, non-challenging nature of the domestic work I was given." Following a six-week convalescence, Hunt was transferred to work that he found more congenial, including recruiting agents in Spain.[20]

When Hunt's revelations were leaked to the press, Senator Goldwater said that during the 1964 campaign, he had come to believe he was being spied on. "I just assumed it was one man or two men assigned at the direction of the President. . . . It never bothered me," he said. "I guess it should have, but knowing Johnson as I did, I never got upset about it."[21] Goldwater did not suggest that the CIA's spying had cost him the election.

After Hunt's departure Continental Press continued to produce propaganda for foreign publications and, presumably, to provide cover for CIA operatives. In 1965, Continental Press hired Enoc Waters, one of America's leading African American reporters, to report from Africa. Waters had traveled to Uganda in 1964 to help set up an English-language newspaper. Three years later he was still working for Continental Press. There is no evidence that he was a witting CIA operative.[22]

When Continental Press closed in 1970, Zusy moved two floors down to the Press Building offices of the CIA-friendly Copley News Service. That year Hunt retired from the CIA. He was hired as a security consultant by the White House in 1971, where he led a unit known as the Plumbers that was dedicated to plugging leaks within the Nixon administration, playing dirty tricks on Nixon's opponents and obtaining political intelligence. Unrestrained by the CIA bureaucrats he loathed, went on to plan a spree of illegal and ill-conceived ventures culminating in the Watergate burglary. Later, he cited the CIA's infiltration of the Goldwater campaign as a precedent for the break-in at the Democratic National Committee's headquarters.[23] His logic was that if it was okay to use surreptitious methods to obtain political intelligence on behalf of one president, it was acceptable to do the same for another president. "Since I'd done it once before for the CIA, why wouldn't I do it again [inside Watergate in June 1972] for the White House?" Hunt explained to the *New York Times* in December 1974.[24]

The Watergate scandal set in motion investigations by Congress and the media of the CIA's illegal domestic activities. The resulting revelations, combined with disillusionment with American policy in Vietnam and revulsion against Nixon's abuses of power turned journalists from willing allies of the CIA into wary adversaries. Reporters who had cooperated with the agency sought to hide or minimize their connections, while senior editors and publishers scrambled to convince staff and the public that American publications and broadcasts were untainted by association with organizations that were dedicated to deception.

Congressional investigations, and reporting by news media, revealed that hundreds, perhaps thousands of reporters in the United States and overseas had close relationships with the CIA from its creation in 1947 through the late 1970s. It paid some reporters to collect information and engaged in informal information exchanges with many more. It bought, subsidized, and manipulated newspapers, magazines, and news services around the world. Major news agencies such as CBS News and the *New*

York Times cooperated extensively with the CIA. The agency slipped its officers into newsrooms, usually with the knowledge and consent of newspaper publishers and television network CEOs. *New York Times* publisher Arthur Hays Sulzberger signed a secrecy agreement with the CIA and allowed it to disguise about ten officers as *Times* journalists, stringers, or clerical staff in the 1950s.[25]

Many of the American journalists and news executives who collaborated with the CIA were motivated by patriotism. They'd seen how intelligence failures had left the United States vulnerable to sneak attack at Pearl Harbor and later witnessed the USSR's ruthless domination of Eastern Europe. Eager to help ensure that the United States wasn't blind-sided by communists at home or abroad, they failed to comprehend or chose to ignore the threat to democracy posed by secret alliances between government and the press. Joseph Alsop, one of the most influential American columnists in the '50s and '60s, said of his extensive cooperation with the CIA, "I'm proud they asked me and proud to have done it."[26]

The CIA vigorously defended its relationship with the press as a logical and necessary tool for fighting the Cold War. In 1977, a year after he resigned as CIA director, Colby told Congress that the conflict with the Soviet Union was a war of ideas that could only be fought through the news media. "We should not disarm ourselves in this contest in the hopes that the rest of the world will be gentlemen," he said. Colby railed against criticism of the CIA's foreign propaganda, arguing that "a larger view of the cultural and intellectual battle which raged in Europe and the less developed world in the 1950's and 1960's would recognize that CIA's support of the voices of freedom in the face of the massive propaganda campaigns of the Communist world contributed effectively to the cohesion of free men during that period." He decried the "ostrich-like tendency to pretend that journalism can be purified by a total separation from CIA."[27]

Colby and other former CIA officials conceded the possibility that foreign propaganda could harm US interests if false news planted overseas returned to the United States and not only misled the American public but was also taken as real by policymakers. Colby said the risk of CIA disinformation corrupting American policy was minimal, but in fact as the world became every more interconnected, it became inevitable.

Ironically, the CIA was a victim of blowback from its own disinformation during the Reagan administration. Secretary of State Alexander Haig read a prepublication galley of *The Terror Network*, a book by the journalist Claire Sterling, and had been impressed by its conclusion that the Soviet Union was responsible for European terrorism. CIA director William Casey was also smitten by Sterling's work. He even held it up in front of a group of CIA analysts and sneered at them that he'd learned more from a book written by a journalist based on publicly available sources than from the agency's secret reports.

When CIA analysts refuted Sterling's conclusions, Casey contracted with an independent scholar to analyze the book. The academic found something startling. Sterling had diligently dug into the archives of obscure newspapers to document her assertions, but the nuggets she'd mined turned out to be fool's gold.[28] Many of the articles she cited were disinformation that had been planted by the CIA. Despite the strong objections of CIA staff, the allegations in Sterling's book were incorporated into a National Intelligence Estimate and used to justify expansion of CIA covert activities in developing countries. Tainted news seeds the agency had planted from Lahore to Lisbon had sprouted and taken root in a book that influenced the Reagan administration's intelligence policy and diplomacy.[29]

CHAPTER SIXTEEN

PROJECT MOCKINGBIRD

The CIA's interactions with American journalists, especially those who have revealed its secrets, have not all been cordial. Project Mockingbird, which was undertaken in 1962, shows that the agency was willing to go to great lengths, including illegal wiretapping, to shut down leaks. Presidents from both parties have leaned on the CIA to tap the phones of American reporters as part of largely futile efforts to identify their sources.

Mockingbird was the first operation conducted by a CIA team formed at President John Kennedy's request that was dedicated to finding and plugging national-security leaks. The team reflected his intense interest in the media, as well as his willingness to use the CIA to tame it.

Kennedy had briefly worked as a reporter after World War II, knew many reporters and publishers personally, and, as president, devoted a great deal of attention to burnishing his public image. Intimate awareness of how the game was played may explain why Kennedy was infuriated by unauthorized leaks. Disclosures of classified information that he hadn't initiated or authorized sometimes helped America's adversaries—but almost always diminished his authority and power.

Throughout his presidency Kennedy trusted journalists to keep secrets that, had they been revealed, could have had dire consequences for both national security and his reputation. He was the first president to routinely grant exclusive interviews to favored reporters, pleasing the few who toed the White House line and angering many more who were excluded. Still, JFK's trust in a handful of reporters and editors didn't reflect confidence in the entire profession, his cultivation of the press didn't immunize him from criticism, and his understanding of the news industry's penchant for exaggeration and controversy didn't thicken his skin.

Kennedy read newspapers as voraciously as he chased women, noting and taking offense at the smallest slights. He also considered himself a master of the art of the leak and the trial balloon. His administration made no apologies for lying to reporters to protect national security. For example, Kennedy's Pentagon spokesman, Arthur Sylvester, told reporters that it was the government's inherent right "to lie to save itself."[1] And Kennedy approved unprecedented steps to prevent unauthorized releases of information. His administration was the first to require that government employees keep track of and systematically report on their interactions with journalists. It was also the first to allow television cameras to cover press briefings, creating new opportunities for the White House to bypass print reporters and to shape the daily news cycle.

The press was incensed by Kennedy's attempts to manipulate news coverage and plug leaks. Arthur Krock, the *eminence grise* of American news, wrote in March 1963 that the administration was managing the news "more cynically and boldly" than had previously been attempted in peacetime. "President Kennedy reads more newspapers regularly than any predecessor appears to have done," reported Krock, who had headed the *New York Times* Washington bureau from 1932 to 1953 and once considered himself a friend of the Kennedy clan. "And his bristling sensitiveness to critical analysis has not been exceeded by that of any previous occupant of the White House."[2]

More ominously, Krock wrote that it was "well known . . . that President Kennedy was prone to turn loose the FBI in a search for the official source of any published information that appeared in a form displeasing to him for one reason or another, especially when the publication was in the nature of an unmanaged 'leak.'" This was a reference to the FBI's heavy-handed investigation of a *New York Times* reporter, Hanson Baldwin, who in a July 1962 scoop had reported classified information about US satellite surveillance of Soviet missiles. Baldwin described details about the construction of Soviet missile silos, and in the process revealed the capabilities of American satellites. This allowed the Red Army to camouflage sensitive military activities or take evasive measures when it knew satellites would be overhead.[3]

Krock didn't know that J. Edgar Hoover had agreed only reluctantly to White House requests to spy on Baldwin and other journalists, or that the president had turned to the CIA to plug leaks. As the FBI's actions against peace activists a decade later demonstrated, Hoover wasn't squeamish about conducting illegal surveillance. He did, however, drag his feet when he felt there was a risk that the FBI's unlawful activities could be exposed.

Kennedy agreed to assign the CIA the task of investigating unauthorized national-security disclosures at an August 1, 1962, meeting of the President's Foreign Intelligence Advisory Board (PFIAB). Details of the meeting are known because in the spring of 1962 Kennedy had secretly ordered installation of a taping system in his office. The president could secretly start and stop the tape recorder, which was located in the White House basement, by activating switches concealed in a pen socket on his desk, in a bookend, or in a coffee table. Beyond the president, the only people who knew about the taping system were Kennedy's private secretary, the Secret Service agents who installed and maintained it, and Robert Kennedy.[4]

Members of the PFIAB told Kennedy that Baldwin's story would cause grave damage to national security. The FBI was trying to find his sources, but based on the bureau's past performance, it was unlikely to succeed, the president was told. The PFIAB had discussed the situation prior to the meeting and decided that the "FBI may not be the best agency to conduct investigations of leaks of this kind," its chairman, James Killian, reported.[5]

The bureau had "never been enthusiastic or successful in dealing with serious security breaches," Killian told Kennedy. "As I am sure you are fully aware, Mr. Hoover apparently doesn't like to get into this field. He feels it is an administrative responsibility rather than an FBI type of responsibility."[6] Furthermore, starting an investigation was a painfully slow process because FBI agents first had to be cleared to receive highly classified information and then educated so they could distinguish between facts that were in public domain and those that were supposed to be secret.

"We would suggest, therefore, that the Director of Central Intelligence be encouraged to develop an expert group that would be available at all times to follow up on security leaks," Killian said.[7]

Clark Clifford, an advisor to the president, chimed in, endorsing the recommendation to create a unit at the CIA dedicated to monitoring journalists, establishing who was supplying them national-security information and plugging the leaks. "Times have changed," Clifford said. "You can't do this anymore on a hit-or-miss basis like we've done in the past because now incidents of this kind are infinitely more important and more damaging than they've ever been."[8] General Maxwell Taylor, at the time an advisor to the president and later chairman of the Joint Chiefs of Staff, also spoke in favor of the idea.

Kennedy was convinced. "That's a very good idea," he said. "We'll do that."

Although Clifford had helped write the CIA charter, which prohibited the agency from undertaking operations inside the United States, he didn't express any concern about investigating journalists working in the United States for American newspapers. The attorney general, Robert Kennedy, failed even to suggest that the government should obtain warrants before investigating American citizens.

CIA director John A. McCone told Kennedy three weeks later that he had formed a group to investigate leaks.[9]

The first reporters targeted for warrantless surveillance by the CIA were Robert S. Allen and his partner, Paul Scott. This was the same Robert S. Allen who had briefly spied for the Soviet Union in 1932 while launching the Washington Merry-Go-Round column with Drew Pearson.

Allen had taken a break from journalism in 1942 to join the Army. In 1945, while serving on General George Patton's staff as an intelligence officer, Colonel Allen was wounded and captured. His right forearm was amputated in a German field hospital. Four days later he was liberated by American forces, and less than three weeks after the surgery was back working on Patton's staff. His wounds had not healed, however, and when the war in Europe was over, Allen spent a year recovering at Walter Reed Army Hospital in Washington.

Allen learned to type with his left hand. Rather than rejoin Pearson, who had reneged on a promise to pay him a royalty on the Merry-Go-Round column's revenues while he served, he started a new syndicated column with Scott. They specialized in military and intelligence scoops.

Allen came to believe that, like in the '30s, the United States and other democracies were sleepwalking into a confrontation with evil. This time the enemy was the USSR. Allen's distrust of the Soviet Union may have been accentuated by personal experience of the ways its intelligence services had infiltrated Washington, or by a sense of guilt over his secret assistance to Stalin.

Allen was convinced that Kennedy's policies toward the Soviet Union amounted to appeasement. He and Scott developed sources in the Pentagon, CIA, Congress, and even the White House who provided a constant stream of classified information that the two reporters fashioned into darts aimed at piercing American complacency. They focused a spotlight on the CIA. Ironically, while their column was shunned by the *New York Times*, *Washington Post*, and other leading American newspapers, TASS, *Izvestia*, and Radio Moscow frequently repeated its allegations of CIA impropriety and incompetence.

An *Izvestia* story in December 1961 quoted "the Washington observer Robert Allen" as revealing that the CIA's $400 million budget included extensive funding of front groups and propaganda. "Allen notes in particular that in West Europe 'the Central Intelligence Agency organized or financed almost all major international conferences of socialists which took place on the continent during the past ten years,'" the Soviet paper reported. It added that the Allen-Scott column "unmasks the faces of the traitor-socialists who have sunk to the role of agents in the pay of the American intelligence service."[10]

Most of the Allen-Scott story about the CIA budget was both true and classified. CIA director McCone wrote a line-by-line analysis of the column as part of an unsuccessful investigation the agency conducted to try to figure out how the columnists had gotten their hands on secret budget documents. CIA security staff's analysis of the story led them to believe that an agency employee was leaking to Allen and Scott as part of a sophisticated attempt to influence policy. Most of the column was an attack on a top CIA official, Cord Meyer Jr. The column included information about Meyer that McCone told CIA security personnel he had no prior knowledge of, such as the fact that before joining the CIA Meyer had been a strong advocate of world government and had led an organization dedicated to creating a global government. These beliefs were an abomination to anti-communists who viewed the United Nations as a plot to subjugate the United States. CIA security staff surmised that the employee who leaked to Scott was "playing a clever game, [by] endeavoring to bring to Mr. McCone's attention these facts or statements through the medium of this column with the possible belief or supposition that some form of inquiry into these matters would be made by Mr. McCone."[11]

In January 1962 Allen and Scott reported about American satellites that had been launched and others that would be deployed over the coming year to keep an eye on Soviet and Chinese military activities.[12] In February, citing a leak from the Defense Intelligence Agency, they told their readers that "an intelligence estimate that Russia has shipped poison gas to Cuba has spread an almost visible chill through the Kennedy administration."[13]

In addition to causing concern about national-security leaks, Allen and Scott irritated the CIA by providing ammunition to the agency's critics in

Congress. For example, under the heading "Another CIA blooper," they wrote in July 1961 that the CIA had "chalked up another in its long line of busts" by failing to anticipate a military coup in South Korea.[14]

A CIA memo describing the reasons for targeting Allen and Scott for surveillance mentioned that the agency was puzzled about how they obtained and reported on classified information. "Although much of the information contained in the columns was garbled, it was apparent that key points were frequently direct quotes from classified reports and summaries of recent vintage."[15]

Everyone involved in arranging for the CIA to tap the telephones at Allen and Scott's National Press Building office and at their homes knew that by involving the agency in a purely domestic operation they were crossing a line, and very likely violating the law. Reflecting concerns about possible legal jeopardy and the certainty of negative publicity should the operation be disclosed, the CIA minimized the Project Mockingbird paper trail. Staff who handled the wiretapping received their instructions verbally. Knowledge of the operation was limited to a small group. Only Robert Kennedy, who had requested the wiretaps, McNamara, McCone, and a handful of other intelligence officials were aware of Mockingbird.[16]

The surveillance started on March 12, 1962, and was halted three months later, on June 15, upon the retirement of the CIA's head of security. It isn't clear why the CIA cut off the project early; internal CIA documents express disappointment that the wiretaps were discontinued prematurely. It is possible that the agency believed its operation had been exposed.

Even in this limited time the CIA learned a lot. The two reporters gathered more secrets in a few months than a pair of KGB officers could have dreamed of collecting in decades of spying in Washington. "Monitors of MOCKINGBIRD were frequently amazed at the sheer bulk of information [Scott] would acquire in the course of a day," according to a CIA memo. "The intercept activity was particularly productive in identifying contacts of the newsmen, their method of operation and many of their sources."[17]

The wiretaps revealed that Allen and Scott were receiving confidential and classified information from a dozen senators and six US representatives, including House Speaker John McCormack, as well as twenty-one congressional staff members. In the executive branch they received classified information from a White House staffer, more than one member of the vice president's staff, an assistant attorney general, and employees of the State Department and NASA.

The CIA was most anxious to determine which of its own employees were leaking to Allen and Scott. Some of the disclosures, a CIA internal report noted, came from a CIA employee "who feels that the policy of the Agency should be shifted to one which would not be harmful to US interests." The report doesn't describe the policy, and although CIA leadership had a suspect, it wasn't able to confirm that he was the leaker.[18]

While it never identified Scott's CIA source, the wiretaps did uncover a White House leaker. It was a clerk who habitually brought documents home, and sometimes shared them with Scott, a neighbor and friend. The clerk's wife once joked on a telephone conversation, which the CIA had intercepted, that if her husband "kept all the papers he brought home from the White House, the home would look like the White House trash room."[19]

This clerk, who is not identified in the CIA documents that have been declassified, once gave Scott a copy of a secret speech that Walt Rostow, Kennedy's deputy national security advisor, had delivered at the Army's Special Warfare School.[20] Rostow outlined a proposal to create an international organization under UN control to combat communist insurgencies in developing countries. According to a story Allen and Scott wrote about the speech, Rostow enlisted Sen. William Fulbright and liberal foundations to support his idea. The proposal "hit the Pentagon like one of Mr. Khrushchev's megaton bombs," Allen and Scott reported. The reporters detailed classified plans the military had crafted for a completely different approach. The idea, which was later implemented, was to set up training schools around the world to give representatives of trusted governments military and propaganda tools to fight communism.[21]

The CIA was surprised to discover that Allen and Scott received several warnings that they were being investigated. Although they weren't specifically informed about Mockingbird, both were told that the Defense Department and CIA had launched investigations into their sources of classified information.[22]

The surveillance solved a riddle that had been puzzling the CIA: although the Allen/Scott columns contained nuggets extracted from sensitive intelligence reports, the accompanying explanations were often inaccurate. "At first it was believed that the garbling was a by-product of [Allen's] regular state of intoxication; however, later it became apparent that the garbling was used to disguise the source."[23]

The CIA learned through its wiretaps that Scott was planning to write a story claiming the agency had contributed money to a political campaign to defeat a congressman; that it had funded a foreign trip to Outer Mongolia by one of Sen. Joseph McCarthy's favorite targets, the scholar Owen Lattimore; and that a dozen communists worked at the CIA. The declassified files do not identify the member of Congress or reveal whether the CIA had actually worked to defeat him. In any case, Allen and Scott never reported this information, nor did they write about Lattimore or reputed communists at the CIA.[24]

The CIA may have exploited its early warning to give Allen and Scott information that cast doubt on the veracity of the leaks. Or the columnists may have decided they couldn't publish them without inadvertently disclosing their sources. Only a small fraction of the information provided to Allen and Scott ever made it into their columns. Some was set aside to protect the identity of a source. Even after sequestering these secrets, they received far more classified information than they could use, so they passed some of it on to other reporters and correspondents, who published the leaks under their own bylines.

Allen continued to be a thorn in the CIA's flesh until illness forced him to stop working in 1980. He committed suicide in 1981 at age 80.[25]

Having been both a Soviet spy and the object of White House–

ordered surveillance in the 1930s and 1960s put Allen in a class by himself, but he was far from being the first or last reporter to have his or her phones tapped. Illegal electronic surveillance of reporters, including those with Press Building offices, didn't start or end with the Kennedy administration, and while Hoover dragged his feet in response to requests from John Kennedy to wiretap reporters, he was more accommodating to other presidents, including Dwight Eisenhower.

In May 1955, the White House requested that the FBI find the source of a leak as soon as possible, and made it clear it didn't care how it did it. A two-man newsletter, *Petty's Oil Letter*, had revealed a confidential discussion between President Eisenhower and the head of the Office of Defense Mobilization about plans to create an oil pipeline from Texas to the Northeast. The pipeline was intended to ensure that an atomic attack wouldn't cut oil supplies to the East Coast.

The head of FBI counterintelligence assembled a team and told them they were "free to do whatever was necessary" to find out who was leaking. It was necessary, the agents decided, to break into *Petty's Oil Letter*'s National Press Building Office and plant a microphone. The head of maintenance for the Press Building, who was already helping the FBI keep tabs on TASS, was happy to assist with the job. The bug caught Milburn Petty and his partner Jim Collins discussing the source of the leak. The FBI confronted the leaker and persuaded him to confess.[26]

Hoover was so concerned about Congress or the public discovering that the agency used illegal bugs and wiretaps that he ordered the bureau to employ euphemisms in all official communications. The agents who handled the *Petty's Oil Letter* operation received commendations from Hoover praising their "very effective utilization of a certain special technique," and internal FBI documents about the operation referred to the bug as a "special technical installation."[27]

National security was used again as a justification for FBI electronic surveillance of reporters during the Nixon administration. Acting on orders from the White House, starting in 1969 the FBI tapped a number of reporters, including Marvin Kalb of CBS television and two *New York Times* reporters, William Beecher and Hedrick Smith. The bureau didn't seek warrants for the taps.[28]

Henry Brandon, the Washington correspondent for the London *Sunday Times*, was also tapped. Brandon, who worked from a Press Building office, was the consummate Washington insider, known and respected by presidents Eisenhower, Kennedy, and Nixon, and the object of envy by rival journalists who lacked his access. The reasons for tapping Brandon are murky and explanations are contradictory. Nixon said on several occasions that he hadn't initiated the tap. Hoover had started listening to Brandon's telephone calls during the Johnson administration and he had simply agreed to continue the practice, Nixon claimed.[29]

In an interview recorded after his resignation, Nixon said that on his first day as president a thick envelope was waiting on his desk marked "Top Secret—Eyes Only—for the President." It was an intelligence report about Brandon. Nixon recalled, "I called Hoover, and I says, 'What the hell is this?' He says, 'Oh, Henry Brandon, he's a British agent.'" Nixon said he threw the envelope in the "out" box with a note asking Kissinger to look into it, and that he never heard another word about it. "I'm sure Brandon thinks I put the tap on, but apparently Johnson had it on all the time."[30] In 1973 Nixon told a White House aide, "Brandon's been zapped for years. That's what Hoover told me."[31]

Justice Department officials denied that Brandon had been tapped during the Johnson administration, and no evidence of a tap prior to 1969 has surfaced. If Hoover had proof that Brandon was a British intelligence officer, he took it to his grave. What is incontrovertible is that Brandon's privacy, along with the privacy of anyone he spoke with on the telephone, was violated for more than two years, and there was no discernable national security justification.[32]

CHAPTER SEVENTEEN
ACTIVE MEASURES

Starting in the late 1950s, Soviet spies who operated from the TASS bureau in the National Press Building engaged in a tense, high-stakes version of cat and mouse with the FBI. Both sides viewed their interactions as a kind of game, but their rivalry wasn't playful. The men Moscow sent to the Press Building were determined to obtain secrets that could give them an edge in the geopolitical conflicts that defined the latter half of the twentieth century—and potentially in the nuclear war that Kremlin leaders believed could break out at any moment.

Unlike its Soviet counterparts, who tracked American spies in Moscow around the clock, the FBI lacked the manpower required to maintain continuous surveillance of all of the known or suspected hostile intelligence operatives in Washington. The bureau compensated by exploiting its home-court advantage: bugging the TASS office, tapping its phones, sifting through its trash—and enlisting volunteers from all walks of life, from Press Club presidents to maintenance workers, to keep an eye on Soviet intelligence officers.

The KGB had its own challenges to overcome. Its American intelligence networks were decimated in the 1950s by the revelations of defectors, the US Army's decryption of KGB World War II intelligence cables, and an increase in American security awareness. Starting in the late 1940s the FBI and the US military instituted background checks on personnel with access to classified information and systematically weeded communists out of sensitive positions. The Soviets had to assume that every one of the assets had been compromised. The chances of a KGB officer finding someone like the true believers who had worked for Soviet intelligence in the past was slim. The FBI had thoroughly infiltrated the Communist Party of the United States, draining a favored Soviet recruiting pool, and following revelations of Stalin's crimes and the death of over 30,000 GIs in the Korean War, almost no Americans outside the party were willing to put their lives on the line to advance the interests of communism. In the absence of ideologically motivated spies, the KGB had to find people with access to secrets who were willing to betray their country for money or, less commonly, who could be entranced through romance or entrapped by blackmail.

The war might have been cold, but in the 1950s and '60s it didn't feel that way for Americans, who lived in fear of nuclear annihilation. The Soviet Union dominated the public imagination. School children were drilled on how to "duck and cover" as if their desks would protect them from a nuclear attack. Newspapers and television were filled with stories that painted Russians as dangerous and duplicitous. In this environment, Soviet reporters and diplomats were widely, and correctly, assumed to be spies. Nonetheless, they were objects of mostly friendly curiosity at the National Press Club, one of the few places in Washington where Americans and Soviets mingled freely.

Valentin Ivanov, a short, pudgy Russian who sported a bushy mustache and thick glasses, didn't cause a stir when he started hanging around the Press Club in the summer of 1957. He was entitled to membership as press attaché at the Soviet embassy. Ivanov's visibility increased in the spring of 1958, when he demolished a series of competitors in preliminary rounds of the club's chess championship and easily won the first two games in the final. He would have taken first prize if he hadn't thrown the last three games; someone in Moscow likely ordered him to avoid the scrutiny that would have been generated by a Soviet victory. Spies are supposed to use activities like playing chess to meet and size up potential recruits, not to call attention to themselves.[1]

Ivanov was less reticent on the evening of May 7, 1960. At 6:18 p.m. Press Club members watched in astonishment as he dashed out of the club crying, "Admitted! Admitted! Admitted! Admitted!"[2] Ivanov had been aroused by an official State Department statement acknowledging that the Eisenhower administration had lied when it claimed that an American weather plane had accidentally strayed into Soviet territory and crashed. In fact, as the government confessed, it had been a U-2 spy plane on an espionage mission.

It was a remarkable moment. The U-2 statement was perhaps the last time journalists and the public were stunned to learn that a US president had been caught perpetrating a bald-faced lie. And it was the first time that the American government publicly acknowledged that it violated borders and sovereignty during peacetime to conduct espionage.

Press Club members were surprised by Ivanov again on August 12, 1960, when they woke up to find a story describing his extracurricular activities on the front page of the *Washington Post*. It wasn't about the Russian's prowess on the chessboard. Instead it was an account of a sleazy and inept attempt at espionage.[3]

Ivanov had befriended a sometime merchant seaman and part-time cook named Roger Foss, whom he had persuaded to move from New York to Washington and to apply for a government job. Ivanov's goal, Foss told the *Post*, was to "infiltrate the Government and society."[4] The story didn't explicitly state that Ivanov was a spy, but it provided details that left little doubt. For example, Foss described how his Russian benefactor set up secret meetings: Foss was instructed to leave a chalk mark on a lamppost near Ivanov's home as a signal that he wanted to meet—a classic technique the KGB used in Washington for decades. They met about fifteen times over the course of a year, usually in Chinatown. "He loved Chinese food; I got so sick of it," Foss moaned. "I'll never touch another bite." Ivanov paid Foss $500 to cover tuition at a business school, plus living expenses to tide him over until a government job opened up.[5]

One hot day in August, while he was waiting for the results of his civil service exam, Foss wandered into the offices of the American Nazi Party in Arlington, Virginia, across the bridge from Washington. After speaking with its leader, George Lincoln Rockwell, he decided fascism suited him better than communism. At Rockwell's urging, Foss told the FBI and later the *Post* about Ivanov's attempts to set him up as a sleeper agent.

The day after Foss's story appeared in the *Post*, the State Department declared Ivanov persona non grata, and he was never again seen in the Press Club.

Ivanov's name reappeared in the newspapers a month later, after two National Security Agency codebreakers, William Martin and Bernon Mitchell, denounced the United States at a dramatic press conference in Moscow. They were the first employees to defect from an organization that was so secret at the time that its initials were said to be short for "No Such Agency." Congressional investigators told reporters that Ivanov had recruited Martin and Mitchell at a Washington area chess club. If true, from the KGB's perspective this would have more than mitigated Ivanov's botched attempt to insinuate a fascist loser into a government job.[6]

With the exception of Martin and Mitchell, and an Army Colonel named William Henry Whalen who sold military secrets to the Soviets, the KGB didn't have much success in Washington in the first half of the '60s. Khrushchev, who had great faith in his own ability to assess international affairs, was far less enthusiastic about foreign intelligence than his predecessors.[7] The KGB's Washington station became a backwater. Its fortunes changed in 1964, when Leonid Brezhnev, who had a more traditional Soviet veneration for espionage and respect for intelligence services, toppled Khrushchev and took over the Soviet government.

The KGB sent a new station chief, Boris Solomatin, to Washington in 1965 to turn things around. He selected a rising star, Oleg Kalugin, as his deputy. Kalugin had studied journalism in New York at Columbia University a decade earlier as part of the first Cold War student exchange program. Like most of the "students" Moscow sent to Ivy League universities, he was a professional intelligence officer. Kalugin had returned to New York in 1960, working undercover in the guise of a correspondent for Radio Moscow.

In his third posting to the "main adversary," as Soviet intelligence agencies called the United States, Colonel Kalugin's cover was as second secretary and press attaché in the Soviet embassy. He was actually in charge of political intelligence, with half of the KGB's forty Washington-based officers reporting to him.[8]

Cultured and quick-witted, Kalugin easily formed bonds with intelligent men and attractive women. In addition to trying to recruit agents with access to the White House, Congress, and the State Department, he focused his considerable charm on journalists. The leading liberal columnists of the day, Walter Lippmann, Joseph Kraft, and Drew Pearson, regularly and openly met with Kalugin, as did reporters like Chalmers Roberts and Murray Marder of the *Washington Post*. Kalugin's circle of friends included the unofficial dean of foreign correspondents, Henry Brandon of the London *Times*. Kalugin was a familiar presence at the Press Club and other watering holes, where prominent journalists exchanged their perspectives on American policy and politics for the insights he provided about the USSR.[9]

Kalugin was far too smooth to try to recruit most American reporters as agents, but he did pitch at least one. Over a series of lunches, Kalugin tried to bring I. F. Stone, who had been a Soviet intelligence operative in the 1930s, back into the fold. Infuriated by the Soviet invasion of Czechoslovakia, Stone broke off contact with Kalugin in the summer of 1969.[10]

Kalugin had more luck with the foreign reporters. His paid recruits in the Press Building included the Washington correspondent for a major European newspaper—as late as 2014 Kalugin refused to identify the journalist or his country—and reporters from developing countries.[11]

In addition to recruiting agents and informants in the Press Building and directing the operations of KGB officers in the TASS bureau, Kalugin found that the building was a perfect spot for evading surveillance and meeting agents. The FBI didn't hide the fact that it was watching Kalugin. He and other KGB officers, however, were convinced that they could detect FBI tails and that intense observation was sporadic, usually lasting a week or two followed by breaks of several weeks.

National Press Club Bar, circa 1965. Women were not permitted to join the National Press Club until 1971. Prior to 1971 women were allowed to enter parts of the club when accompanied by members, but were strictly excluded from the bar, card room, and other male sanctuaries.
    Credit: National Press Club archives

According to the FBI's unwritten rules of engagement, its agents might tail Kalugin to the lobby of the Press Building, but they wouldn't get on the elevator with him and they couldn't easily follow him into the Press Club. Once he was in the club, Kalugin could take advantage of stairwells to descend to lower floors. There, long corridors arranged in a rectangle with uninterrupted sightlines were perfect for covert meetings.

About once a month for several years, a diplomat from a Western European country slipped unnoticed through the Press Building lobby. He got off on one of the middle floors and walked down the corridor at a prearranged time. Just as he rounded one of the corners, he would see Kalugin walking toward him. If anyone else was in sight, they would walk past each other and wait for another day to rendezvous. If the coast was clear, they would duck into a stairwell, where the diplomat passed Kalugin a package. The contents ranged from copies of diplomatic cables and top-secret reports to recordings of the diplomat's ambassador's conversations. Kalugin handed his agent an envelope with cash and a note indicating the date, time, and floor number for their next assignation. Following an exchange that took less than a minute, Kalugin jogged back upstairs to the Press Club bar for a drink with a reporter. He'd been absent from the bar for about the amount of time it would have taken to visit the bathroom.[12]

While Kalugin had recruited a handful of foreign reporters and was on friendly terms with scores of American journalists, his closest collaborators were KGB subordinates who worked from the cramped TASS office on the third floor of the Press Building. The TASS bureau chief, Mikhail Sagatelyan, and most of his staff were KGB officers. There were also a few military intelligence (GRU) officers at TASS who worked completely independently of the KGB. Like every foreign TASS bureau, the Press Building office had a couple of "clean" staff, real reporters who had to carry the load for the spooks, who did as little work for the news agency as they could get away with. In addition to KGB officers working undercover at TASS, all Soviet journalists in Washington, including those working for *Izvestia*, the Novosti news agency, and Soviet radio and television networks, were obliged to cooperate with and obey instructions from the KGB. The sole exception was employees of *Pravda*, the Communist Party newspaper, which was completely off-limits to the intelligence services. In the Soviet hierarchy the only body more privileged than the intelligence services was the party.[13]

In 1967 Kalugin hatched a plot with Viktor Kopytin, a KGB officer working under TASS cover, which reflected the Washington station's appetite for risk. The idea was to plant a bug in a congressional hearing room and listen in on closed sessions where classified and sensitive military information was discussed. Kopytin cased the Senate Armed Services Committee room, decided that security was too tight, and advised Kalugin that the House Armed Services Committee room would be a better target.[14]

A KGB unit in Moscow that specialized in spy tech—like poison dart guns camouflaged in umbrellas—created a custom bug. The battery-powered microphone and transmitter were concealed in a piece of wood that matched a table in the committee room. There were metal spikes on one side so it could be stuck onto the table.

On a summer afternoon, Kopytin lingered in the room after a hearing, waited until he believed that no one was watching, and casually slipped his hand under the table and firmly attached the bug. KGB officers in a car parked on Capitol Hill huddled anxiously over a receiver, but they never heard a peep from the bug. It turned out that Kopytin was overly confident in his ability to detect surveillance. He'd been seen planting the microphone. The FBI neutralized the device and kept the room under observation, hoping to catch a KGB officer attempting to retrieve it. The Soviets, however, didn't take the bait.[15]

Kopytin's congressional caper had probably been seen by a member of an FBI unit that specialized in counterintelligence against the KGB. It operated from the FBI's Washington Field Office, three blocks from the Press Building in the Old Post Office building. (The building was renovated and repurposed as a Trump Hotel in 2017.) Once the FBI suspected that someone was a KGB spy, an agent from the unit was assigned to keep track of him.

An FBI agent named W. Peyton George was assigned to Kopytin in 1968. He learned that his target, like most TASS reporters, gave a high priority to establishing relationships with American journalists. George was eager to find out what Kopytin was discussing with reporters because learning what kind of information the KGB was fishing for could shed light on its priorities. This wasn't a straightforward task because FBI director J. Edgar Hoover, obsessed with preventing negative publicity, had laid down strict rules governing his agents' contacts with the media. Prior to contacting a reporter, an FBI agent had to conduct a background investigation and receive approval from FBI headquarters, a process that could take a month.[16]

Under Hoover's rules, there were no restrictions on agents speaking with reporters who volunteered to help the FBI. This loophole led George to come up with a pragmatic solution. When he learned through FBI electronic surveillance of the TASS office that Kopytin was planning to have lunch with a reporter, George would call Alan Cromley, Washington bureau chief of the *Daily Oklahoman* and, in 1968, president of the National Press Club. In some cases, Cromley would tell George to steer clear of a reporter who was a "leftist" and therefore unlikely to cooperate with the FBI. In other cases, Cromley would make a discreet telephone call, and ten minutes later one of Kopytin's sources would call George to offer to keep the FBI informed about their conversations. In addition to consulting Cromley about his own cases, George called Cromley on behalf of other FBI counterintelligence agents. After Cromley's term was over, the FBI agent established a similar working arrangement with another Press Club president, Michael Hudoba, an editor at *Sports Afield Magazine*.[17]

George ran a classic operation against Kopytin. As in the best counterintelligence operations, the KGB had no idea it had been snared and, in fact, believed it was scooping up valuable secrets under the FBI's nose. Appropriately, it all began in a bar, when Kopytin overheard two men talking about "multiple reentry vehicles" and other bits of arcane defense terminology. It turned out that they were analysts at a think tank that worked for the Department of Defense. Kopytin joined in the conversation, telling the Americans that he was a Soviet journalist. Before long the Russian found a common interest with one of his new acquaintances— the man's grandfather had emigrated from Russia.[18]

The American, who has not been publicly identified, reported his contact with Kopytin to the FBI, and George encouraged him to develop the relationship under the FBI's direction, as a double agent. Kopytin ran the recruitment according to the standard KGB playbook. He started by asking the American for innocuous information, gradually upping the ante until he was requesting and paying for classified information. To the intense irritation of the American intelligence community, Senator J. William Fulbright had publicly released a list of classified projects that the Defense Department was funding. The list gave Kopytin and other KGB officers a carryout menu to order secret documents from. The FBI and the National Security Council set up a process to vet Kopytin's requests and determine which reports could be given to him without damaging national security.[19]

Kopytin met with the American about once every six weeks to receive the classified reports, usually over dinner. The KGB officer would punch his finger in the double agent's chest and say, "We want to know what your President is thinking!" Between courses, he slipped his informant an envelope with three to six thousand dollars in crisp twenty-dollar bills. When the defense analyst moved to Massachusetts, the FBI paid for his travel back to DC for the meetings and put him up at the Hilton or the Watergate Hotel, covering the expenses with the KGB's twenty-dollar bills.[20]

Based on the information Kopytin was requesting, it became clear to Pentagon officials that the Soviet government had obtained the complete US negotiating strategy for nuclear disarmament talks that were being conducted in Geneva. Kopytin "even had the United States' Position Points in chronological order," George recalled.[21]

The State Department expelled Kopytin in May 1969, ostensibly in retaliation for the Soviet Union's expulsion of a *Washington Post* reporter. The FBI was proud of the way it had handled the TASS reporter and KGB officer. The bureau didn't discover for another eighteen years that even as it was playing Kopytin it had failed to detect one of the KGB's most successful espionage operations.

One of the worst security leaks in American history started on a cold day in October 1967 at the Soviet embassy, an old mansion that had a quirk that made it especially easy for the FBI's surveillance teams: there was a single front entrance and no back door. Nonetheless, the FBI didn't notice when John Anthony Walker, a chief warrant officer in the US Navy, walked up to the front door and rang the bell. He stepped inside and asked to speak with "someone connected with intelligence." Walker told a KGB officer that he wanted to strike up a business relationship with the USSR, and he handed over a sheaf of Xeroxed papers to prove that he had access to valuable information. The documents were brought to Kalugin and his boss Solomatin, who quickly realized they were real—and that they were extraordinary. Walker had handed over information that could help the Soviets decrypt the most secret American Navy communications.[22]

Kalugin spent hundreds of hours over the following months scouting "dead drops," sites where Walker could deposit documents and pick up money and instructions without meeting face-to-face with a KGB officer, and poring over the material Walker sold the KGB. Walker was one of the most effective Soviet Cold War spies, providing high-level intelligence about American Navy codes, technology, strategy, and tactics. Information he supplied allowed the USSR to track American ships, submarines, and war planes in real time, and to know in advance where they were going.

In addition to giving Moscow secrets that could have provided it a decisive military advantage in a war with the United States, Walker gave a career boost to Kalugin, who left Washington in December 1969 to start a new job in Moscow as the KGB's deputy chief of foreign counterintelligence.

Besides stealing secrets, while in Washington Kalugin had engaged in what the KGB called "active measures," intelligence operations designed to advance Soviet objectives and influence events in foreign countries. Active-measures techniques included creating forged documents, disseminating disinformation, recruiting "agents of influence," as the KGB called individuals who could shape policy or public opinion, organizing political influence operations, and creating and funding front groups.[23] Soviet propaganda thrived on "whataboutism," pointing to supposed moral equivalencies between the Soviet Union and its adversaries. When there was no real evidence, the KGB was tasked with using active measures to create it.

One of Kalugin's small contributions to the KGB's massive active-measures campaigns involved creating disinformation to divert attention from entirely accurate accounts of Soviet discrimination against Jews. His first move was to flood American Jewish organizations with anonymous anti-Semitic materials. Then Kalugin found individuals who were willing, for a fee, to desecrate Jewish graves and paint swastikas on synagogues. He sent photographers to document the wave of hatred that the Soviet press claimed was sweeping across America.[24]

After Kalugin's departure, the KGB revisited the theme. In 1971, KGB chief Yuri Vladimirovich Andropov personally approved the distribution in New York of pamphlets presented as if they had been written by the Jewish Defense League that attacked African Americans as "black mongrels." The Jewish Defense League staged a more overt, and colorful, operation at the Press Building the same year. To protest unfair "scapegoating" of Jews in Leningrad, they chained a sedated goat to the door of the TASS office. The goat wore a sign indicating that he was a "Jewish scapegoat." Other "gifts" left at the TASS office have included an effigy with a noose affixed to its neck and a sticker modifying the word TASS to UNITASS, which sounds like "unitaz," or toilet in Russian.[25]

During the Democratic primaries for the 1976 presidential campaign, the KGB forged FBI files that accused Senator Henry "Scoop" Jackson, a hardline opponent of the Soviet Union, of being a homosexual. The documents were sent to the *Chicago Tribune*, *Los Angeles Times*, and other newspapers, but none of them fell for the ruse.[26]

The KGB's Washington station, most likely including officers working in the TASS office, had more success with a provocation intended to stir up racial tensions ahead of the 1984 Olympics. The KGB printed up flyers that appeared to be products of the Ku Klux Klan and sent them to the Olympic committees of African and Asian countries. The flyers announced that the Olympics were "for whites only" and warned "African monkeys" that rewards would be paid to Americans for lynching or shooting them. Newspapers around the world ran stories about the flyers. Some of them followed up with stories noting the US State Department's assertion that they were KGB disinformation.[27]

KGB active-measures activities in Washington included more subtle, and more effective initiatives. For example, Yuri Shvets, a KGB officer who was posted to the TASS Press Building office in 1985, successfully targeted an influential journalist, Claudia Wright, the Washington correspondent for *New Statesman*, a British magazine. Wright, an Australian who was strongly pro-Soviet and vehemently anti-American, had been unwittingly serving as a vehicle for KGB fabrications for several years. In 1982 she wrote a story claiming that Jeane Kirkpatrick, the US ambassador to the United Nations, had a clandestine relationship with apartheid South Africa's military intelligence. The story was based on a letter the KGB had forged.[28]

Shvets decided in October 1985 to kick it up a notch by meeting Wright and offering her an ongoing working relationship with the KGB. She immediately agreed and became a classic agent of influence. Rather than steal secrets for the KGB, she slipped its disinformation into her stories. After her recruitment, Wright's stories appeared regularly in *New Statesman*, and occasionally in the *Washington Post*, *New York Times*, and *Foreign Affairs*. They always favored Moscow's interpretation of events, were anti-Israeli, and expressed great confidence in the wisdom of the Libyan leader Muammar Gaddafi. For example, Wright repeated Soviet disinformation in a story printed in the Dublin, Ireland, *Sunday Tribune* on September 3, 1989, asserting that "the Korean Airlines jumbo jet, shot down by the Soviet Air Force six years ago today, was on a spy mission for the US."[29]

The KGB and GRU continued to send officers to work as TASS reporters in the National Press Building up until the final days of the

Soviet Union and, according to defectors, the Russian Federation continued the practice.

One of the last Soviet intelligence officers to work in the National Press Building, Stanislav Lunev, a colonel in the GRU, arrived in Washington in 1988. He was working in the TASS Washington bureau on Christmas in 1991 when Mikhail Gorbachev turned the lights out on the Soviet Union and transferred power to the first Russian president, Boris Yeltsin.

Lunev met one of his most valuable agents at a press conference for the environmental advocacy group National Resources Defense Council. In a memoir published in 1998, Lunev described one adventure involving the agent, whom he did not identify. On a sunny evening in the summer of 1990 Lunev drove to Northern Virginia, and pulled over near a pay phone, lifted the hood of his Mercury Sable and waited. If the phone had rung three times, and then three times a few minutes later, he would have aborted the mission. That would have been a signal that his compatriots, who were monitoring radio frequencies used by FBI agents, had detected surveillance. Relieved by the phone's silence, Lunev drove to secluded spot, parked, and stooped down to pick up a Coca Cola can. Inside the can, which was rigged to destroy its contents if someone tried to open it improperly, Lunev's agent had placed undeveloped film. It was a transcript of a closed Senate Intelligence Committee hearing about US strategy on the disintegration of the USSR, and included sensitive details about agents and operations against the Soviet Union.[30]

Lunev defected in March 1992 and spent a year at a safe house in Maryland briefing American intelligence officials. Among other things, he told them that he'd spent a great deal of time scouting locations where small nuclear bombs, so-called suitcase nukes, could be pre-positioned in advance of a war between the United States and the USSR.

TASS was not the only organization in the National Press Building that carried out active measures for the KGB. Soviet intelligence backed another active-measures project based there, which seriously damaged the CIA.

CHAPTER EIGHTEEN

CovertAction

The CIA had previously experienced damaging and embarrassing leaks, but these were droplets compared to the torrent that poured out of *CovertAction Information Bulletin*, a publication dedicated to using disclosures of secret information to cripple America's capacity for conducting intelligence operations. For a time it was surprisingly successful.

A low-budget magazine with an erratic publishing schedule, *CovertAction* wasn't much to look at, but it packed a punch. Its power came from exposing the identities of CIA officers and operatives, and describing some of the agency's most sensitive operations. *CovertAction* also educated its readers around the world about CIA tradecraft, provided lessons on spotting spooks, as well as detecting and evading electronic surveillance, and encouraged citizens to apply this knowledge to mount vigilante attacks on American spies and their operations.

The CIA viewed *CovertAction* and books published by its staff as an existential threat.

Ronald Reagan's CIA director, William Casey, told Congress that the individuals who produced *CovertAction* "understand correctly that secrecy is the life blood of an intelligence organization and that disclosures of the identities of the individuals whose intelligence affiliation is deliberately concealed can disrupt, discredit and—they hope—ultimately destroy an agency such as the CIA."[1]

While its *raison d'être* was exposing secrets, *CovertAction* held tightly onto its most important secret: its founder's close collaboration with communist intelligence services.

CovertAction was created by Philip Agee, a renegade former CIA officer who was devoted to destroying the institution he had once served. It was secretly supported by the *Dirección General de Inteligencia* (DGI), Cuba's intelligence service, and by the KGB, which considered the publication one of its most effective "active measures" against the United States.[2]

The pages of *CovertAction* and books produced by its staff disclosed the identities of over two thousand undercover CIA officers, impairing and in some cases destroying their ability to collect intelligence or conduct secret operations. Along with publishing accurate depictions of CIA activities, including some that many Americans would find abhorrent, such as the subversion of democratically elected governments and complicity in torture, the magazine also served as a conduit for Soviet propaganda and disinformation.

According to the CIA, while they were working for *CounterSpy*, a precursor of *CovertAction*, the magazine's staff published revelations that directly led to the murder of a CIA station chief in Athens. The CIA also blamed *CovertAction* for an attack on the top CIA officer in Jamaica. Agee and *CovertAction*'s staff denied that they inspired either incident.

Agee also denied any connection to communist intelligence services.

Like anything viewed through the rearview mirror of history, the competition between the United States and the USSR seems to shrink in importance over time, especially as living connections to the Soviet Union pass away. But as he looked out into the world in 1957, when he joined the CIA, all Agee could see was the Cold War and the proxy hot wars it inspired. He was an uncritical supporter of American foreign policy at a time when all other goals were subordinate to containing and rolling back communism.

For a dozen years Agee recruited agents and ran covert operations in Ecuador, Uruguay, and Mexico. He witnessed and participated in the CIA's incitement of armed uprisings, plotting of coups, subversion of elections, and tainting of the media with propaganda. Agee came to believe, much like Smedley Butler four decades earlier, that American activities in Latin America were not intended to promote democracy but rather to advance the financial interests of American capitalists. Echoing Butler's disillusionment, Agee later wrote that the CIA was "nothing more than the secret police of American capitalism, plugging leaks in the political dam night and day so that shareholders of US companies operating in poor countries can continue enjoying the rip-off."[3]

Searching for explanations for the economic inequality and poverty he witnessed, Agee, who had been educated by Jesuits, shed his Catholicism and adopted Marxism. The failure of his marriage may have contributed to his crisis of faith. In 1968, while stationed in Mexico City, he submitted his resignation to the CIA, effective early the next year. Agee remained in Mexico City and, seeking an outlet for his anger, and an instrument of retribution against the CIA, started writing a book about his experiences. Agee contacted publishers in New York seeking a contract and advance, but was rebuffed by editors who wanted a spectacular exposé, not the Marxist treatise he pitched.[4]

Undeterred, Agee traveled to Havana in May 1971 determined to write his book. He later acknowledged that he had received assistance from Cuban officials in researching his book in exchange for pledges that it would be "politically acceptable to the Cubans."[5] Given the de facto state of war between the DGI and CIA, it is inconceivable that he would have been able to enter Cuba, or to retain his freedom there, without collaborating with its intelligence service.

Agee maintained a low profile and apparently stayed off the CIA's radar until October 1971, when a newspaper in Montevideo published a letter to the editor he had sent from Havana. It warned that the CIA was likely to mount covert operations to prevent a leftist party from winning Uruguay's upcoming national elections. Publication of the letter tipped off the CIA that Agee had turned against it, sparking an investigation that revealed his plans to write a book about the agency. By the time the CIA started looking for him, Agee had traveled to Paris. CIA agents posing as leftists befriended him and tried to obtain a copy of his manuscript. To help the agency keep tabs on Agee, they lent him a typewriter in which he found a concealed microphone and transmitter. The CIA pressured Agee's family to entice him to return the United States, presumably so that he could be arrested, but he stayed in Europe. Decades later, Agee claimed he had evidence that the CIA was so anxious to quash his book that it had plotted to kill him before it could be published.[6]

Inside the Company: CIA Diary was published in Britain in April 1975 and was an immediate sensation. The public, and especially journalists, were fascinated by firsthand accounts of the agency's use of bribery, forgery, bugging, wiretapping, and blackmail throughout Latin America. And they were appalled to learn that the CIA was abetting torture.

In one of the most dramatic passages, Agee described how he and his colleagues had come up with a scheme to drive a wedge between the government of Uruguay and the Soviet Union. It involved fabricating a plot by four Soviet diplomats to conspire with leftist labor unions to overthrow the government. As part of the operation, Agee recommended that the police place a young labor leader named Oscar Bonaudi in protective detention. A few days later, on December 12, 1965, Agee was visiting a police station when he heard agonized screams emanating from a nearby cell. Agee immediately suspected that it was Bonaudi, the man he had falsely accused. A few days later he learned that this was correct, and that the torture had continued for three days.[7]

The horror, Agee asserted, went far beyond the CIA abetting the brutalizing innocent individuals. CIA subversion, he wrote, was directly responsible for the seizure of power across Latin America by corrupt, authoritarian dictators who oppressed and impoverished millions of people.

To the extreme consternation of his former employer, unlike previous books that criticized the CIA, Agee's made no attempt to mask the identities of intelligence officers or their agents. *Inside the Company* featured an appendix that named 250 CIA officers and provided detailed information about government officials and private citizens they had recruited. For example, Agee accused the future president of Costa Rica, Jose Figueres, of being a "front man for CIA operations." The book listed hundreds of organizations from newspapers to labor unions that, Agee claimed, had been penetrated or coopted by the CIA.

Published in the United States six months after its release in London, *Inside the Company* was a bestseller.

The CIA assumed that Agee, who had spent considerable periods in Havana, must have been in touch with the DGI. It also suspected he was cooperating with the KGB. For decades, however, there was no evidence to support these suspicions. The first confirmation came from a remarkable source—notes secreted from the Lubyanka by a former KGB employee named Vasili Mitrokhin.

The journey that brought those notes to the CIA's attention started in 1956, when Mitrokhin was a foreign intelligence officer. He participated in a discussion at work about Nikita Khrushchev's famous speech revealing Stalin's crimes. While his colleagues denounced Stalin, Mitrokhin asked, "Where was Khrushchev when all these crimes were taking place?"[8] This impertinent question helped derail his career as a spy. The young skeptic was relegated to working in the service's dusty archives, where having learned his lesson, he kept his growing disillusionment with the KGB and the Soviet Union to himself. In 1972 Mitrokhin was put in charge of moving 300,000 foreign intelligence files from the Lubyanka in downtown Moscow to a new building in the suburbs. He spent his days alone in the archives and hatched an audacious plan: At tremendous risk, over a decade the archivist took detailed notes and smuggled them out of KGB offices. He hid them under the mattress in his apartment, and on weekends took them to his family's *dacha*, stuffed them into containers, and buried them beneath the floorboards. His plan was to find a way to alert the world to the KGB's actions—especially its crimes.

Taking advantage of the chaos following the breakup of the Soviet Union, Mitrokhin contacted representatives of British intelligence in late 1991, and a year later he, his family, and his extraordinary notes were "exfiltrated"—surreptitiously moved—to Britain. The British shared the information with the CIA.[9]

Among the many revelations buried in the exhumed notes are excerpts from files indicating that Agee worked closely with the DGI in researching and writing *Inside the Company*. Furthermore, Mitrokhin's records indicate that the KGB played a major role in the project. An internal KGB memo took full credit for the book, claiming that it was "prepared by Service A, together with the Cubans."[10] Service A was the KGB's "active measures" department.

One of Mitrokhin's conditions for turning over his treasure trove to British intelligence was that the information would be released to the public. *The Sword and the Shield*, the first of two books based on the files, was published in 1999. It described Agee's collaboration with the DGI and KGB. Later, Mitrokhin's raw notes were made available to the public.

In 1994, prior to publication of the *Sword and the Shield* or any other public discussion of Mitrokhin's allegations about Agee, the former KGB general Oleg Kalugin published a memoir that included a description of the provenance of *Inside the Company*. Kalugin, who headed KGB counterintelligence during the time that Agee was completing his book, reported that the CIA defector initially approached the KGB in Mexico City offering damaging information about the CIA. He was turned away by officers who thought he was a "dangle," or false defector.

The threat of dangles wasn't hypothetical, as Agee knew. While he was working for the CIA, Agee learned that an American master sergeant had been dangled to the KGB in Mexico City in 1968. The soldier met with twenty-six KGB case officers over eight years in Mexico, West Germany, Switzerland, Japan, and Austria, giving the United States tremendous insight into KGB operations and, presumably, opportunities to feed its rival disinformation. The operation lasted until 1976, when Agee tipped off the KGB.[11]

The KGB approached Agee only after reviewing secrets he'd spilled to the Cubans and realizing that his defection was genuine. "The Cubans shared Agee's information with us. But as I sat in my office in Moscow reading reports about the growing list of revelations coming from Agee, I cursed our officers for turning away such a prize," Kalugin wrote.[12] While Agee was finishing his manuscript, the KGB kept in touch with him through

Edgar Anatolyevich Cheporov, the London correspondent of the Novosti news agency and of the Soviet literary weekly *Literaturnaya Gazeta*. Agee complied with a request from Cheporov to remove references in his manuscript to the CIA's penetration of Latin American communist parties. This information presumably would have tarnished the parties' reputations.[13]

A review in a CIA journal concluded that *Inside the Company* "will affect the CIA as a severe body blow does any living organism: some parts obviously will be affected more than others, but the health of the whole is bound to suffer."[14] Agee and his backers in the DGI and KGB must have been pleased by the impact. They were, however, aiming for more than a body blow.

The next punch was thrown in August 1978 at the Eleventh World Festival of Youth and Students in Havana. Agee and a small group of supporters distributed copies of a new book, *Dirty Work*, which identified seven hundred CIA staff who were at the time or had previously been stationed in Western Europe. Agee had never been posted to Europe, so the information must have come either from research he and his collaborators conducted, from the KGB, or a mix of the two.

The co-author of *Dirty Work* was Louis Wolf. A Quaker and conscientious objector to the Vietnam War, Wolf had become radicalized while performing alternative service in Laos where, he believed, the CIA had turned him into an unwittingly pawn in its clandestine war against communists.[15]

In addition to rolling out *Dirty Work*, Agee and his comrades used the festival to announce the launch of *CovertAction*. As with *Inside the Company*, the KGB privately took credit, claiming in an internal memo that the magazine was founded "on the initiative of the KGB."[16]

The inaugural issue of *CovertAction* included a Naming Names column. The magazine explained that as a "service to our readers, and to progressive people around the world, we will continue to expose high-ranking CIA officials whenever and wherever we find them." It apologized for including only one name, Dean J. Almy, the CIA chief of station in Jamaica, and promised to provide longer lists in future issues.[17]

The lead article, written by Agee and Wolf, presented *CovertAction*'s philosophy. It called the CIA the "Gestapo and SS of our time" and asserted that "exposure of its secret operations—and secret operatives—remains the most effective way to reduce the suffering they cause." Agee and Wolf proposed a "novel form of international cooperation" in which opponents of the CIA would scour lists of Americans working as diplomats or on aid projects, identify likely CIA operatives using techniques described in a chapter in *Dirty Work* called "How to Spot a Spook," then send the information to *CovertAction*. The magazine promised to check the research and publish all the information it could confirm. It estimated that the CIA had about five thousand officers experienced in running clandestine operations and suggested that it should be possible to identify almost all of those who had ever worked under diplomatic cover. The article concluded with a call to action: "We can all aid this struggle, together with the struggle for socialism in the United States itself."[18]

After the youth festival, Agee returned to London. While he was listed on the masthead and contributed articles, most of the work of producing *CovertAction* was undertaken by Wolf; Ellen Ray, a journalist; and Bill Schaap, a lawyer. Newspaper and magazine articles about *CovertAction* and its staff invariably highlighted its location in the Press Building, a setting that had clearly been chosen to bolster its claim to protection under the First Amendment to the US Constitution. A profile of Wolf distributed by the *New York Times* news service described a "miasma of suspicion about the office" and stated that "Wolf believes the telephones are tapped by the National Security Agency on behalf of the CIA."[19]

Another article about the *CovertAction* team, printed in the *Village Voice*, set the scene by reporting that it was based on an interview the author had conducted in the Press Club bar with Ray, Schaap, and Wolf. It described how the turmoil of the '60s, and especially the Vietnam War, shaped the outlook of *CovertAction*'s staff. While Wolf was working with peasants in Laos, Schaap and Ray were in Okinawa, "organizing workers at the big air base and helping GI's get out of going to Vietnam," the *Village*

Voice reported. And, the story continued, "they had these kites . . . these kites to bring down B-52s, kites with tinfoil stringing from them that they'd fly right up there in front of these huge jets loaded with 10,000-pound bombs lofting off the runways of Okinawa on another run to the Mekong Valley. Bill and Ellen, standing there at the end of the runway with their kites, trying to lasso a goddamn B-52!"[20]

There is no evidence that Wolf, Ray, Schaap, or anyone else connected with *CovertAction* wittingly collaborated with intelligence services, or that they were aware of Agee's connections to the DGI and KGB. It didn't take much imagination, however, to guess where Agee obtained the secret CIA documents and biographies of undercover CIA officers he provided to the magazine. Like Agee, Wolf, Ray, and Schaap were driven by a visceral hatred for American covert operations, affinity for the Soviet Union—at least their fantasy of the Soviet Union—and a fervent desire to help socialism triumph over capitalism.

The denunciations of human rights abuses in the pages of *CovertAction* never extended to those committed by the Soviet Union, China, or their allies. The magazine trained a spotlight on government surveillance activities but failed to aim it at East Germany's Stasi, which was tapping, bugging, and spying on its population. And *CovertAction*'s sympathy for the plight of the oppressed didn't extend to the millions of innocent people whose lives were destroyed in the Soviet prison camps or their analogues in China, North Korea, and other workers' paradises.

Inside the second issue of *CovertAction* there was an account by a former CIA finance officer, James Wilcott, of techniques the CIA used to target and recruit foreign diplomats. Wilcott and his wife, Elsie, a former CIA secretary, were advisors and frequent contributors to *CovertAction*. Wilcott's article was accompanied by a guide to identifying CIA officers working undercover as diplomats, an interview with a Cuban intelligence officer who claimed he had infiltrated the CIA for ten years, and the Naming Names column revealing the identifies of CIA personnel in France, Italy, India, Venezuela, El Salvador, and Jordan.[21]

The KGB created a task force dedicated to supplying *CovertAction* with material that would harm the CIA. In addition to providing names of agency officers, Soviet intelligence gave the magazine classified documents. For example, in 1979 the KGB provided *CovertAction* with "Director of Central Intelligence: Perspectives for Intelligence, 1976–1981," a classified document that had been mailed anonymously to the KGB's Washington *rezident*.[22]

Also in 1979, according to Mitrokhin's notes, two KGB officers "met Agee in Cuba and gave him a list of CIA officers working on the African continent." Some of this information was featured in the fourth issue of *CovertAction*, which provided extensive information about CIA activities in Africa, including a Naming Names column with the identities of sixteen CIA station or base chiefs on the continent.[23]

CovertAction's coverage of Africa was expanded into a book, *Dirty Work 2: The CIA in Africa*. In the introduction Agee addressed critics who had called out the one-sided nature of the *CovertAction* team's reporting. "There is no pretense of trying to 'balance' this book by describing similar, or different, activities of socialist nations," Agee wrote.[24] He argued that although the USSR and its allies "may well employ clandestine operations, the frequency and depth of such activities have been modest in comparison with secret intervention by Western powers." Assistance to African countries from the Soviet bloc "tends to be public, well-known, and without the stigma attached to political support, overt or covert, from the US and the former colonial powers," Agee claimed.

CovertAction got its hands on a manual used in CIA training called "The Principles of Deep Cover," and reproduced the ten-page document in its August 1980 issue. While the magazine presented the manual as a contemporary document, it had actually been written in 1961. Despite its vintage, the insights were relevant twenty years later and remain so today.[25]

The manual described the lengthy, detailed planning that went into establishing "deep cover," defined as the ability of intelligence officers to live "as legitimate private citizens with such authenticity that their intelligence sponsorship would not be disclosed even by an intensive and determined investigation."[26] It advised that CIA officers consider employing "natural cover," by recruiting individuals who were working for a private company and teaching them to be intelligence officers. "Some companies are willing to furnish information on all the young men they recruit for their foreign branches and to make those selected as potential agents available for training with reasonable assurances that they will eventually be assigned where the service wants them."

The manual also explained why elaborate measures to create and maintain deep cover were necessary. "The simplest and therefore the most used device an intelligence service has for getting its unwelcome officers covertly into other countries is to assign them to cover jobs in its government's diplomatic missions, consulates, and other official representations there," it explained. While simple, this practice, which the Soviets called "legal" and Western intelligence services called "official" cover, has the "disadvantage that the disguise is a pretty shabby one. It requires no Herculean counterintelligence effort to determine which foreign officials probably have intelligence connections; they can be kept deniable, but not really secret."[27]

Peeling off the thin layer of subterfuge covering CIA officers posted under official cover was one of *CovertAction*'s core activities. While it wasn't difficult for the KGB or other sophisticated intelligence service's to spot CIA officers working abroad under official cover, their jobs became far more difficult when their identities had been made public. The KGB, fearing reciprocal unmasking by the CIA of its officers working under legal cover, rarely did this. Kalugin and his comrades were delighted, however, to help Agee and Wolf make the lives of CIA officers miserable. This happened when a newspaper, say in Ouagadougou, ran a story based on data from *CovertAction* pointing out that a local US Agency for International Development representative was a spook. This often led to demonstrations in front of the outed agents' homes, threats to their families, and the disruption of their ability to recruit and run agents.

In some cases, *CovertAction* didn't restrict itself to "naming names" in print. It actively publicized the identities of CIA employees and tried to get them run out of town. In the most dramatic incident, Wolf traveled to Kingston, the capital of Jamaica, and on July 2, 1980, read out the names of fifteen reputed CIA officers at a press conference. He also provided their home addresses, telephone numbers, and car license-plate numbers. In case anyone missed the press conference, which was televised live in Jamaica and later rebroadcast, Prime Minister Michael Manley's party printed the information on handbills.[28]

The performance was intended, according to Wolf, to counteract a destabilization campaign that the CIA was running against Manley's socialist government.[29]

Two days later, at 2:30 a.m. on the night of July 4, the home of the CIA chief of station, Richard Kinsman, was raked by machine-gun bullets. A small bomb exploded on his front lawn. The bullets missed the bedroom where Kinsman was sleeping; his family was traveling outside of Jamaica. American newspapers immediately blamed Wolf and *CovertAction*.

Wolf issued a press release and held a press conference denying any responsibility for provoking the violence. He suggested that it had been staged by the CIA to smear *CovertAction* and revive stalled efforts to pass legislation criminalizing the disclosure of the identities of intelligence officers.

The CIA seized the opportunity. On July 8 deputy director Frank Carlucci sent a package of press clippings about the attack to members of congressional intelligence committees and the Senate and House leadership. "The incident exemplifies most vividly the potential for harm which flows from activities of organizations like CovertAction Information Bulletin, and why I continue to believe such activities should be restricted under the law," he wrote in a cover letter. "I further believe we can ill afford to wait until another member of a US overseas mission comes home in a casket before the Congress addresses this pressing problem."[30]

Publicity about the attack revived interest in the Intelligence Identities Protection Act (IIPA), a bill that had been first introduced in 1975 after the murder of Richard Welch, the CIA chief of station in Athens. As in case of the 1980 incident in Jamaica, the CIA and its supporters attributed Welch's murder to an article in *CounterSpy*, the Washington-based magazine that was launched and had folded prior to the establishment of *CovertAction*. Agee, Ray, and Schaap, who all worked for *CounterSpy* at the time, blamed CIA security lapses, not their disclosure of his identity, for Welch's assassination.

The IIPA, widely referred to as the "get Agee bill," stalled over objections that it would be impossible to outlaw the outing of CIA staff without violating the First Amendment's guarantee of freedom of speech. These objections were based in part on the fact that official cover could be breached without access to classified information, simply by using the tools of journalism. Wolf or anyone else who had been trained to detect the tracks of a covert CIA career could dive into the National Archives, immerse themselves in obscure government documents, and emerge with lists of putative CIA officers.

Wolf and his comrades tried to persuade American journalists that an attack on *CovertAction* was an attack on the right of all publications to report about intelligence operations. The IIPA, according to Wolf, was a "serious threat, not only to the *Bulletin*, but also to freedom of the press, investigative journalism, and reform of government abuses here in the United States."[31]

Whatever sympathy mainstream news media had for this view was blasted away by Agee's and *CovertAction*'s pro-Soviet orientation, the joy they took in naming names, and their indiscriminate disruption of CIA operations. After the shooting and bombing of Kinsman's home, the *New York Times* and *Washington Post* editorial pages endorsed the need for legislation to protect the identities of intelligence officers. They also pushed for limitations that would not restrict what they considered legitimate journalism.

The *Post* excoriated Wolf and those who emulated his practice of naming names of CIA operatives: "Though they work with a pen rather than a gun, they are terrorists in spirit, and their true purpose is to destroy democracy."[32]

Responding to the *Post* editorial, Wolf, Ray, and Schaap called themselves "journalists in the traditional sense, with good faith, just as much as your reporters are, and there is no way a law can distinguish between us." They challenged the *Post*'s accusation that they sought to destroy democracy with the assertion that the "CIA represents the least democratic aspect of the entire US government."[33]

The *Times* branded Agee a "villain for all seasons" and wrote that he had "abused his former access to intelligence methods by systematically publicizing the names of those he knows or suspects to be secret operatives."[34] Its editorial board wrote that imposing harsh penalties on "those who so callously violate their oaths of secrecy" wasn't sufficient:

> Mr. Agee is contagious. He has inspired Louis Wolf and others who never worked for the CIA to spot the names of US agents and to name them in publications like Mr. Wolf's *CovertAction Information Bulletin*. They have a common purpose: to blow the agents' cover and thus destroy vital intelligence functions. They are indifferent to the safety of the agents. They don't even pretend to distinguish between useful and questionable spy projects.[35]

The *Times* nonetheless urged caution, noting that "several of the bills aimed at Mr. Wolf would punish the publication even of widely known facts."[36] Proposals to require prosecutors to prove a sinister intent provided little reassurance, it added: "Since Government is all too quick to equate criticism with treason, and to consider all public discussion of intelligence as harmful, the requirement to prove a hostile intent may be no protection whatever." The self-appointed voice of mainstream journalism concluded, "Congress should pass only the most tightly drawn identities bill and then get on with more pressing matters: the quiet but smart management of the spy service, for instance."

Wolf, Schaap, and Ray responded to the *Times* by asking: who made *you* the arbiter of what disclosures are acceptable? The staff of *CovertAction* and their supporters, including the American Civil Liberties Union, wondered aloud why newspapers, including some like the *Times* that had long histories of collaboration with the CIA, should be permitted to decide that publication of the Pentagon Papers was in the public interest while details of CIA operations published in *CovertAction* were not.

By September 1981 the IIPA was advancing and the *Times* and other newspapers were concerned that in trying to suppress disclosures by individuals who mined their scoops from open sources, Congress would violate the First Amendment and chill legitimate journalism. By "outlawing what Louis Wolf does," a version of the bill under consideration in the House "strikes at every reporter and scholar who would publish facts that Government prefers to keep concealed," the Gray Lady warned. The paper's complaint was language subjecting a publisher to criminal penalties if it "had reason to believe" disclosure would harm national security.[37]

Congress eventually convinced itself that it had threaded the needle. The final version of the IIPA makes unauthorized intentional disclosure of information identifying a covert agent a crime if the person responsible for the disclosure knows that the United States is trying to conceal the agent's association with American intelligence. Disclosures by individuals who did not have access to classified information can be punished only if the perpetrator participated in a pattern of activity designed to discover and reveal the identities of covert agents with the intent to harm US intelligence operations. President Ronald Reagan signed the bill into law on June 23, 1982, at a ceremony at CIA headquarters.[38]

Wolf and his collaborators had seen the writing on the wall. "Because of the imminent passage of the Intelligence Identities Protection Act, this will be our last Naming Names column until such time as the constitutionality of the Act has been decided by the courts," *CovertAction* announced in its October 1981 issue.[39] Realizing that judges and juries were unlikely to be sympathetic to activists promoting a worldwide socialist revolution, they decided to wait for someone else to challenge the law in court. The magazine vowed, however, "to continue our struggle against covert operations and US secret intervention around the world." It went out with a bang, listing the identities and biographical details of sixty-nine CIA officers in forty-five countries, from Bangladesh to Zambia.

While *CovertAction* was waging war on the CIA from the National Press Building, the CIA was keeping Agee on the move. CIA pressure prompted the United Kingdom, France, and the Netherlands to deport Agee. He eventually found refuge in Germany. In 1979 the US State Department revoked Agee's passport. The decision was provoked by reports that Ayatollah Khomeini's revolutionary government had invited him to travel to Iran to serve on a tribunal judging American actions in the country. There were also news reports that he had been asked to help student militants who were holding fifty-two American diplomats hostage prove that they were CIA spies. Agee publicly said that he'd recommended to the Iranian government that it demand complete CIA documents on the agency's operations in Iran as a condition for releasing the hostages. Agee also said that he would not travel to Iran until the hostages were released.[40]

Agee sued in US courts to recover the right to use his passport. The case made its way to the Supreme Court. In agreeing to consider the case, the court stated that the "right to hold a passport is subordinate to national security and foreign policy considerations, and is subject to reasonable governmental regulation."[41] In 1981, the Supreme Court ruled against Agee. Revoking his passport was legal because he had "jeopardized the security of the United States" and endangered the interests of other countries, according to the decision. Grenada and Nicaragua provided him passports until communist regimes in those countries were overthrown. Agee ended up with a German passport, granted because he was married to a German citizen. The US government never charged him with a crime and Agee eventually traveled to the United States several times without incident.

With *CovertAction* shorn of its ability to name names, the frisson of excitement that accompanied publication of each new issue dissipated. Its stories detailing the CIA's paramilitary attacks on communist regimes throughout the developing world rippled across the mainstream media, but they didn't stir of waves of outrage. The magazine became more polemical, and even more obviously pro-Soviet. Mirroring the KGB's and the Kremlin's darkest fantasies, *CovertAction* continually warned its readers that the United States was on the verge of launching an unprovoked nuclear war. It also distributed Soviet disinformation that was so crude that no other American publication would touch it.

CovertAction falsely accused the CIA of responsibility for a Cuban outbreak of dengue fever, saying it was "only the latest in a long line of outrageous, immoral and illegal CBW [chemical and biological warfare] attacks against Cuba."[42] It repeated old, discredited allegations that the United States had dropped "germ bombs" on North Korea during the Korean War, and repeated phony Soviet stories that the United States. was spreading dengue and yellow fever in Afghanistan under cover of malaria-eradication efforts.[43]

Of all of the Soviet propaganda *CovertAction* regurgitated, perhaps the most pernicious was dissemination of lies about the origins and nature of AIDS. It ran lengthy articles presenting pseudoscientific theories about AIDS, many of them involving nefarious plots by the American government. These stories laid out numerous ways in which AIDS could have been an intentional or inadvertent product of American CBW activities. *CovertAction*'s preferred theory was that the CIA had plotted to contaminate pig vaccines in order to impoverish Third World peasants, that something had gone wrong with the vaccine, and that the mistake somehow inadvertently led to the worldwide AIDS epidemic. *CovertAction* suggested that its readers take seriously the views of Peter Duesberg, a UCLA researcher whose denial that HIV is pathogenic had influenced South Africa's President Thabo Mbeki to reject drugs that could have saved millions of lives.[44]

In 1988, summing up the morass of nonsense about AIDS it had served up in series of stories, *CovertAction* stated that "one conclusion is clear: Western institutions—military, governmental, corporate and especially medical—played a major role in the origin and spread of AIDS. This was probably more through their 'normal' functioning than by a specific CBW 'conspiracy,' though that cannot be ruled out."[45]

The editors of *CovertAction* did not applaud the demise of the Soviet Union. Searching for explanations for what it clearly considered a catastrophe, the magazine constructed an elaborate conspiracy in which the National Endowment for Democracy, a private, US government-financed foundation, was the tip of the spear for "one of the largest coordinated covert operations ever set in motion." It pointed to the endowment's leader, Allen Weinstein, a historian then little-known outside academe, as the mastermind behind the plot. Boris Yeltsin's rise to power was not a democratic revolution, *CovertAction* informed its readers, but rather a "victory in a new kind of warfare." Anticipating arguments adopted by Yeltsin's successor, Vladimir Putin, *CovertAction* warned its readers that the success of America's project to destroy the USSR by promoting democracy "is bound to be reproduced and exported around the world."[46]

The shuttering in 2005 of *CovertAction*, by then a fringe publication that hadn't made the leap into cyberspace, was little noticed. The debates it provoked in the first half-dozen years of its existence, however, are as relevant today as they were in the final decade of the Cold War. The *CovertAction* experience foreshadowed the way governments and society have responded to dumps of classified data by WikiLeaks, disclosures of the former NSA contractor Edward Snowden, and reporting on emails associated with Hillary Clinton's presidential campaign. Like *CovertAction*'s naming of names, these events raised questions about the definition of journalism, and the responsibilities of reporters and publications to their readers and to society. They also challenged governments to defend the ethics and legality of covert intelligence operations, and revived old concerns about the ability of open societies to protect themselves against attempted subversion by totalitarian states.

EPILOGUE

The National Press Building is no longer the focal point for Washington journalism or for the nexus between journalism and espionage. The business of reporting in the nation's capital has grown so large that it cannot be contained within the walls of a single building. There may still be spies roaming the Press Building's corridors, but they are more likely to be found in the newsrooms scattered across Washington and its suburbs that feed cyberspace's insatiable demand for political news and gossip.

Regardless of its role in today's covert dramas, the history of eight decades of espionage in the Press Building provides valuable insights into the secret connections between journalists and spies that drive events today. Advances in technology have changed the tactics, but many aspects of the game endure. Governments and individuals continue to use press credentials as shields for espionage. The practice of spilling secrets in the hope that disclosures will change policies, and perhaps alter the course of history, has become routine. "Fake news," once a topic of discussion only among professional propagandists, has entered the contemporary lexicon.

British intelligence's organized campaign to spread rumors during World War II could be considered a precedent for Russia's twenty-first-century troll factories. Like their British predecessors, executives at the Internet Research Agency in St. Petersburg craft lies, inject them into news feeds, and then track them as they fly around the globe, watching rumors mutate into more potent formulations or crumble into Twitter dust. And Britain's campaign of dirty tricks against American interventionist politicians has obvious echoes in activities undertaken by Russia and other entities in the 2016 elections.

There are, however, critically important differences between covert attempts to influence the American public in 1940 and 1941 and twenty-first-century intervention in American politics.

Britain's intervention in the American press was effective because most people trusted newspapers and radio broadcasts. The idea was to slip a stream of plausible but fake stories, along with accurate stories that were obtained using clandestine, illegal methods, into the river of real news. The last thing British Security Coordination or its collaborators in the United States wanted was to make readers and listeners believe their newspapers were irredeemably tainted by lies and propaganda. That would have rendered the British-inspired stories useless. This principle is at work today. For example, the entities behind the release of hacked emails during the 2016 American presidential election, as well as those responsible for disclosures like the Panama and Paradise papers leaks of confidential offshore banking data, relied on the mainstream news media to provide context and credibility.

Attempts by governments to manipulate mainstream news media continue unabated. At the same time, the press—and the public who rely on it—are facing a different threat. Vladimir Putin's government, and public actors like Donald Trump who emulate its tactics, have moved beyond adulterating the news with calibrated doses of information derived from clandestine sources and carefully prepared disinformation. Rather than use the news as a vehicle to influence the public, they have another goal. This is to undermine confidence in the news media, to create so much cacophonous noise that people believe there is no such thing as truth, or that it is impossible to distinguish between truth and lies. The Russian government's success in shaping its citizens' thinking stems in large part from its domination of domestic television networks, and America's ability to resist a similar fate will depend on the strength of its independent news media. When a bogus story can bounce from a bedroom in Montenegro, Montevideo, or Mar-a-Lago to millions of smartphones in an instant, and elected officials remain silent in the face of torrents of lies spewing out of the White House, traditional journalism may be the only defense against autocracy and nihilism.

It is neither possible nor desirable to return to a time when three television networks and a handful of publications controlled what Americans saw and read. It is, however, useful to recall the successes and failures of the press in insulating America from Soviet disinformation. A handful of active measures, such as false accounts of the origins and nature of AIDS, penetrated the United States. These were exceptions. The Soviets had little success in spreading fake news in the United States. That's why the KGB, like the CIA, focused fake-news initiatives on developing countries.

Another thing that has changed since World War II and the early decades of the Cold War, at least in the United States, is the attitude of journalists and editors toward intelligence services. Partnering with British intelligence in 1940 and 1941 to battle isolationists and Nazi sympathizers seemed noble and natural to principled American reporters. The transition from fighting Nazis to confronting communists was, for many, a natural progression. The cachet of the CIA in the decades before the Vietnam War, combined with the inherent allure of sharing secrets, made cooperating with the agency irresistible to many journalists.

When stories emerged of ABC television reporter John Scali's secret meetings with a KGB officer during the Cuban missile crisis, Scali was hailed as a patriot and a hero. A reporter who stumbled into circumstances similar to Scali's today would probably not be celebrated. Collaboration with the FBI, CIA, or any other intelligence service has come to be considered a mark of shame.

The CIA has also changed. Responding to the backlash against post-Watergate revelations of deep ties between the CIA and journalists, the agency vowed to cut its ties to the news media. Arrangements that were routine during the early decades of the Cold War, a time when the CIA could count on cooperation from senior management of newspapers and television networks in placing its officers on their payrolls, are gone.

The CIA has, however, left the door open to receiving information from reporters who volunteer their assistance, and acknowledges it would use journalism as a cover in an emergency.[1] Moreover, the CIA has made no commitments to steer clear of reporters working for foreign news media. And intelligence services of other countries have not made comparable commitments. This ambiguity creates dangers for reporters who are falsely accused of being spies, and for the public who cannot be sure that the information they receive is free of government-sponsored propaganda.

There are many reasons why arm's-length dealings between journalists and spies are best for both professions, and for society. One of them is the impossibility of geographically containing propaganda. In an era when the most obscure publications in distant countries are never more than a click away, and Facebook can spread news at the speed of light, "blow back," or contamination of US government decision-making from fake news disseminated overseas, is no longer a hypothetical possibility. It is a certainty.

It also seems inevitable that governments and individuals will see more of their secrets spilled into cyberspace. Responses by governments and the news media to disclosures by WikiLeaks and Edward Snowden resemble those Philip Agee and *CovertAction* provoked more than two decades ago. The Supreme Court's 1981 decision to uphold the State Department's right to revoke Agee's passport set a precedent that facilitated the revocation of Snowden's passport in 2013. Like *CovertAction*'s disclosures of the identities of CIA officers, disclosures by Snowden and WikiLeaks have raised questions about what constitutes the news media and the boundaries of the First Amendment to the US Constitution. And the activities of Snowden and WikiLeaks leader Julian Assange, like those of Agee, raise the specter that individuals and organizations that present themselves as whistleblowers could be manipulated by intelligence services. Revelations of secret partnerships between reporters or their employers and intelligence services would only add to the public's distrust of the media.

At a time when lives are ruled, and more than occasionally ruined, by frictionless electronic exchanges of information, it is important to remember that the most advanced devices will never supplant the oldest and most important form of communication, talking face-to-face. The National Press Club remains a place where reporters and sources meet to solve humanity's problems over a beer. That, ultimately, is the National Press Building's greatest legacy, and a sign that even in dark times decency may prevail.

NOTES

Introduction: Spying between the Lines in the National Press Building

1. *National Press Club Yearbook* (Washington, DC: National Press Club, 1932), p. 28.
2. Ibid., p. 30.
3. Ibid., p. 31.
4. Ibid., p. 32.
5. *Reliable Sources: 100 Years at the National Press Club* (Nashville, TN: Turner, 2008), p. 42.
6. Advertisement in the *Evening Star* (Washington, DC), December 9, 1925, p. 31.
7. "Concrete in Press Building Would Build 15-Mile Road," *Evening Star* (Washington, DC), September 4, 1926, p. 13.
8. "National Press Building Opens September First," *Evening Star* (Washington, DC), August 21, 1927, p. 10.
9. "The National Press Club," *Washington Post*, December 30, 1927, p. 6.
10. Theodore Tiller, "Bareheaded Men in Elevators," *Washington Post*, October 2, 1927, p. M13.
11. "National Press Building Houses Capitol Newsmen," *Holland* (MI) *Evening Sentinel*, April 20, 1948, p. 10.
12. Karl Schriftgiesser, "European News Hardest to Get, 3 Tell Editors: Brains, Courage, Spying Needed, Correspondents Declare Here," *Washington Post*, April 20, 1935, p. 7.
13. *Reliable Sources*, p. 8.

Chapter One: Washington Merry-Go-Round

1. "Vassiliev Yellow Notebook, No. 4, 1923–1950," 2009, Alexander Vassiliev Papers, Manuscript Division, Library of Congress, Washington, DC, pp. 24–25, http://digitalarchive.wilsoncenter.org/document/112859 (accessed April 11, 2018); Charles Fisher, *The Columnists* (New York: Howell, Soskin, 1944), p. 241.
2. "Vassiliev Yellow Notebook, No. 4," p. 24.
3. "Leaders in Capital Twitted in a Book," *New York Times*, July 16, 1931, p. 25.
4. "Vassiliev Yellow Notebook, No. 4," p. 25.
5. Ibid.
6. "Biography: Robert S. Allen: Co-Author of 'Daily Washington Marry-Go-Round'

(1932?)," (Washington, DC: American University Special Collections, Digital Research Archive), http://auislandora.wrlc.org/islandora/object/pearson%3A25554#page/1/mode/1up (accessed April 11, 2018); Sam G. Riley, *Biographical Dictionary of American Newspaper Columnists* (Westport, CT: Greenwood, 1995), p. 7.

7. Dan Nimmo and Chevelle Newsome, *Political Commentators in the United States in the 20th Century: A Bio-Critical Sourcebook* (Westport, CT: Greenwood, 1997), p. 270.

8. [Robert S. Allen], "Guilt Admitted by Adolf Hitler," *Christian Science Monitor*, February 27, 1924, p. 1.

9. Riley, *American Newspaper Columnists*, pp. 7–8.

10. "Vassiliev Yellow Notebook, No. 4," p. 24.

11. Walter F. Jones, "Espionage System at White House Revealed in Book," *Modesto* (CA) *News-Herald*, October 6, 1931, p. 11.

12. Robert Sharon Allen and Drew Pearson, *More Merry-Go-Round* (New York: Liveright, 1932), pp. 299–300.

13. Samuel Nicholson, "A Most Unlikely Agent: Robert S. Allen," Washington Decoded, September 11, 2010, http://www.washingtondecoded.com/site/2010/09/a-most-unlikely -agent.html (accessed April 11, 2018); Fisher, *Columnists*, p. 230; Nimmo and Newsome, *Political Commentators*, p. 270.

14. Drew Pearson and Robert S. Allen, Daily Washington Merry-Go-Round, December 8, 1932, American University Digital Research Archives, http://islandora.wrlc.org/islandora/object/pearson%3A25481#page/1/mode/1up/search/december+8%2C+1932 (accessed April 11, 2018); Pearson and Allen, Daily Washington Merry-Go-Round, December 19, 1932, http://auislandora.wrlc.org/islandora/object/pearson%3A27042?solr_nav%5Bid%5D=cf04c4 a293b162039007&solr_nav%5Bpage%5D=0&solr_nav%5Boffset%5D=7#page/1/mode/1up (accessed April 11, 2018).

15. "Vassiliev Yellow Notebook, No. 4," p. 25.

16. Dennis J. Dunn, *Caught between Roosevelt & Stalin: America's Ambassadors to Moscow* (Lexington, KY: University Press of Kentucky, 1998), pp. 6–7; Nikolai Sivache and Nikolai Yakovlev, *Russia and the United States* (Chicago: University of Chicago Press, 1979), p. 103.

17. Christopher Andrew and Julie Elkner, "Stalin and Foreign Intelligence," *Totalitarian Movements and Political Religions* 4, no. 1 (2003); John Haynes, Harvey Klehr, and Alexander Vassiliev, *Spies: The Rise and Fall of the KGB in America* (New Haven, CT: Yale University Press, 2009).

18. "Vassiliev Yellow Notebook, No. 4," p. 25.

19. Ibid., pp. 25–26.

20. "Vassiliev Black Notebook, 1932–1954," 2009, Alexander Vassiliev Papers, p. 4, http://digitalarchive.wilsoncenter.org/document/112860 (accessed April 11, 2018).

21. "Vassiliev Yellow Notebook, No. 4," p. 27.

22. Donald Ritchie, *Reporting from Washington: The History of the Washington Press Corps* (New York: Oxford University Press, 2005), p. 136.

Chapter Two: A Popular Spy

1. Theodore R. Weeks, "From 'Russian' to 'Polish': Vilna-Wilno 1900–1925," (paper; Washington, DC: National Council for Eurasian and East European Research, 2004), http://www.ucis.pitt.edu/nceeer/2004_819-06g_Weeks.pdf (accessed April 11, 2018).

2. Kazuo Nakai, "Soviet Agricultural Policies in the Ukraine and the 1921–1922 Famine," *Harvard Ukrainian Studies* 6, no. 1 (March 1982): 43–61.

3. Julius Wachtel, *Stalin's Witnesses* (New York: Knox Robinson, 2012), pp. 375–404.

4. Andrew Meier, *The Lost Spy: An American in Stalin's Secret Service* (London: Orion, 2010), p. 161; Christopher Andrew and Julie Elkner, "Stalin and Foreign Intelligence," in *Redefining Stalinism*, ed. Harold Shukman (London: Frank Cass, 2003).

5. John T. Whitaker, *We Cannot Escape History* (New York: Macmillan, 1943), p. 340.

6. Constance Drexel, "Spotlight on Foreign Affairs," *Brooklyn* (NY) *Daily Eagle*, January 26, 1937, p. 7.

7. Harold Denny, "Soviet to Send First Permanent Reporter; Americans Tell Him There Is Freedom Here," *New York Times*, June 2, 1934, p. 19.

8. *Goldfish Bowl* 4, no. 6, National Press Club newsletter, July 1934, p. 3.

9. "Dictatorships Temporary, Says Soviet Envoy Who Sees Russians Turning to Democracy," *New York Times*, June 27, 1935, p. 1.

10. George Durno, "The National Whirligig," *Detroit Free Press*, June 15, 1934, p. 6.

11. Ernie Pyle, "Party First, Soviet Writer Considers Self Secondary in Importance," *The Toledo* (OH) *News-Bee*, February 6, 1936, p. 13.

12. "President Gives Talk at Dinner of Press Club," *Washington Post*, May 10, 1936, p. M15.

13. *San Francisco Chronicle*, January 1, 1937, p. 2, cited in Institute of Pacific Relations, *Hearings Before the Subcommittee to Investigate the Administration of the Internal Security Act and Other Internal Security Laws of the Committee on the Judiciary*, US Senate, 82nd Cong., 2nd session (May 2 and June 20, 1952), https://archive.org/stream/instituteofpacif14unit/instituteofpacif14unit_djvu.txt (accessed April 11, 2018).

14. Robert Whymant, *Stalin's Spy: Richard Sorge and the Tokyo Espionage Ring* (London: I. Tauris, 1996), p. 93; "Red I. P. R. Delegate in Attack on Japan: Lauds Red Army, Raps Nippon Trade Policy," *China Press*, August 23, 1936, p. 1.

15. Whymant, *Stalin's Spy*, p. 93.

16. "American Writers Attempt to Save Romm," *New York Times*, January 24, 1937; Walter G. Krivitsky, *In Stalin's Secret Service* (New York: Harper & Brothers, 1939), p. 28.

17. Walter Duranty, "Radek Wins Tilt of Wits at Trial," *New York Times*, January 25, 1937, p. 3.

18. "American Writers Attempt to Save Romm."

19. Joseph B. Phillips, "Radek Flaunts Story of Plot, Blames Trotsky," *New York Herald Tribune*, January 25, 1937, p. 6.

20. "Old & New Bolsheviks," *Time*, February 1, 1937, http://content.time.com/time/magazine/article/0,9171,788639,00.html (accessed April 11, 2018); Leon Trotsky, "Trotsky Gives His Proof of Moscow Trial Falsity," *New York Times*, February 16, 1937.

21. Duranty, "Radek Wins Tilt of Wits."

22. Ibid.

23. Ibid.""

24. Joseph Davies, "Mission to Moscow," *Times Herald* (Olean, NY), June 10, 1942, p. 4.

25. "Friends Act Again in Romm's Behalf," *New York Times*, January 27, 1937, p. 10; "Reporters Visit Troyanovsky in Plea for Romm," *New York Herald Tribune*, January 27, 1937, p. 13.

26. "Friends Act Again in Romm's Behalf," *New York Times*.

27. Isidor Feinstein, "????????????" *New York Post*, January 26, 1937, p. 6, as quoted in D. D. Guttenplan, *American Radical: The Life and Times of I. F. Stone* (Evanston, IL: Northwestern University Press, 2012), p. 109.

28. Robert K. Landers, "Iffy Izzy," *Commonweal*, February 12, 2010, pp. 22–23.

29. D. D. Guttenplan, "Red Harvest: The KGB in America," *Nation*, May 6, 2009, p. 25.

30. Max Holland, "I. F. Stone: Encounters with Soviet Intelligence," *Journal of Cold War Studies* 11, no. 3 (Summer 2009): pp. 144–205, https://www.mitpressjournals.org/doi/pdf/10.1162/jcws.2009.11.3.144 (accessed April 11, 2018); "Vassiliev Black Notebook, 1932–1954," 2009, Alexander Vassiliev Papers, Manuscript Division, Library of Congress, Washington, DC, p. 23 http://digitalarchive.wilsoncenter.org/document/112860 (accessed April 11, 2018); Oleg Kalugin, personal interview with author, March 7, 2014.

31. "Vassiliev Black Notebook," p. 24.

32. Ibid., p. 23.

33. Ernst Hanfstaengl, *Hitler: The Missing Years* (New York: Arcade, 1994), pp. 153–54; William E. Dodd, letter to FDR, March 20, 1935, FDR Library Digital Collections, http://docs.fdrlibrary.marist.edu/psf/box32/t299t03.html (accessed April 11, 2018).

34. "Vassiliev Black Notebook," p. 24; "Vassiliev White Notebook, No. 2, 1927–1975," Alexander Vassiliev Papers, p. 69, http://digitalarchive.wilsoncenter.org/document/112565 (accessed April 11, 2018).

35. Rodney Dutcher, "Behind the Scenes in Washington," *Ogden* (UT) *Standard-Examiner*, January 30, 1937, p. 4.

36. Davies, "Mission to Moscow," p. 4.

37. Julius Wachtel, "Vladimir Georgievich Romm (1896–1937)" (unpublished paper, 2001).

38. Photo caption, "Newsmen Hear Russian Ambassador. Washington, DC," LC-H22-D-1322, April 22, 1937, Library of Congress Prints and Photographs Division, http://www.loc.gov/pictures/resource/hec.22609/ (accessed April 11, 2018); "Romm, Ex-DC Correspondent, Feared Shot in Russian Purge," *Washington Post*, March 1, 1938, p. 1.

39. Wachtel, "Vladimir Georgievich Romm."

Chapter Three: "Kike Killer"

1. United Press, "Hour of Triumph Strikes for F. D. Roosevelt Today," March 4, 1933, *Piqua* (OH) *Daily Call*, p. 1.

2. United Press International, "Zangara Says Crowd Kept Him from Killing Roosevelt," February 16, 1933, https://www.upi.com/Archives/1933/02/16/Zangara-says-crowd-kept -him-from-killing-Roosevelt/7871007408139/ (accessed May 15, 2018).

3. Arthur Krock, "100,000 at Inauguration," *New York Times*, March 5, 1933, p. 1.

4. "The Presidency," *Time*, March 13, 1933, http://content.time.com/time/magazine/ article/0,9171,745289,00.html (accessed April 11, 2018).

5. Arthur Sears Henning, "For Dictatorship if Necessary," *Chicago Daily Tribune*, March 5, 1933, p. 1.

6. George Wolfskill and John Hudson, *All But the People: Franklin D. Roosevelt and His Critics, 1933–39* (London: Macmillan, 1969), p. 69.

7. James True, Policeman's Truncheon, US Patent 2,026,077, "" filed September 30, 1935, issued December 31, 1935.

8. Wolfskill and Hudson, *All But the People*, p. 69.

9. Ibid., pp. 66, 69.

10. Charles P. Stewart, "Dies and Ickes Exaggerate," *New Castle* (PA) *News*, December 7, 1938, p. 4; Charles P. Stewart, "What's What at a Glance," *Nevada State Journal* (Reno, NV), June 23, 1935.

11. "Better Luck Next Time," *Goldfish Bowl* 7, no. 48 (first quarter 1940), p. 9.

12. *Investigation of Un-American Propaganda Activities in the United States, Hearings Before a Special Committee on Un-American Activities*, House of Representatives, 77th Cong., p. 2743; *Industrial Control Report*, Washington, DC, November 23, 1935.

13. Wolfskill and Hudson, *All But the People*, p. 92.

14. *Investigation of Un-American Propaganda Activities*, p. 2747; John Roy Carlson, *Under Cover: My Four Years in the Nazi Underworld of America—The Amazing Revelation of How Axis Agents and Our Enemies Within Are Now Plotting to Destroy the United States* (New York: E. P. Dutton, 1943), p. 145; Drew Pearson, Washington Merry-Go-Round, July 18, 1944, American University Digital Research Archives, http://hdl.handle.net/1961/2041-20579 (accessed April 11, 2018).

15. *Investigation of Un-American Propaganda Activities in the United States*, vol. 5, May 18, May 22–24, May 31–June 1, 1939, Special House Committee on Un-American Activities, p. 3470.

16. James True trading as the James True Associates, US Bureau of Investigation file no. 62-2930, September 18, 1934; Acting Attorney General William Stanley, correspondence to Louis McHenry Hoew, secretary to the president, August 17, 1934; Memorandum for the Secretary of the Treasury, October 19, 1937; all in the James True folder, FDR archives, Hyde Park, NY.

17. Regin Schmidt, *Red Scare: FBI and the Origins of Anticommunism in the United States* (Copenhagen: Museum Tusculanum Press, 2004), p. 34; Paul Rosier, *Serving Their Country: American Indian Politics and Patriotism in the Twentieth Century* (Cambridge, MA: Harvard University Press, 2009), p. 75; Timothy Dowling, ed., *Personal Perspectives: World War II*, vol. 2 (Santa Barbara, CA: ABC-Clio, 2005), pp. 233–34; Charles J. Weeks, "The Eastern Cherokee and the New Deal," *North Carolina Historical Review* 53, no. 3 (July 1976): pp. 303–19, http://www.jstor.org/stable/23529643 (accessed April 11, 2018).

18. "Blind Senator Thomas D. Schall of Minnesota Uses a Revolver for Target Practice, Guided by Sound as a Wand Taps the Bulls Eyes," December 1935, ed. danielharden44, Critical Past, April 12, 2012, http://www.criticalpast.com/video/65675060566_Senator-Thomas-D-Schall_blind-Senator_making-score-with-revolver_bulls-eye (accessed May 25, 2018).

19. Wolfskill and Hudson, *All But the People*, pp. 69–70; "Death of Schall," *Time*, December 30, 1935.

20. "America First! Incorporated: Confidential Statement," FDR archives, James True folder.

21. "Oust 24 Aides, America First! Asks Roosevelt," *New York Herald Tribune*, September 17, 1934, p. 6; James True, "Seeks Dismissal of Those 'Prolonging Depression,'" *Register* (Sandusky, OH), September 16, 1934, p. 3.

22. Edward A. Williams, "Washington's 'Big Leagues' Take a Hand in Political Game," *Washington Post*, October 28, 1934, p. B2; John L. Spivak, "Plotting the American Pogroms, Part I: Organization of the Anti-Semitic Campaign," *New Masses*, October 2, 1934, pp. 9–13, http://www.unz.org/Pub/NewMasses-1934oct02?View=PDF (accessed May 25, 2018).

23. John Earl Haynes, Harvey Klehr, and Alexander Vassiliev, *Spies: The Rise and Fall of the KGB in America* (New Haven, CT: Yale University Press, 2009), p. 160; "Whalen Offers Secret Proof of Soviet Plot," *New York Herald Tribune*, July 19, 1930, p. 1; Harvey Klehr, John Haynes, and Fridrikh Firsov, *The Secret World of American Communism* (New Haven, CT: Yale University Press, 1995), p. 26.

24. "Vassiliev White Notebook, No. 2, 1927–1975," 2009, Alexander Vassiliev Papers, Manuscript Division, Library of Congress, Washington, DC, p. 33, http://digitalarchive.wilsoncenter.org/document/112565 (accessed April 11, 2018).

25. Ibid.; "Vassiliev Black Notebook, 1932–1954," Alexander Vassiliev Papers, p. 11, http://digitalarchive.wilsoncenter.org/document/112860 (accessed April 11, 2018).

26. "Vassiliev Black Notebook," p. 14.

27. Raymond Lonergan, "Wild Yarns Broadcast," *Labor*, September 15, 1935, p. 1.

28. Wolfskill and Hudson, *All But the People*, p. 69.

29. United Press, "Dies Hears Evans, Moseley Named: Atlantans Mentioned in Letter to Goebbels on Proposed Newspaper," *Atlanta Constitution*, October 22, 1939, p. 14A.

30. "The Sedition Trial: A Study in Delay and Obstruction," *University of Chicago Law Review* 15, no. 3 (Spring 1948): 691–702; James E. Chinn, "Court Removes Two From Trial," *Washington Post*, July 14, 1944, p. 1.

Chapter Four: American Liberty League

1. Ranjit Dighe, "Pierre S. du Pont and the Making of an AntiProhibition Activist," *Social History of Alcohol & Drugs: An Interdisciplinary Journal* 24, no. 2 (Summer 2010): 97–118.

2. Ibid.

3. Ibid.; Daniel Okrent, "No Closing Time for Income Taxes," *New York Times*, June 12, 2010, p. WK11.

4. Sheldon Richman, "A Matter of Degree, Not Principle: The Founding of the American Liberty League," *Journal of Libertarian Studies* 6, no 2 (Spring 1982).

5. Arthur Krock, "AAPA, Its Work Well Done, Passes Out of Existence," *New York Times*, December 31, 1933, p. E1.

6. *Investigation of Lobbying Activities, Special Committee to Investigate Lobbying Activities*, US Senate, 74th Congress, 2nd Session (Washington, DC: Government Printing Office, 1936), p. 2059.

7. Frederick Rudolph, "The American Liberty League, 1934–1940," *American Historical Review* 56, no. 1 (October 1950): 19–33.

8. Blanche Wiesen Cook, *The Defining Years, 1933–1938*, vol. 2, *Eleanor Roosevelt* (New York: Viking Penguin, 1999), chap. 17.

9. Elliott Thurston, "Leaders of 2 Parties Set to Sift New Deal," *Washington Post*, August 23, 1934, p. 1.

10. Associated Press, "President Cool on Liberty Body," *Washington* (DC) *Star*, August 25, 1934, p. 1; David Kyvig, *Repealing National Prohibition* (Chicago: University of Chicago Press, 1979), p. 191.

11. Smedley Butler, "On War," The Religious Society of Friends (Quakers), 1933, http://quaker.org/legacy/co/Writings/SmedleyButler.htm.

12. "Investigation of un-American propaganda activities in the United States. Hearings before a Special Committee on Un-American Activities, House of Representatives, Seventy-fifth Congress, third session-Seventy-eighth Congress, second session," US Government Printing Office, Washington, DC, 1935, p. 20.

13. Paul Comly French, "$3,000,000 Bid for Fascist Army Bared," *Philadelphia Herald*, November 20, 1934, p. 1.

14. Ibid.

15. Special Committee on Un-American Activities, "Investigation of Nazi Propaganda Activities ad Investigation of Certain Other Propaganda Activities, House of Representatives, Seventy-third Congress, second session" US Government Printing Office, Washington, DC, 1935, p. 10.

16. Sally Denton, *The Plots against the President: FDR, A Nation in Crisis, and the Rise of the American Right* (London: Bloomsbury, 2012), p. 215.

17. "*Investigation of Lobbying Activities, Special Committee to Investigate Lobbying Activities*," pp. 1948–49, 1958, 2051–52, 2094; Jared A. Goldstein, "The American Liberty

League and the Rise of Constitutional Nationalism," *Temple Law Review* 86, no. 2 (Winter 2014): 287–330.

18. Robert Burk, *The Corporate State and the Broker State: The Du Ponts and American National Politics, 1925–1940* (Cambridge, MA: Harvard University Press, 1990), p. 158; Patrick C. Patton, "Standing at Thermopylae: A History of the American Liberty League" (PhD diss., Temple University, 2015), pp. 177–88.

19. Roger Biles, *The South and the New Deal* (Lexington: University Press of Kentucky, 1994), p. 140.

20. Patton, "Standing at Thermopylae," p. 188.

21. Franklyn Waltman Jr., "Happy Warrior 'Looks at Record,' Sees 'Debts, but No Progress,'" *Washington Post*, January 26, 1936, p. M1.

22. "Smith's Oratory Dominates 2,000 Hilarious New Deal Foes," *Washington Post*, January 26, 1936, p. M1.

23. Ibid.

Chapter Five: We, the People

1. John Franklin Carter, *Murder in the State Department* (London: J. Cape & H. Smith, 1930.), p. 19.

2. Bruce Rae, "New Mystery Stories," *New York Times*, October 19, 1930, p. 70.

3. John Franklin Carter, *What We Are About to Receive* (New York: Covici, Friede, 1932), p. 21.

4. John Franklin Carter, "The Year of Crisis," John Franklin Carter Papers, University of Wyoming, Laramie, WY.

5. John Franklin Carter, interview by Charles T. Morissey, John Franklin Carter Papers, FDR Library, Hyde Park, NY.

6. Ibid.

7. Ernst Hanfstaengl, *Hitler: The Missing Years* (New York: Arcade, 1994), p. 188.

8. "US All Set for Welcome to Hanfstaengl," Jewish Telegraphic Agency, June 15, 1934, http://www.jta.org/1934/06/15/archive/u-s-all-set-for-welcome-to-hanfstaengl (accessed April 12, 2018); Scott Christianson, *The Last Gasp: The Rise and Fall of the American Gas Chamber* (Berkeley, CA: University of California Press, 2010), p. 127.

9. Ernst Hanfstaengl, *Hitler: The Missing Years* (London: Eyre & Spottiswoode, 1957), p. 100.

10. Christof Mauch, *The Shadow War against Hitler: The Covert Operations of America's Wartime Secret Intelligence Service* (New York: Columbia University Press, 2003), p. 49.

11. "Back Channels," *Washingtonian* 31 (June 1996).

12. Jay Franklin, We, the People, *Evening Star* (DC), October 6, 1939, p. A-13.

13. FDR PSF files, subject file, "Carter, John F., 1939," box 97, http://www.fdrlibrary.marist.edu/_resources/images/psf/psfc0214.pdf (accessed April 12, 2018).

14. Jay [John Franklin] Carter, *1940* (New York: Viking, 1940), p. 9.

15. Carter, interview by Morissey.

16. The chapters were serialized in *Liberty* magazine in 1935 and assembled into a book, *The President's Mystery Story* (New York: Farrar & Rinehart, 1936).

17. Joseph E. Persico, *Roosevelt's Secret War: FDR and World War II Espionage* (New York: Random House, 2001), pp. 8–11. In addition to Astor, the Room's members included the three other companions who accompanied FDR on the *Nourmahal*: Kermit Roosevelt, Teddy Roosevelt's son; William Rhinelander Stewart, a wealthy philanthropist; and Frederic Kernochan, a member of the Roosevelt clan and a state judge.

18. "Memo from Miss Tully," John Franklin Carter, April 24, 1945, in JFC papers, http://www.fdrlibrary.marist.edu/_resources/images/psf/psfc0244.pdf (accessed April 12, 2018).

19. Mauch, *Shadow War against Hitler*, p. 63.

20. "Raw Material Situation in Belgium," John Franklin Carter, March 1, 1941, in JFC papers, http://www.fdrlibrary.marist.edu/_resources/images/psf/psfc0215.pdf (accessed March 16, 2018)

21. "Nazi Activities in the Union of South Africa," John Franklin Carter, March 8, 1941, in JFC papers, http://www.fdrlibrary.marist.edu/_resources/images/psf/psfc0215.pdf (accessed March 16, 2018)

22. Carter, interviewed by Morissey.

23. Ibid.

24. "Navy Department, 1940–1941," Box 44, Franklin D. Roosevelt Library, Files of Dr. Henry Field, p. 6, http://www.fdrlibrary.marist.edu/archives/pdfs/findingaids/findingaid_field.pdf (accessed April 12, 2018).

25. Executive Office of the White House, transcription of press conference, April 25, 1941, p. 35, http://www.fdrlibrary.marist.edu/_resources/images/pc/pc0116.pdf (accessed April 12, 2018).

26. Ibid., p. 43.

27. Ibid.

28. Associated Press, "President Defines Lindbergh's Niche," New York Times, April 26, 1941, p. 5.

29. Unsigned, "Lindbergh Quits Air Corps," New York Times, April 29, 1941, p. 1.

30. Albert Fried, *FDR and His Enemies* (New York: St. Martin's, 1999), p. 196.

31. Franklin D. Roosevelt, "Memorandum for Nelson Rockefeller," May 19, 1941, in JFC papers, http://www.fdrlibrary.marist.edu/_resources/images/psf/psfc0215.pdf (accessed April 12, 2018).

32. "Memorandum on Report From Stockholm to a Chicago Investment Trust," May 16, 1941, in JFC papers, http://www.fdrlibrary.marist.edu/_resources/images/psf/psfc0215.pdf (accessed May 16, 2018)

33. Christopher Andrew and Julie Elkner, "Stalin and Foreign Intelligence," *Totalitarian Movements and Political Religions* 4, no. 1 (2003): 78–79.

34. Franklin D. Roosevelt, "Memorandum for John Franklin Carter," June 7, 1941, in JFC papers, http://www.fdrlibrary.marist.edu/_resources/images/psf/psfc0215.pdf (accessed April 12, 2018).

35. John Franklin Carter, "Memorandum on Martinique," June 23, 1941, in JFC papers, http://www.fdrlibrary.marist.edu/_resources/images/psf/psfc0215.pdf (accessed April 16, 2018).

36. Transcription of FDR press conference, August 22, 1941, http://www.fdrlibrary .marist.edu/_resources/images/pc/pc0122.pdf (accessed April 16, 2018).

37. Byron Fairchild, "Chapter 3: Decision to Land United States Forces in Iceland, 1941," in *Command Decisions*, ed. Kent Roberts Greenfield (Washington, DC: Center of Military History, Department of the Army, 1958), http://www.history.army.mil/books/70-7_03.htm (accessed April 16, 2018).

38. "Says Wheeler Put Troops in Danger," *New York Times*, July 9, 1941, p. 12.

39. "Mr. Whitley Tele. from New York," Federal Bureau of Investigation, January 30, 1937, FBI File 62-47509-1; "Memorandum for Mr. Joseph," January 7, 1937, FBI File 62-47509-2.

40. Ibid.

41. "Memorandum for Mr. Tolson," Federal Bureau of Investigation, September 5, 1941, FBI File 62-47509-6.

42. C. B. Munson, "Japanese on the West Coast," in *Asian American Studies: A Reader*, ed. Jean Yu-wen Shen Wu and Min Song (New Brunswick, NJ: Rutgers University Press, 2000).

43. John Franklin Carter, "Memorandum Concerning Japanese Situation on the West Coast," October 22, 1941, in JFC papers, http://www.fdrlibrary.marist.edu/_resources/images/ psf/psfc0215.pdf (accessed April 16, 2018).

44. Ibid.

45. Ibid.

46. Ibid.

47. Ken Ringle, "What Did You Do Before The War, Dad?," Washington Post, December 6, 1981, p. SM54.

48. John Franklin Carter, "Memorandum Concerning Japanese Situation on the West Coast," October 22, 1941, in JFC papers, http://www.fdrlibrary.marist.edu/_resources/images/ psf/psfc0216.pdf (accessed April 16, 2018).

49. John Franklin Carter, "Memorandum Concerning Japanese Situation on the West Coast (Supplementary)" November 10, 1941, in JFC papers, http://www.fdrlibrary.marist .edu/_resources/images/psf/psfc0216.pdf (accessed April 16, 2018).

50. John Franklin Carter, "Memorandum Concerning Japanese Situation on the West Coast (Supplementary)" November 10, 1941, in JFC papers, http://www.fdrlibrary.marist .edu/_resources/images/psf/psfc0216.pdf (accessed April 16, 2018).

51. Franklin D. Roosevelt, "Dear Jack," November 11, 1941, in JFC papers, http://www .fdrlibrary.marist.edu/_resources/images/psf/psfc0216.pdf (accessed April 16, 2018).

52. Report of the Joint Committee on the Investigation of the Pearl Harbor Attack, Congress of the United States, Pursuant to S. Con; Res; 27, 79th Cong., pp. 453, 455.

53. David A. Pfeiffer, "Sage Prophet or Loose Cannon?" *Prologue Magazine* 40, no. 2 (Summer 2008), https://www.archives.gov/publications/prologue/2008/summer/zacharias .html (accessed April 6, 2018).

54. Munson, "Japanese on the West Coast."

Chapter Six: British Security Coordination

1. Ernest Cuneo, "CIA's British Parentage," Cuneo papers, Franklin D. Roosevelt Library.

2. Curt Gentry, *J. Edgar Hoover: The Man and His Secrets* (New York: Norton, 2001), p. 265.

3. Nigel West, *The Secret History of British Intelligence in the Americas, 1940–1945* (Mt. Prospect, IL: Fromm International, 1999), p. 1.

4. H. Montgomery Hyde, *Room 3603: The Incredible True Story of Secret Intelligence Operations during World War II* (New York: Lyons, 2001), pp. 26–27.

5. West, *Secret History of British Intelligence*, p. 3.

6. Ibid., p. 20.

7. Thomas Mahl, *Desperate Deception: British Covert Operations in the United States, 1939–44* (London: Brassey's, 1999), p. 50.

8. West, *Secret History of British Intelligence*, p. 11.

9. West, *Secret History of British Intelligence*, p. 9; Joseph E. Persico, *Roosevelt's Secret War: FDR and World War II Espionage* (New York: Random House, 2003), p. 64; Christof Mauch, *The Shadow War against Hitler: The Covert Operations of America's Wartime Secret Intelligence Service* (New York: Columbia University Press, 2003), p. 21.

10. Kermit Roosevelt, "War Report of the OSS (Office of Strategic Services)" (Washington, DC: US Government Printing Office, 1949), p. 26.

11. Mauch, *Shadow War against Hitler*, pp. 20–21; Associated Press, "Edgar Ansel Mowrer Dies at 84," *New York Times*, March 4, 1977, p. 32.

12. Edgar Mowrer, *Triumph and Turmoil: A Personal History of Our Time* (New York: Weybright & Talley, 1968), pp. 314–15.

13. Ibid.

14. Persico, *Roosevelt's Secret War*, pp. 65–66; West, *Secret History of British Intelligence*, p. 9; "Colonel Donovan Leaves on the Atlantic Clipper," *New York Times*, July 16, 1940, p. 30.

15. Mowrer, *Triumph and Turmoil*, pp. 316–17.

16. Mauch, *Shadow War against Hitler*, p. 21;

17. "British Plane Here on Regular Flight," *New York Times*, August 5, 1940, p. 1.

18. West, *Secret History of British Intelligence*, p. 10.

19. Persico, *Roosevelt's Secret War*, p. 68.

20. "Radio Today," *New York Times*, February 19, 1941, p. 42; "Today's Radio Programs," *New York Herald Tribune*, February 19, 1941, p. 36; "Radio Today," *New York Times*, December 31, 1942, p. 31.

21. Hyde, *Room 3603*, p. 41.

22. Mauch, *Shadow War against Hitler*, pp. 14–15; Edgar Mowrer, "Donovan Bares 5th Column Acts in Europe and Warns America," *New York Herald Tribune*, August 20, 1940, p. 7.

23. Ibid.

24. Ibid.

25. Ibid.

26. Franklin D. Roosevelt, "Message to Congress on Exchanging Destroyers for British Naval and Air Bases," Washington, DC, September 3, 1940, http://www.presidency.ucsb.edu/ws/?pid=16004 (accessed April 16, 2018).

27. Sanford Levinson and Jack M. Balkin, "Constitutional Crises," *University of Pennsylvania Law Review* 157, no. 3 (February 2009): 707–53.

28. "USA: Liaison with Authorities in USA and London," June 6, 1940–January 29, 1943, FO 1093/238, UK National Archives.

29. Cuneo, "CIA's British Parentage."

30. Mowrer, *Triumph and Turmoil*, p. 323.

31. Ibid., pp. 325–426.

32. Jon Lellenberg, "The Secret War, 1939–45," "Churchill's North America," 29th International Churchill Conference, Toronto, October 13, 2012 http://www.bsiarchivalhistory.org/BSI_Archival_History/Toronto.html (accessed April 12, 2018)

33. Mark Chadwin, *The Hawks of World War II* (Chapel Hill, NC: University of North Carolina Press, 1968), pp. 44–45.

34. Ibid., p. 178; Carl Bernstein, "The CIA and the Media," *Rolling Stone*, October 20, 1977, p. 3.

35. Betty Houchin Winfield, *FDR and the News Media* (Champaign, IL: University of Illinois Press, 1990), p. 58; "May 24, 1935," Franklin D. Roosevelt Day by Day, FDR Presidential Library, http://www.fdrlibrary.marist.edu/daybyday/daylog/may-24th-1935/ (accessed April 16, 2018); "May 16, 1937," Franklin D. Roosevelt Day by Day, FDR Presidential Library, http://www.fdrlibrary.marist.edu/daybyday/daylog/may-16th-1937/ (accessed April 16, 2018); and "April 9, 1938," Franklin D. Roosevelt Day by Day, FDR Presidential Library, http://www.fdrlibrary.marist.edu/daybyday/daylog/april-9th-1938/ (accessed April 16, 2018).

36. Chadwin, *Hawks of World War II*, pp. 51–52; Lynne Olson, *Those Angry Days: Roosevelt, Lindbergh, and America's Fight Over World War II, 1939–1941* (New York: Random House, 2014), p. 324.

37. Chadwin, *Hawks of World War II*, p. 205.

38. Ibid., p. 74.

39. Bernard Kilgore, "G.O.P. Convention: Roosevelt's Cabinet Changes May Make G.O.P. the 'Peace Party,' Help-Allies Group Weakened by Stimson and Knox Action, Observers Feel Effect on Candidates Unclear," *Wall Street Journal*, June 21, 1940, p. 1; Turner Catledge, "Republicans Confused on Eve of Convention," *New York Times*, June 23, 1940, p. E10.

40. "Delegate Poll Says 60% Favor Help for Allies," *New York Herald Tribune*, June 26, 1940, p. 1;

41. Ibid; "Opinion Poll at the Republican National Convention," June 19–25, 1940, Francis Henson folder, Ernest Cuneo papers, FDR Library, Hyde Park, NY.

42. Mahl, *Desperate Deception*, p. 87; "Sanford Griffith, Internal Security Act Investigation," Francis J. Galiant, March 10, 1952, FBI NY 65-4098.

43. Mahl, *Desperate Deception*, p. 91.

44. August 9, 1940, correspondence in Francis Henson folder, Ernest Cuneo papers, FDR Library, Hyde Park, NY.

45. "Opinion Poll at the Republican National Convention," Francis Henson folder.

46. "Francis Henson to Ernest Cuneo," December 27, 1948, in Francis Henson folder, Ernest Cuneo papers, FDR Library, Hyde Park, NY.

47. Mowrer, *Triumph and Turmoil*, p. 318.

48. William Allen White, "G.O.P. Convention Clash Between Old and New Party Ideas," *Boston Globe*, June 28, 1940, p. 10.

49. "Poll Shows Delegates Fear Nazi Peril to US," *New York Herald Tribune*, July 15, 1940, p. 34; Sanford Griffith to Ernest Cuneo, July 22, 1940, Francis Henson folder, Ernest Cuneo papers, FDR Library, Hyde Park, NY.

50. "Poll Shows Delegates Fear Nazi Peril to US."

51. Mahl, *Desperate Deception*, p. 93.

52. Chadwin, *Hawks of World War II*, p. 105.

Chapter Seven: Frying Fish and Fixing Franks

1. Thomas Mahl, *Desperate Deception: British Covert Operations in the United States, 1939–44* (London: Brassey's, 1999), p. 107.

2. Francis Henson to Ernest Cuneo, October 18, 1940, in Francis Henson folder, Ernest Cuneo papers, FDR Library, Hyde Park, NY.

3. Mahl, *Desperate Deception*, p. 111.

4. Drew Pearson and Robert S. Allen, Daily Washington Merry-Go-Round, October 21,1940, American University Digital Research Archives, http://islandora.wrlc.org/islandora/object/pearson%3A25481#page/1/mode/1up/search/october+21%2C+1932 (accessed April 11, 2018).

5. Mahl, *Desperate Deception*, p. 110.

6. Sanford Griffith to Ernest Cuneo, November 13, 1940, in Francis Henson folder, Ernest Cuneo papers, FDR Library, Hyde Park, NY.

7. Henry Hoke, *Black Mail* (New York: Reader's Book Service, 1944), p. 4.

8. Ibid., p. 5.

9. Ibid., p. 6.

10. Mahl, *Desperate Deception*, p. 124; "Nazi Propaganda in US and Abuse of the US Congressional Frank," November 10, 1941, Report No. S.O. 517, Kew, Richmond, Surrey, British National Archives, http://discovery.nationalarchives.gov.uk/details/r/C11029414

(accessed April 16, 2018); Mark Chadwin, *The Hawks of World War II* (Chapel Hill, NC: University of North Carolina Press, 1968), p. 213.

11. Nigel West, *The Secret History of British Intelligence in the Americas, 1940–1945* (Mt. Prospect, IL: Fromm International, 1999), pp. 75–80.

12. "Nazi Propaganda in US" British National Archives; West, *Secret History of British Intelligence*, pp. 75–80.

13. "Nazi Propaganda in US," British National Archives.

14. Ibid.

15. Ibid.

16. West, *Secret History of British Intelligence*, p. 78–79.

17. "Dennett, Fish Deny Knowing Secret of Wandering Files," *Washington Post*, September 26, 1941, p. 1.

18. "Nazi Propaganda in US," British National Archives.

19. Dillard Stokes, "8 Bags of Evidence in Nazi Probe 'Turn Up' at Rep. Fish's Bin," *Washington Post*, September 28, 1941, p. 1.

20. "Nazi Propaganda in US," British National Archives.

21. "Fish Is Linked to Removal of Dennett's Files," *New York Herald Tribune*, September 26, 1941, p. 8; "Mail Bags Linked to No-War Groups Are Investigated," *New York Times*, September 27, 1941, p. 1; West, *Secret History of British Intelligence*, p. 79.

22. "Nazi Propaganda in US," British National Archives.

23. "Anti-Semitic Propaganda Carried in Franked Envelopes of Congressman Fish," Jewish Telegraphic Agency, August 28, 1941, https://www.jta.org/1941/08/28/archive/anti-semitic -propaganda-carried-in-franked-envelopes-of-congressman-fish (accessed April 16, 2018); Edward Willards, "Fish Assails Smear Drive by War Mongers: Tells Foes' Tactics in House Speech," *Chicago Daily Tribune*, September 30, 1941, p. 1; Chadwin, *Hawks of World War II*, p. 214.

24. Mahl, *Desperate Deception*, p. 131.

25. West, *Secret History of British Intelligence*, p. 80.

Chapter Eight: Zapping Zapp

1. Nigel West, *The Secret History of British Intelligence in the Americas, 1940–1945* (Mt. Prospect, IL: Fromm International, 1999), p. 68.

2. *Investigation of Un-American Propaganda Activities in the United States. Hearings before a Special Committee on Un-American Activities*, House of Representatives, 75th Cong., 3rd Session, and 78th Second Session, on H. Res. 282 (Washington, DC: Government Printing Office, 1940), http://www.archive.org/stream/investigationofu194102unit/ investigationofu194102unit_djvu.txt (accessed April 16, 2018).

3. George E. Sterling, *The History of the Radio Intelligence Division Before and During World War II*, ed. Albert A. Evangelista and E. Merle Glunt, http://users.isp.com/danflan/ sterling/ridhist.pdf (accessed May 25, 2018).

4. Donald Ritchie, *Reporting from Washington: The History of the Washington Press Corps* (Oxford: Oxford University Press, 2005), p. 98; *Investigation of Un-American Propaganda Activities*.

5. B. N. Timmons, "Nazi Newsman Is Captured," *Amarillo* (TX) *Daily News*, April 27, 1945, p. 10.

6. "Horrors of War," *Goldfish Bowl* 7I, no. 47, p. 1.

7. "News Service Bureau Chief to Accept Subpoena Dies," *Washington Evening Star*, September 17, 1940, p. 1.

8. *Investigation of Un-American Propaganda Activities*.

9. Ibid.

10. Ibid.

11. "Letter by Zapp Tells Woes of a Propagandist," *New York Herald Tribune*, June 17, 1941, p. 6.

12. Drew Pearson and Robert S. Allen, Washington Merry-Go-Round, November 15, 1940, American University Digital Research Archives, http://auislandora.wrlc.org/islandora/object/pearson%3A8150?solr_nav%5Bid%5D=5e2f233f6371cb367541&solr_nav%5Bpage%5D=0&solr_nav%5Boffset%5D=5#page/1/mode/1up/search/zap (accessed April 16, 2018).

13. "*Investigation of Un-American Propaganda Activities*," p. 1054.

14. Philip Jenkins, *Hoods and Shirts: The Extreme Right in Pennsylvania, 1925–1950* (Chapel Hill, NC: University of North Carolina Press, 1997), p. 154; FDR Press Conference no. 630, March 19, 1940, White House transcription, p. 19, http://www.fdrlibrary.marist.edu/_resources/images/pc/pc0095.pdf (accessed April 16, 2018).

15. Dillard Stokes, "Jurors Want Fish to Face Widened Quiz," *Washington Post*, November 22, 1941, p. 1.

16. Franklin D. Roosevelt, "Address at the Annual Dinner of White House Correspondents' Association," March 15, 1941, American Presidency Project, http://www.presidency.ucsb.edu/ws/index.php?pid=16089 (accessed April 16, 2018).

17. "Propaganda Trial," *Time*, August 4, 1941, http://content.time.com/time/magazine/article/0,9171,884360,00.html (accessed April 16, 1941).

18. Associated Press, "US Jury Convicts Nazi News Agency: Transocean Found Guilty," *Baltimore Sun*, July 26, 1941, p. 1.

19. *PR Blue Book* and supplement to the *International Who's Who in Public Relations, 1960* (Meriden, NH: PR Pub. Co., 1960–70).

Chapter Nine: Fake News

1. "News Agency Set Up," *New York Times*, July 15, 1940, p. 32.

2. "Czechs Charge Girls Transported to Reich for White Slavery," *Overseas News Agency* 1, no. 2 (August 15, 1940).

3. For example, in British National Archives, "America: Fortnightly Progress Reports—

SOE Activities in America," November 22, 1941: "ONA Cover Provided for Hacswnski, New Agent of G4000," http://discovery.nationalarchives.gov.uk/details/r/C11029664 (accessed April 17, 2018).

4. Foxworth to Hoover, FBI file 62-67633-1, April 23, 1942.

5. Ibid.

6. Moscow to Mexico City, September 7, 1944 (cable), *Mexico City KGB–Moscow Center Cables: Cables Decrypted by the National Security Administration's Venona Project*, arr. John Earl Haynes (Washington, DC: Library of Congress, 2011), p. 216, https://www.wilsoncenter.org/sites/default/files/Venona-Mexico-City-KGB.pdf (accessed April 24, 2018); New York to Moscow, February 2, 1944 (cable), *New York KGB Station–Moscow Center Cables, 1944*, p. 7, https://www.wilsoncenter.org/sites/default/files/Venona-New-York-KGB-1944.pdf (accessed April 24, 2018); Mexico City to Moscow, January 15, 1944 (cable), p. 17.

7. Nigel West, *The Secret History of British Intelligence in the Americas, 1940–1945* (Mt. Prospect, IL: Fromm International, 1999), pp. 58–59.

8. Ibid.

9. Zbynek Zeman, *Selling the War: Art and Propaganda in World War II* (Ossining, NY: Orbis, 1978), p. 132.

10. Pat Frank, "US Navy Alert; Hint Nazis May Man Warplanes: Where US Navy Keeps Watch," *Boston Globe*, November 14, 1940, p. 1.

11. Ibid.

12. Ibid.

13. Pat Frank, "US Defense Imperiled by Fascist Bands in Puerto Rico, Haiti," *Oakland* (CA) *Tribune*, February 11, 1941, p. 2.

14. Overseas News Agency, "Bedouin Chief Dies at 130," New York Times, August 31, 1941, p. 22.

15. Associated Press, "Hitler's Star Setting, Declare Astrologers in Convention," *Los Angeles Times*, August 7, 1941, p. 1.

16. West, *Secret History of British Intelligence*, p. 125.

17. Political Warfare Executive Correspondence, Underground Propaganda Committee Minutes (SIBS) MS/42/XI/4a, British National Archives.

18. Nicholas Cull, *Selling War: The British Propaganda Campaign Against American "Neutrality" in World War II* (Oxford: Oxford University Press, 1996), p. 132.

19. Political Warfare Executive, "The Meaning, Techniques, and Methods of Political Warfare," File 462/88G, Political Warfare Executive paper, Kew, Richmond, Surrey, British National Archives, p. 4, http://discovery.nationalarchives.gov.uk/details/r/d2df6ab4-71c4-4ccc-933b-65a1dbfe7d20 (accessed April 24, 2018).

20. Ibid.

21. "Underground Propaganda Committee: Meetings, Minutes, and Reports," FO 898/69, Minutes 1940–1945, Kew, Richmond, Surrey, British National Archives, http://discovery.nationalarchives.gov.uk/details/r/C257620 (accessed April 24, 2018).

22. Overseas News Agency, "Report Hitler in Collapse." *New York Post*, August 15, 1941, p. 1.

23. Overseas News Agency, "Mind of Hitler Slipping, Rumor in Geneva," *Boston Globe*, August 17, 1941, p. B1; Overseas News Agency, "Report Hitler in Collapse," *New York Post*, August 15, 1941.

24. Lee Richards, *Whispers of War: Underground Propaganda Rumour-Mongering in the Second World War* (East Sussex, UK: Psywar.org, 2010), pp. 26–27, https://books.google.com/books?id=Q4CBDJIW-ZwC&printsec=frontcover&source=gbs_ge_summary_r&cad=0#v=onepage&q&f=false (accessed April 24, 2018); Associated Press, "Japan Said to Fear Soviet," *New York Times*, July 12, 1941, p. 2.

25. Joseph S. Evans Jr., "Purge of Nazi Minor Officials? Division between Party and Army Over," *Baltimore Sun*, August 18, 1941, p. 1.

26. FO 898/70, Memo, Underground Propaganda Committee, September 27, 1940, Kew, Richmond, Surrey, British National Archives.

27. Richards, *Whispers of War*, p. 16.

28. West, *Secret History of British Intelligence*, p. 112; Associated Press, "British Using Deadly New Sea Explosive: Secret Weapon Reported 47 Times as Powerful as TNT in Depth Charge," *New York Herald*, November 2, 1941, p. 1; Associated Press, "New High Power British Explosive May Be Decisive in Atlantic Battle," *Boston Globe*, November 2, 1941, p. B21.

29. "Super-Explosive Tales," *New York Times*, November 3, 1941, p. C18.

30. FO 898/70, Memo, Underground Propaganda Committee, December 5, 1940, Kew, Richmond, Surrey, British National Archives.

31. Ibid.

32. Ibid.

33. Propaganda: Underground Propaganda Committee Minutes Correspondence, February 1942, Kew, Richmond, Surrey, British National Archives.

Chapter Ten: Battling the French and Irish

1. Mary Lovell, *Cast No Shadow: The Life of the American Spy Who Changed the Course of World War II* (New York: Pantheon Books, 1992), pp. 198–99.

2. Nigel West, *The Secret History of British Intelligence in the Americas, 1940–1945* (Mt. Prospect, IL: Fromm International, 1999), p. 198.

3. Ansel E. Talbert, "Vichy Embassy in US Shown as Heading Clique of Agents Aiding Nazis," *New York Herald Tribune*, August 31, 1941, p. 1.

4. Ansel E. Talbert, "Vichy Agents in US Tried to Steal Plans for Improved Bren Machine Gun," *Washington Post*, September 2, 1941, p. 2.

5. Talbert, "Vichy Embassy in US Shown as Heading Clique of Agents."

6. Nigel West, *The Secret History of British Intelligence*, p. 201.

7. Drew Pearson and Robert S. Allen, Washington Merry-Go-Round, May 15, 1941,

American University Digital Research Archives, https://auislandora.wrlc.org/islandora/object/pearson%3A9858?solr_nav%5Bid%5D=86297a489a747019dd5b&solr_nav%5Bpage%5D=0&solr_nav%5Boffset%5D=6#page/1/mode/1up/search/Schering (accessed April 24, 2018).

8. West, *Secret History of British Intelligence*, p. 136–43.

9. Ibid.

10. Ibid.

11. Lee Rashall, "Federal Men Air Financial Blitzkrieg," *(Cincinnati) Enquirer*, April 11, 1941, p. 2.

12. William Stevenson, *A Man Called Intrepid: The Incredible WWII Narrative of the Hero Whose Spy Network and Secret Diplomacy Changed the Course of History* (Guilford, CT: Lyons, 2000), p. 132.

13. Menzies to Cadogan, April 1, 1941, FO 1093/238, Kew, Richmond, Surrey, British National Archives.

14. "Wheeler Blasts Irish-American War Propaganda," *Chicago Daily Tribune*, November 11, 1941, p. 17; *Congressional Record*, November 10, 1941, pp. 8692–94.

15. Ibid.

16. "Wheeler Blasts Irish-American War Propaganda," *Chicago Daily Tribune*.

17. West, *Secret History of British Intelligence*, pp. 84–86.

18. Mark Chadwin, *The Hawks of World War II* (Chapel Hill, NC: University of North Carolina Press, 1968), p. 148.

19. West, *Secret History of British Intelligence*, p. 85.

20. Albert Fried, *FDR and His Enemies* (New York: St. Martin's, 1999), p. 161.

21. Fred Warner Neal, "John L. Lewis: He Hates Roosevelt; He Hates War; He Wants a Showdown," *Wall Street Journal*, November 19, 1941, p. 1.

22. West, *Secret History of British Intelligence*, pp. 82–83.

23. George Tagge, "CIO Delegates Put Approval on Mine Strike," *Chicago Daily Tribune*, November 18, 1941, p. 2.

24. Paul Tobenkin, "C.I.O. Votes All Aid to Defense as Murray Backs Coal Strike," *New York Herald Tribune*, November 19, 1941, p. 1.

25. West, *Secret History of British Intelligence in the Americas*, p. 84.

26. Wendell Willkie met with William Stephenson, the head of British Security Coordination, in January 1941 to strategize on tactics for getting Congress to approve lend-lease. Willkie briefed Stephenson on a confidential meeting with President Roosevelt, FO 1093_238-6.

Chapter Eleven: Eight Days in December

1. Amanda Smith, *Newspaper Titan: The Infamous Life and Monumental Times of Cissy Patterson* (New York: Alfred A. Knopf, 2011), p. 392.

2. Frank C. Waldrop, "A 'Scoop' Gave Axis Our World War II Plans: Called 'Rainbow Five,'" *Washington Post*, January 6, 1963, p. E5.

3. Chesly Manly, "FDR's War Plans!: Goal Is 10 Million Armed Men," *Chicago Daily Tribune*, December 4, 1941, p. 1.

4. Ibid.

5. Waldrop, "'Scoop' Gave Axis Our World War II Plans."

6. Smith, *Newspaper Titan*, p. 394.

7. George H. Tinkham, "The American Republic Betrayed," *Congressional Record*, December 4, 1941, p. A5448.

8. William Lambertson, *Congressional Record*, December 4, 1941, p. 9449.

9. James C. Gaston, *Planning the American Air War: Four Men and Nine Days in 1941* (Washington, DC: National Defense University Press, 1982), p. 100.

10. *Documents on German Foreign Policy*, series D, vol. 13 (Washington, DC: US Government Printing Office, 1954), p. 950, https://archive.org/details/Documents OnGermanForeignPolicy-SeriesD-VolumeXiii-June23- (accessed April 25, 2018).

11. Gaston, *Planning the American Air War*, p. 101.

12. Paul Dull, *A Battle History of the Imperial Japanese Navy, 1941–1945* (Annapolis, MD: Naval Institute Press, 2007), p. 7.

13. William Strand, "Nation Stirred by AEF Plan: House in Uproar Over FDR War Aims," *Chicago Daily Tribune*, December 5, 1941, p. 1.

14. Burton Wheeler with Paul Healy, *Yankee from the West: The Candid, Turbulent Life Story of the Yankee-Born US Senator from Montana* (London: Octagon Books, 1977), p. 32.

15. Ibid.

16. Thomas Fleming, *The New Dealers' War: FDR and the War Within World War II* (New York: Basic Books, 2001), pp. 22–23.

17. Smith, *Newspaper Titan*, p. 395.

18. Masuo Kato, *The Lost War: A Japanese Reporter's Inside Story* (New York: Alfred A. Knopf, 1946), p. 39.

19. John Hughes-Wilson, *Military Intelligence Blunders* (New York: Carroll & Graf, 1999), p. 110.

20. Kato, *Lost War*, p. 22.

21. Peter de Mendelssohn, *Japan's Political Warfare* (Crow's Nest, New South Wales, Australia: George Allen & Unwin, 1944), p. 67.

22. H. R. Baukhage, "Popular Mr. Kato," *Atlanta Constitution*, October 14, 1937, p. 6.

23. Hugh Byas, "Japan Sends US an Admiral," *New York Times*, February 9, 1941, p. SM14.

24. *The "Magic" Background of Pearl Harbor*, vol. 1 (Washington, DC: Department of Defense, 1978), p. 4, https://archive.org/stream/MagicBackgroundOfPearlHarbor/Magic backgroundofPearlHarborvolumeI%28February141941-May121941%29#page/n1/mode/2up (accessed April 25, 2018).

25. Ibid., p. 9.

26. "Red and Purple," *Pearl Harbor Review*, May 3, 2016, https://www.nsa.gov/about/cryptologic-heritage/center-cryptologic-history/pearl-harbor-review/red-purple.shtml (accessed April 25, 2018).

27. Office of Naval Intelligence, "Japanese Intelligence and Propaganda in the United States During 1941," December 4, 1941, http://www.mansell.com/eo9066/1941/41-12/IA021.html (accessed April 25, 2018).

28. Ladislas Farago, *Burn After Reading: The Espionage History of World War II* (Annapolis, MD: Naval Institute Press, 2003), p. 180.

29. *"Magic" Background of Pearl Harbor*, vol. 3, p. 32.

30. Ibid., vol. 1. pp. A-75–76.

31. "Magic" Background of Pearl Harbor, vol. 1, p. A-87.

32. Drew Pearson and Robert S. Allen, Washington Merry-Go-Round, October 8, 1941, http://auislandora.wrlc.org/islandora/object/pearson%3A2934#page/1/mode/1up (accessed April 25, 2018).

33. Tom Treanor, "The Home Front," *Los Angeles Times*, June 30, 1941, p. 1A.

34. Roger B. Jeans, *Terasaki Hidenari, Pearl Harbor, and Occupied Japan: A Bridge to Reality* (Lanham, MD: Lexington Books, 2011), p. 83; *"Magic" Background of Pearl Harbor*, vol. 1, p. A-73.

35. *"Magic" Background of Pearl Harbor*, vol. 1, p. A-87.

36. Kato, *Lost War*, p. 28.

37. Ibid., p. 27.

38. Ibid., p. 29.

39. Ibid., p. 32.

40. Kato, The Lost War, p. 37.

41. David Kahn, *The Codebreakers: The Comprehensive History of Secret Communication from Ancient Times to the Internet* (New York: Scribner's and Sons, 1997), p. 44.

42. Kato, *Lost War*, p. 36.

43. Ibid., p. 38.

44. Ibid., p. 56.

45. Ibid., p. 57.

46. Ibid., p. 59.

47. Lyle C. Wilson, "Recalls Pearl Harbor Day in Washington on Sabbath," *Chicago Defender*, December 7, 1959, p. 5.

48. Drew Pearson and Robert S. Allen, Washington Merry-Go-Round, December 14, 1941, https://auislandora.wrlc.org/islandora/object/pearson%3A8383#page/1/mode/1up (accessed April 25, 2018).

49. Adolf Hitler, "Speech Declaring War against the United States," December 11, 1941, Jewish Virtual Library, http://www.jewishvirtuallibrary.org/hitler-s-speech-declaring-war-against-the-united-states (accessed April 25, 2018).

Chapter Twelve: Carter Goes to War

1. Memorandum for Mr. Nichols, March 4, 1947, FBI HQ File 62-47509-70.

2. John Franklin Carter to FDR, "Report on the Organization or Development of a World-Wide Intelligence," January 9, 1942, PSF, John Franklin Carter, box 122, FDRL.

3. Ibid.

4. Memo for Mr. Tolson, Mr. Tamm, Mr. Ladd, January 16, 1942, FBI 62-49507-21, 62-49507-22.

5. Vannevar Bush to John Franklin Carter, January 1, 1942, PSF, John Franklin Carter, box 122, FDRL, http://www.fdrlibrary.marist.edu/_resources/images/psf/psfc0217.pdf (accessed April 25, 2018).

6. Tully to John Franklin Carter, January 2, 1942, PSF, John Franklin Carter, box 122, FDRL.

7. "Report on Interview with C. C. Smith," January 3, 1942, PSF, John Franklin Carter, box 122, FDRL, http://www.fdrlibrary.marist.edu/_resources/images/psf/psfc0217.pdf (accessed April 25, 2018).

8. "Report on Stalin's Secret Board of Strategy," January 7, 1942, PSF, John Franklin Carter, box 122, FDRL, http://www.fdrlibrary.marist.edu/_resources/images/psf/psfc0217.pdf (accessed April 25, 2018).

9. "Report on Confidential Soviet Intelligence," PSF, John Franklin Carter, box 122, FDRL, http://www.fdrlibrary.marist.edu/_resources/images/psf/psfc0217.pdf (accessed April 25, 2018).

10. Memorandum for Jack Carter, January 9, 1942, PSF, John Franklin Carter, box 122, FDRL, http://www.fdrlibrary.marist.edu/_resources/images/psf/psfc0217.pdf (accessed April 25, 2018).

11. "Report on Polish Prisoners of War," January 9, 1942, PSF, John Franklin Carter, box 122, FDRL.

12. Memorandum for Mr. Carter, January 13, 1942, PSF, John Franklin Carter, box 122, FDRL.

13. "Report on Japanese Activities along the West Coast of Mexico from Nogales, Sonora, South to Manzanillo," January 16, 1942, John Franklin Carter, box 122, FDRL.

14. "Report on Alleged Intrigue between Free French and John L. Lewis," October 8, 1942, PSF, John Franklin Carter, box 123, FDRL.

15. John Franklin Carter, "Poland and Lithuania," July 1942, box 128, FDRL; PSF, John Franklin Carter, box 123, FDRL.

16. Ibid.

17. C. B. Munson to Grace Tully, undated, PSF, John Franklin Carter, box 122, FDRL.

18. J. Franklin Carter, "Memorandum on Summary of West Coast and Honolulu Reports by Munson Etc.," December 16, 1941, John Franklin Carter, box 121, FDRL.

19. Memorandum for Mr. Ladd, November 17, 1941, FBI 62-47508-7; Memorandum for the Director, December 13, 1941, FBI 62-47509-14; Hoover to Carter, January 7, 1942,

62-47509-19; J. Franklin Carter, "Memorandum on Summary of West Coast and Honolulu Reports by Munson Etc.," December 16, 1941, John Franklin Carter, box 121, FDRL; "Progress Report on the West Coast Japanese Problem," January 13, 1942, PSF, John Franklin Carter, box 122, FDRL; Stimson to FDR, February 5, 1942, PSF, Stimson, Henry L, box 84, FDRL.

20. John Franklin Carter, oral history interview, February 9, 1966, John Franklin Carter Papers, FDRL, http://www.fdrlibrary.marist.edu/archives/collections/franklin/index .php?p=collections/findingaid&id=345 (accessed April 25, 2018).

21. "'Memorandum for the Director," February 13, 1942, FBI 62-47509-30.

22. Carter, oral history interview, February 9, 1966.

23. Peter Conradi, *Hitler's Piano Player: The Rise and Fall of Ernst Hanfstaengl: Confidant of Hitler, Ally of FDR* (Boston: Da Capo, 2009), p. 267; Jay Franklin [pseud.], *The Catoctin Conversation*, with an introduction by Sumner Welles (New York: C. Scribner's Sons, 1947), p. xiii.

24. Carter, oral history interview.

25. "Memorandum on the Hanfstaengl Case," January 31, 1943, PSF, John Franklin Carter, box 123, FDRL, http://www.fdrlibrary.marist.edu/_resources/images/psf/psfc0223.pdf (accessed April 25, 2018).

26. Jay Franklin, "Hess for 'German' Germany, Hitler for World Conquest: Rift Seen Nearing Climax," *Boston Globe*, May 14, 1941, p. 7.

27. David George Marwell, "Unwonted Exile: A Biography of Ernst 'Putzi' Hanfstaengl" (PhD dissertation, SUNY Binghamton, 1988), p. 509.

28. Memorandum on Ernst Hanfstaengl, Henry Field, October 29, 1965, Files of Henry Field, box xx1, FDRL; Conradi, *Hitler's Piano Player*, p. 259.

29. Carter, oral history interview.

30. Ibid.

31. Conradi, *Hitler's Piano Player*, p. 302.

32. Ibid., pp. 297–98.

33. "Report on 'Sedgwick's' Answer to Your Question," December 1, 1942, PSF, John Franklin Carter, box 123, FDRL, http://www.fdrlibrary.marist.edu/_resources/images/psf/ psfc0221.pdf (accessed April 25, 2018).

34. Memorandum on Hitler's Speech, November 8, 1943, "Franklin D. Roosevelt, Papers as President: The President's Secretary's File," (PSF), box 99, FDRL.

35. File Note, June 28, 1944, PSF, John Franklin Carter, FDRL, http://www.fdrlibrary .marist.edu/_resources/images/psf/psfc0239.pdf (accessed April 25, 2018); "Analysis of the Personality of Hitler," President's Secretary's File (Franklin D. Roosevelt administration), October 1943, FDRL.

36. Conradi, *Hitler's Piano Player*, p. 283.

37. "Report on Public-Relations Technique in the Hanfstaengl News-Release," February 1, 1943, PSF, John Franklin Carter, box 123, FDRL.

38. North American Newspaper Alliance, "Hanfstaengl Is Now Aiding US," *New York Times*, January 28, 1943, p. 1.

39. Memorandum on the Hanfstaengl Case, January 31, 1943, PSF, John Franklin Carter, box 123, FDRL.

40. John Franklin Carter, "The Year of Crisis—1943," diary in the American Heritage Center, University of Wyoming.

41. File Memo, Grace Tully, June 28, 1944, PSF, John Franklin Carter, box 100, FDRL.

42. "Report on Turning Putzi Hanfstaengl Over to the British," July 7, 1944, PSF, John Franklin Carter, FDRL, http://www.fdrlibrary.marist.edu/_resources/images/psf/psfc0239.pdf (accessed April 25, 2018).

43. Carter, oral history interview.

44. Memorandum for John Franklin Carter, July 30, 1942, http://www.fdrlibrary.marist .edu/_resources/images/psf/psfc0219.pdf (accessed April 25, 2018).

45. Greg Robinson, *After Camp: Portraits in Midcentury Japanese American Life and Politics* (Berkley: University of California Press, 2012).

46. Report on Interview with Dr. Ales Hrdlička, July 30, 1942, PSF, John Franklin Carter, FDRL, http://www.fdrlibrary.marist.edu/_resources/images/psf/psfc0219.pdf (accessed April 25, 2018).

47. Memorandum for Dr. Hrdlička, July 30, 1942, PSF, John Franklin Carter, FDRL, http://www.fdrlibrary.marist.edu/_resources/images/psf/psfc0219.pdf (accessed April 25, 2018).

48. "As Roosevelt Sees It," *Macon* (GA) *Telegraph*, April 21, 1925, http://georgiainfo .galileo.usg.edu/topics/history/article/franklin-d.-roosevelts-editorials-for-the-macon -telegraph#april21 (accessed April 25, 2018).

49. Memorandum for Dr. Hrdlička, August 7, 1942, PSF, John Franklin Carter, FDRL; Memorandum for Dr. Hrdlička, July 30, 1942, PSF, John Franklin Carter, FDRL.

50. Ibid.

51. Memorandum for Miss Tully: Hrdlička correspondence, August 7, 1942, PSF, John Franklin Carter, FDRL, http://www.fdrlibrary.marist.edu/_resources/images/psf/psfc0221.pdf (accessed April 25, 2018).

52. Jason Kalman, "Dark Places Around the University: The Johns Hopkins University Admissions Quota and the Jewish Community, 1945–1951," *Hebrew Union College Annual* 81 (2010): 233–79, http://www.jstor.org/stable/23509958 (accessed April 25, 2018).

53. FDR to Bowman, November 2, 1938, in FDRL, President's Personal File 5575, http:// www.fdrlibrary.marist.edu/_resources/images/hol/hol00107.pdf (accessed May 22, 2018).

54. Rafael Medoff, "What FDR Said about Jews in Private," *Los Angeles Times*, April 7, 2013, p. A26.

55. Franklin, *Catoctin Conversation*.

56. John Franklin Carter, oral history interview by Jerry N. Hess, October 7, 1966, Harry S. Truman Presidential Library and Museum, Washington, DC, https://www.trumanlibrary .org/oralhist/carter.htm (accessed April 25, 2018).

57. "John F. Carter Dead; News, Political Figure," *Washington Post*, November 29, 1967, p. C9; "John Franklin Carter, 70, Dies," *New York Times*, November 29, 1967.

Chapter Thirteen: TASS: The Agency of Soviet Spies

1. Biography of Roland Abbiate, School of Karl May [in Russian], http://www.kmay.ru/sample_pers.phtml?n=5 (accessed May 25, 2018).

2. E. L. Spencer to Deputy Assistant Commissioner, Special Branch (memo), September 1, 1946, KV 2/2389, p. 80, Soviet Intelligence Agents and Suspected Agents, Records of the Security Service, National Archives, Kew, Surrey, UK, http://discovery.nationalarchives.gov.uk/details/r/C11287909 (accessed April 25, 2018); M. J. Lynch to Mr. R. H. Hollis (memo), October 25, 1944, KV 2/2389, p. 96.

3. Christopher Andrew and Vasili Mitrokhin, *The Sword and the Shield: The Mitrokhin Archive and the Secret History of the KGB* (New York: Basic Books, 2000), p. 75.

4. "Vassiliev White Notebook, No. 1, 1930–1947," 2009, Alexander Vassiliev Papers, Manuscript Division, Library of Congress, Washington, DC, pp. 61–62, http://digitalarchive.wilsoncenter.org/document/112564 (accessed April 11, 2018).

5. Gary Kern, *A Death in Washington: Walter G. Krivitsky and the Stalin Terror*, rev. ed. (New York: Enigma Books, 2004), p. 129.

6. Ibid., pp. 127–30, 440.

7. Case No. 14, September 3, 1938, KV 2/2389.

8. Lynch to Hollis, KV 2/2389; H. Shillito to H. A. R. Philby, August 10, 1945, KV 2/2389, p. 96.

9. H. A. R. Philby to H. Shillito, August 25, 1945, KV 2/2389; "Re. Olga Pravdina," n.d. (memo), KV 2/2389.

10. "Briton and TASS Writer Lead Field as Prophets," *Baltimore Sun*, November 5, 1936, p. 2; Drew Pearson and Robert S. Allen, Washington Merry-Go-Round, March 23, 1941, American University Digital Research Archive, https://auislandora.wrlc.org/islandora/object/pearson%3A45450#page/1/mode/1up (accessed May 22, 2018).

11. "Vassiliev Black Notebook, 1932–1954," Alexander Vassiliev Papers, pp. 172–73, http://digitalarchive.wilsoncenter.org/document/112860 (accessed April 25, 2018).

12. New York to Moscow, May 17, 1944 (cable), *New York KGB Station–Moscow Center Cables, 1944: Cables Decrypted by the National Security Administration's Venona Project*, arr. John Earl Haynes (Washington, DC: Library of Congress, 2010), p. 127, https://www.wilsoncenter.org/sites/default/files/Venona-New-York-KGB-1944.pdf (accessed May 22, 2018).

13. "Vassiliev Black Notebook," pp. 174–76.

14. John Haynes, Harvey Klehr, and Alexander Vassiliev, *Spies: The Rise and Fall of the KGB in America* (New Haven, CT: Yale University Press, 2009), p. 176.

15. "Vassiliev White Notebook, No. 1," p. 60.

16. Dayna L. Barnes, *Architects of Occupation: American Experts and Planning for Postwar Japan* (Ithaca, NY: Cornell University Press, 2017), p. 180.

17. New York to Moscow, May 16, 1944 (cable), *New York KGB Station–Moscow Center Cables, 1944*, p. 117.

18. New York to Moscow, December 23, 1944 (cable), *New York KGB Station–Moscow Center Cables, 1944*, p. 748.

19. Ronald Steel, *Walter Lippmann and the American Century* (London: Bodley Head, 1980), pp. 193–94.

20. New York to Moscow, October 23, 1944 (cable), *New York KGB Station–Moscow Center Cables, 1944*, p. 599.

21. "Vassiliev Black Notebook," pp. 23–24, 101; "Vassiliev White Notebook, No. 1," p. 56; "Vassiliev White Notebook, No. 3, 1934–1951," Alexander Vassiliev Papers, pp. 73, 76, http:// digitalarchive.wilsoncenter.org/document/112566 (accessed April 25, 2018); "Vassiliev Yellow Notebook, No. 2, 1934–1971," Alexander Vassiliev Papers, p. 40–41, http://digitalarchive .wilsoncenter.org/document/112857 (accessed April 25, 2018); *New York KGB–Moscow Center Cables, 1944*, pp. 488, 599, 748.

22. "Vassiliev White Notebook, No. 1," p. 77.

23. Ibid.

24. Ibid.

25. Ibid., pp. 77, 78.

26. Ibid., p. 78.

27. Moscow to New York, March 28, 1945, *New York KGB Station–Moscow Center Cables, 1945: Cables Decrypted by the National Security Administration's Venona Project*, arr. John Earl Haynes (Washington, DC: Library of Congress, 2010), p. 123, https://www.wilsoncenter.org/ sites/default/files/Venona-New-York-KGB-1945.pdf (accessed April 25, 2018).

28. Haynes, Klehr, and Vassiliev, *Spies*, p. 276.

29. Ibid., p. 509–13.

30. "Vassiliev White Notebook, No. 1," pp. 71–73.

31. Ben Macintyre, *A Spy Among Friends: Kim Philby and the Great Betrayal* (Oxford: Isis, 2015), p. 144.

32. Andrew and Mitrokhin, *Sword and the Shield*, p. 126.

33. Haynes, Klehr, and Vassiliev, *Spies*, p. 260.

34. San Francisco to Moscow, May 5, 1945, *San Francisco KGB Station–Moscow Center Cables, 1943–46: Cables Decrypted by the National Security Administration's Venona Project*, arr. John Earl Haynes (Washington, DC: Library of Congress, 2010), p. 228, https://www .wilsoncenter.org/sites/default/files/Venona-San%20Francisco-KGB.pdf (accessed May 22, 2018).

35. "Vassiliev Black Notebook," p. 53.

36. Ibid., p. 86.

37. Ibid., pp. 163–64.

38. Ibid.

39. Haynes, Klehr, and Vassiliev, *Spies*, p. 183.

40. Ibid.

41. Preface, *Venona: Soviet Espionage and the American Response, 1939–1957*

(Washington, DC: National Security Agency and Central Intelligence Agency, 1996), https://www.cia.gov/library/center-for-the-study-of-intelligence/csi-publications/books-and-monographs/venona-soviet-espionage-and-the-american-response-1939-1957/preface.htm (accessed April 25, 2017).

42. "Re. Olga Pravdina," KV 2/2389, p. 69.

43. "Vassiliev White Notebook, No. 2, 1927–1975," Alexander Vassiliev Papers, p. 32, http://digitalarchive.wilsoncenter.org/document/112565 (accessed April 25, 2018); Kathryn Olmsted, *Red Spy Queen: A Biography of Elizabeth Bentley* (Chapel Hill: University of North Carolina Press, 2014), pp. 93–94.

44. "Vassiliev White Notebook, No. 2," p. 30.

45. Ibid., p. 31.

46. "Vassiliev White Notebook, No. 1," p. 79.

47. Andrew and Mitrokhin, *Sword and the Shield*, p. 145.

48. FBI File No. 100-17076, "TASS News Agency," July 31, 1951.

49. Ibid.; FBI File No. 100-17076-159, Hotel to Springston, September 21, 1950; FBI File No. 100-17076-226, September 6, 1951, USSR Information Bulletin Internal Security.

50. Sam Roberts, "Judith Coplon, Haunted by Espionage Case, Dies at 89," *New York Times*, March 2, 2011, p. A22.

51. "Procedure Followed in Preparing Oatis for Trial" (information report), August 10, 1951, Central Intelligence Agency, Washington, DC, https://www.cia.gov/library/readingroom/docs/CIA-RDP83-00415R008700120007-5.pdf (accessed April 26, 2018).

52. A. H. Raskin, "Report on Moscow's Reporters in America," *New York Times*, November 4, 1951, p. 188; NYHT News Service, "FBI Is Probing TASS Bureau," *Washington Post*, October 24, 1951, p. A6.

53. Christy Wise, "Oral History Interview with Frank Holeman," transcript (Washington, DC: National Press Club, October 21, 1991), https://www.press.org/sites/default/files/Holeman21Oct91.pdf (accessed April 26, 2018).

54. Aleksandr Fursenko and Timothy Naftali, *"One Hell of a Gamble": Khrushchev, Castro, and Kennedy, 1958–1964* (New York: Norton, 2001), p. 111.

55. Michael Beschloss, *The Crisis Years: Kennedy and Khrushchev, 1960–63* (London: Faber & Faber, 1991), p. 132.

56. Ibid.

57. Ibid.

58. Ibid., p. 153.

Chapter Fourteen: Back Channels

1. Steve Smith, Amelia Hadfield, Tim Dunne, *Foreign Policy: Theories, Actors, Cases* (Oxford: Oxford University Press, 2012), p. 272.

2. John R. Cauley, "A Calm Career Man at Heart of Cuban Missile Crisis," *Kansas*

City (MO) *Times*, April 24, 1963, p. 32, quoted in Robert Anthony Waters Jr., "Only Ninety Miles Away: A Narrative History of the Cuban Missile Crisis" (PhD dissertation, University of Mississippi, 1994).

3. Roger Hilsman, *To Move a Nation: The Politics of Foreign Policy in the Administration of John F. Kennedy* (New York: Doubleday, 1967), p. 194.

4. Georgi Bolshakov, "Goryachaya Linaya" [Hot Line], *Novoye Vremya*, no. 5 (1989).

5. Ibid.

6. Ibid.

7. Ibid.

8. Aleksandr Fursenko and Timothy Naftali, *"One Hell of a Gamble": Khrushchev, Castro, and Kennedy, 1958–1964* (New York: Norton, 2001), p. 112.

9. Bolshakov, "Goryachaya Linaya."

10. Ibid.

11. Michael Beschloss, *The Crisis Years: Kennedy and Khrushchev, 1960–63* (London: Faber & Faber, 1991), p. 133.

12. Bolshakov, "Goryachaya Linaya."

13. Frederick Kempe, *Berlin 1961: Kennedy, Khrushchev, and the Most Dangerous Place on Earth* (New York: Berkley, 2011), p. 19.

14. Pierre Salinger, *With Kennedy* (New York: Avon Books, 1967), p. 200.

15. Ibid., p. 198.

16. Christopher Andrew and Vasili Mitrokhin, *The Sword and the Shield: The Mitrokhin Archive and the Secret History of the KGB* (New York: Basic Books, 2000), p. 182.

17. Bolshakov, "Goryachaya Linaya."

18. Ibid.

19. Ibid.

20. President Kennedy news conference no. 43, State Department Auditorium, Washington, DC, September 13, 1962, https://www.jfklibrary.org/Research/Research-Aids/Ready-Reference/Press-Conferences/News-Conference-43.aspx (accessed April 26, 2018).

21. Robert Kennedy, *Thirteen Days: A Memoir of the Cuban Missile Crisis*, with introductions by Robert S. McNamara and Harold Macmillan (New York: Norton, 1969), pp. 22–23.

22. "The High Point in a Notable Week," *Life*, December 19, 1960, p. 29; Charles Bartlett, oral history interview by Fred Holborn, JFK Presidential Library, no. 2, February 20, 1965, https://www.jfklibrary.org/Asset-Viewer/Archives/JFKOH-CLB-02.aspx (accessed April 26, 2018).

23. Warren Rogers, "Eyewitness at the Missile Brink," *Washington Times*, October 23, 2002, https://www.washingtontimes.com/news/2002/oct/23/20021023-093448-8558r/ (accessed April 26, 2018).

24. Warren Rogers, "Capital Secrecy Hints New Crisis," *Boston Globe*, October 22, 1962, p. 1.

25. John F. Kennedy, "Radio and Television Address to the American People on the Soviet Arms Build-Up in Cuba," October 22, 1962, John F. Kennedy Presidential Library and Museum, https://www.jfklibrary.org/Asset-Viewer/sUVmCh-sB0moLfrBcaHaSg.aspx (accessed April 26, 2018).

26. Ibid.

27. Evan Thomas, *Robert Kennedy: His Life* (New York: Simon & Schuster, 2013), p. 222; Fursenko and Naftali, *One Hell of a Gamble*, pp. 249–50; "Discussion between President Kennedy and Robert Kennedy on 23 October 1962," Tapes 36.1 and 36.2, John F. Kennedy Library, President's Office Files, Presidential Recordings Collection, Digital Edition (Philip Zelikow and Ernest May, eds., *The Great Crises*, vol. 3 [Charlottesville: University of Virginia Press, 2014], http://prde.upress.virginia.edu/conversations/8030012 (accessed April 26, 2018).

28. Fursenko and Naftali, *One Hell of a Gamble*, p. 251.

29. Bolshakov, "Goryachaya Linaya."

30. "Discussion between President Kennedy and Robert Kennedy on 23 October 1962."

31. Llewellyn King, in telephone interview with the author on September 24, 2017; Johnny Prokoff memorial plaque, Fourth Estate bar, National Press Building, text written by Llewellyn King.

32. King, in telephone interview with the author; Fursenko and Naftali, *One Hell of a Gamble*, p. 258.

33. Ibid.

34. Ibid., p. 260–61.

35. Ibid., p. 261.

36. Ibid., p. 262.

37. Andrew and Mitrokhin, *Sword and the Shield*, pp. 182–83.

38. Fursenko and Naftali, *One Hell of a Gamble*, p. 264.

39. "John Scali, ABC News," ABC transcript, August 13, 1964.

40. John Scali's notes on his first meeting with Alexander Fomin during the missile crisis, confidential, memorandum of conversation, October 26, 1962, p. 1, DNSA collection: Cuban Missile Crisis.

41. "Report on Meeting between John Scali and Aleksandr Fomin on October 26, 1962, 7:35 p.m.," Digital National Security Archive collection: Cuban Missile Crisis.

42. Report on meeting between John Scali and Aleksandr Fomin on October 26, 1962.

43. Michael Dobbs, *One Minute to Midnight: Kennedy, Khrushchev, and Castro on the Brink of Nuclear War* (Waterville, ME: Thorndike Press, 2008), pp. 167–68.

44. Ibid., p. 168.

45. Ibid., p. 167–68.

46. Salinger, *With Kennedy*, p. 278.

47. Occidental restaurant plaque, http://www.occidentaldc.com/history/, accessed April 26, 2018.

48. Rogers, "Eyewitness at the Missile Brink."

Chapter Fifteen: Continental Press

1. Seymour M. Hersh, "Hunt Tells of Early Work for a CIA Domestic Unit," *New York Times*, December 31, 1974, p. 1.

2. Will Lester, "Former AP Correspondent Fred Zusy Dies," Associated Press, June 4, 2010, http://archive.boston.com/news/local/massachusetts/articles/2010/06/04/former_ap _correspondent_fred_zusy_dies/ (accessed April 26, 2018).

3. Frank Holeman, interviewed by Christy Wise of the NPC Oral History Committee, October 21, 1991, at the National Press Club, https://www.press.org/sites/default/files/ Holeman21Oct91.pdf; Llewellyn King, in telephone interview with the author, September 24, 2017.

4. "Veil Ripped from Ugly Face of Jap Monster," *Los Angeles Times*, December 31, 1944, p. B4; Associated Press, "Calls Enemy Torture Deliberate," *New York Times*, January 30, 1944, p. 28.; "Copley News Head Named," *Los Angeles Times*, May 23, 1960, p. 11; Official Congressional Directory, 88th Cong., 1st session (1963).

5. Joe Trento and Dave Roman, "The Spies Who Came in from the Newsroom," *Penthouse*, July 1977, p. 45.

6. Herbert Foerstel, *From Watergate to Monicagate: Ten Controversies in Modern Journalism and Media* (Westport, CT: Greenwood, 2001), p. 76; Stephen Kinzer, *The Brothers: John Foster Dulles, Allen Dulles, and Their Secret World War* (New York: St. Martin's Griffin, 2014), p. 125; Memorandum for Henry Kissinger from Brent Scowcroft, "Proposed New Membership of the PFIAB," June 26, 1975.

7. Howard Hunt CIA file 104-10194-10023, pp. 197–200.

8. Hersh, "Hunt Tells of Early Work."

9. "Praeger Discusses CIA Book Ties," *Publisher's Weekly*, March 6, 1967, p. 48; "Praeger Published '15 or 16' Books at CIA Suggestion," *New York Times*, February 24, 1967, p. 16.

10. Howard Hunt CIA file, pp. 196–200.

11. US Intelligence Agencies and Activities, Hearings Before the Select Committee on Intelligence, US House of Representatives, Ninety-Fourth Congress, First Session, November 6, 1975, Statement of William Colby (Washington, DC: US Government Printing Office, 1976).

12. Howard Hunt CIA file, pp. 197–200.

13. E. Howard Hunt, *American Spy: My Secret History in the CIA, Watergate, and Beyond* (Hoboken, NJ: John Wiley & Sons, 2007), p. 155;

14. William J. Middendorf II, *Potomac Fever: A Memoir of Politics and Public Service (Annapolis, MD: Naval Institute Press, 2011)*, pp. 100–101.

15. Lee Edwards, "Johnson's 'Watergate,'" *National Review*, June 7, 2005, http://www .nationalreview.com/article/214628/johnsons-watergate-lee-edwards (accessed April 26, 2018); "Partial Text of Goldwater's Seattle Coliseum Walk: Look at the Record," *Washington Post*, September 10, 1964, p. A22.

16. Lyndon B. Johnson, The President's Press Conference, transcript, Washington, DC, September 9, 1964.

17. Robert Semple Jr., "Johnson Selects Foreign Advisors," *New York Times*, September 10, 1964, p. A1.

18. Arthur Krock, "It's a Bit Easier for the President," *Atlanta Constitution*, September 12, 1964, p. 4.

19. Hunt, *American Spy*, p. 155.

20. Howard Hunt CIA file.

21. Lawrence Meyer and John Hanrahan, "Hunt Tells Senate Panel He Spied On Goldwater in '64 on LBJ Order," *Washington Post*, December 20, 1973, p. A1.

22. "Enoc P. Waters Gets Africa Assignment," *Chicago Daily Defender*, June 10, 1965, p. 16; Doris E. Saunders, "Confetti," *Chicago Daily Defender*, January 3, 1968, p. 12.

23. Hunt, *American Spy*, p. 155.

24. Seymour M. Hersh, "Hunt Tells of Early Work For a C.I.A. Domestic Unit," *New York Times*, December 31, 1974, p. 1.

25. John M. Crewdson, "The CIA's 3-Decade Effort to Mold the World's Views," *New York Times*, December 25, 1977, p. 1; Carl Bernstein, "The CIA and the Media," *Rolling Stone*, October 20, 1977, p. 3.

26. Bernstein, "CIA and the Media," p. 3.

27. Ibid.; *The CIA and the Media, Hearings Before the Subcommittee on Oversight of the Permanent Select Committee on Intelligence, House Of Representatives*, 95th Cong., 1st and 2nd Sessions, December 27, 28, 29, 1977, January 4, 5, and April 20, 1978, p. 20.

28. Claire Sterling, *The Terror Network* (New York: Holt, Rinehart, and Winston, 1981)

29. George Lardner Jr. and Walter Pincus, "Former Analyst's Testimony Could Be Crucial for Gates: Hill Hearing Tuesday to Review CIA Tenure," *Washington Post*, September 30, 1991, p. A1; Melvin A. Goodman, "Ending the CIA's Cold War Legacy," *Foreign Policy* no. 106 (Spring 1997): 128–43; Garry Wills, "CIA's Planted Falsehoods Complete the Circle: The Amazing Mindset of Bill Casey," *Chicago Sun-Times*, October 10, 1987, p. 17; Robert Pittman, "CIA's Planted Falsehoods Complete the Circle," *St. Petersburg* [FL] *Times*, October 25, 1987.

Chapter Sixteen: Project Mockingbird

1. "US Aide Defends Lying to Nation," *New York Times*, December 7, 1962, p. 5.

2. Arthur Krock, "Mr. Kennedy's Management of the News," *Fortune*, March 1963, p. 82.

3. Hanson Baldwin, "Soviet Missiles Protected in 'Hardened' Positions," *New York Times*, July 26, 1962, p. A1.

4. "Meeting of the President's Foreign Intelligence Advisory Board," Washington, DC, August 1, 1962, John F. Kennedy Library.

5. Timothy Naftali, ed., "The Presidential Recordings, John F. Kennedy," *The Great Crises*, vol. 1 (New York: W. W. Norton, 2001), p. 195.

6. Ibid.

7. Ibid.

8. Ibid.

9. Tim Weiner, "JFK Turns to the CIA to Plug a Leak," *New York Times*, July 1, 2007, p. 4.

10. "CIA-Socialist Deals," *Izvestia*, December 4, 1961.

11. Ibid.

12. Robert Allen and Paul Scott, "More Spy-in-the-Sky Satellites," *Los Angeles Times*, January 8, 1962, p. B5.

13. Robert Allen and Paul Scott, "US Checks into Report of Soviet Poison Gas Shipments to Castro," *Los Angeles Times*, February 14, 1962, p. A5.

14. Robert S. Allen and Paul Scott, "Shakeup of the CIA Will Keep a Civilian at Its Helm," *Miami News*, July 13, 1961, p. 8.

15. "Project Mockingbird," CIA memo, Box 3, folder "O-R (IV-FF), Project MOCKINGBIRD - Telephone Tap of Newspaper Columnists" of the US President's Commission on Central Intelligence Agency Activities within the United States Files at the Gerald R. Ford Presidential Library, p. 9.

16. Ibid. p. 4.

17. Ibid. pp. 10–11.

18. Ibid. p. 17.

19. "Memorandum for the Record," December 29, 1961, Box 3, folder "O-R (IV-FF), Project MOCKINGBIRD - Telephone Tap of Newspaper Columnists" of the US President's Commission on Central Intelligence Agency Activities within the United States Files at the Gerald R. Ford Presidential Library; "Project Mockingbird," CIA memo, p. 25; Robert S. Allen and Paul Scott, "McCone Set to Curb Free Spending by CIA," *Los Angeles Times*, December 4, 1961, p. B5.

20. "Memorandum for the Record," December 29, 1961.

21. Robert S. Allen and Paul Scott, "Officials Battle Over War Plan," *Los Angeles Times*, October 1, 1961, p. B5.

22. "Project Mockingbird," CIA memo, pp. 11–12.

23. Ibid., p. 9.

24. Ibid., p. 17.

25. "Robert S. Allen, Political Columnist," *New York Times*, February 25, 1981, p. B6.

26. John T. Conway, interview by Stanley A. Pimentel, June 9, 2009, Society of Former Special Agents of the FBI, http://www.nleomf.org/assets/pdfs/nlem/oral-histories/FBI_Conway_interview.pdf (accessed April 26, 2018); Edward L. Beach, Memorandum of Conference with the President, May 26, 1955, https://www.eisenhower.archives.gov/research/online_documents/declassified/fy_2012/1955_05_26.pdf (accessed April 26, 2018).

27. Conway interview by Pimentel; L. V. Boardman to A. H. Belmont, July 20, 1955, FBI file 65-63450.

28. David Binder, "How the Wiretapping Program Began," *New York Times*, September 11, 1973, p. 10.

29. Nicholas M. Horrock, "Hoover Defended on 1969 Wiretaps," *New York Times*,

January 25,1976, p. 23; Nicholas M. Horrock, "Nixon Testifies Kissinger Picked Wiretap Targets," *New York Times*, March 11, 1974, p. 1.

30. Richard Nixon, interview by Frank Gannon, transcript, June 13, 1983, Nixon/Gannon Interviews, Walter J. Brown Media Archives & Peabody Awards Collection, http://www.libs .uga.edu/media/collections/nixon/nixonday8.html (accessed April 26, 2018).

31. President Richard M. Nixon, Alexander M. Haig, and Stephen B. Bull, conversation 442-8, June 4, 1973, Secret White House Tapes, Miller Center, University of Virginia, https:// millercenter.org/the-presidency/secret-white-house-tapes/442-8 (accessed April 26, 2018).

32. John Crewdson, "US Aides Dispute Nixon on Wiretapping of British Newsman," *New York Times*, March 11, 1976, p. 28; Seymour Hersh, "Nixon and Kissinger in the White House," *Atlantic Monthly*, May 1982, p. 35.

Chapter Seventeen: Active Measures

1. *Shrdlu: An Affectionate Chronicle* (Washington, DC: National Press Club, 1958).

2. David Wise, Thomas B. Ross, "US Admits Spy Flight Over Russia," *Washington Star*, June 10, 1962, p. A3.

3. Leslie H. Whitten, "American 'Nazi' Reveals Trysts, $500 Aid from Russian Attaché," *Washington Post*, August 12, 1960, p. A1.

4. Ibid.

5. Warren Rogers Jr., "Red Embassy Official Ousted by US as Spy: Russian First Secretary," *New York Herald Tribune*, August 14, 1960, p. 1.

6. Robert S. Allen, "House Probers Are Probed," *Abilene* (TX) *Reporter-News*, September 30, 1960, p. 51; Jack Anderson, "The Near Arm of Soviet Espionage," *Washington Post*, September 4, 1960, p. E5.

7. Associated Press, "Retired Colonel Pleads Guilty in Soviet Agent Plot," *New York Times*, December 7, 1966, p. 14.

8. Oleg Kalugin, *The First Directorate: My 32 Years in Intelligence and Espionage against the West* (New York: St. Martin's, 1994), p. 72; Oleg Kalugin, in personal interview with the author, March 7, 2014.

9. Kalugin, *First Directorate*, p. 73.

10. Ibid., p. 74; Kalugin, in personal interview with the author.

11. Kalugin, in personal interview with the author.

12. Kalugin, *First Directorate*, p. 78; Kalugin, in personal interview with the author.

13. Kalugin, in personal interview with the author.

14. Kalugin, *First Directorate*, p. 91.

15. Kalugin, *First Directorate*, p. 91; W. Peyton George, interview by Brian R. Hollstein, June 29, 2009, transcript, Society of Former Special Agents of the FBI, http://www.nleomf.org/ assets/pdfs/nlem/oral-histories/FBI_George_interview.pdf (accessed May 24, 2018).

16. George, interview.

17. Ibid.

18. Ibid.

19. Ibid.

20. Ibid.

21. Ibid.

22. Kalugin, *First Directorate*, pp. 84–85.

23. C. W. Young, "Soviet Active Measures in the US: An Updated Report by the FBI," *Congressional Record*, December 9, 1987, pp. E-4716–17.

24. Kalugin, *First Directorate*, p. 93.

25. Tom Trede, "Vigilantes Keep an Unauthorized Eye on Soviet Spies," *Daily Intelligencer* (Montgomery, Pennsylvania), July 7, 1983, p. 3.

26. Lurma Rackley, "Goat Is Chained to TASS Door," *Washington Star*, May 18, 1971, p. 10; Christopher Andrew and Vasili Mitrokhin, *The Sword and the Shield: The Mitrokhin Archive and the Secret History of the KGB* (New York: Basic Books, 2000), pp. 238, 240.

27. Andrew and Mitrokhin, *Sword and the Shield*, p. 238.

28. Christopher Andrew and Oleg Gordievsky, *KGB: The Inside Story of Its Foreign Operations from Lenin to Gorbachev* (New York: HarperCollins, 1992), p. 587.

29. Yuri Shvets, *Washington Station: My Life as a KGB Spy in America* (New York: Simon & Schuster, 1995), pp. 40–46; Yuri Shvets, C-SPAN Booknotes interview, June 18, 1995; "*Soviet Active Measures in the 'Post-Cold War' Era 1988–1991*," report prepared at the request of the United States House of Representatives Committee on Appropriations (Washington, DC: United States Information Agency, June 1992), http://intellit.muskingum.edu/russia_folder/pcw_era/sect_16a.htm (accessed April 26, 2018).

30. Shvets, *Washington Station*, pp. 134, 144, 159.

Chapter Eighteen: *CovertAction*

1. William J. Casey, "Statement for the Record," before the Senate Committee on the Judiciary Subcommittee on Security and Terrorism, May 8, 1981.

2. Christopher Andrew and Vasili Mitrokhin, *The Sword and the Shield: The Mitrokhin Archive and the Secret History of the KGB* (New York: Basic Books, 2000), p. 230.

3. Philip Agee, *Inside the Company: CIA Diary* (New York: Farrar, Straus, & Giroux, 1975), pp. 558, 562.

4. Ibid. pp. 562–63.

5. Ibid., pp. 567–73.

6. Philip Agee, "Philip Agee on CIA Role," letter to the editor, *Los Angeles Times*, August 22, 1992, http://articles.latimes.com/1992-08-22/local/me-5142_1_florintino-aspillaga-cia-diary-cia-money (accessed April 26, 2018).

7. Agee, *Inside the Company*, p. 389.

8. Andrew and Mitrokhin, *Sword and the Shield*, p. 3.

9. Ibid., pp. 3–15.

10. Ibid., p. 230.

11. Ibid., p. 206.

12. Oleg Kalugin, *The First Directorate: My 32 Years in Intelligence and Espionage against the West* (New York: St. Martin's, 1994), p. 192.

13. Andrew and Mitrokhin, *Sword and the Shield*, p. 231.

14. "Inside the Company: CIA Diary," Studies in Intelligence, Vol. 19 No. 2, Summer 1975, p. 35.

15. Philip Taubman, "Gadfly Exposes CIA's Covert Activities and Agents," *New York Times*, July 10, 1980, p. A12.

16. Andrew and Mitrokhin, *Sword and the Shield*, p. 233.

17. Naming Names, *CovertAction Information Bulletin*, no. 1 (July 1978): 23.

18. Philip Agee, "Where Myths Lead to Murder," *CovertAction Information Bulletin*, no. 1 (July 1978): 7.

19. Philip Taubman, "CIA Foe Blows Agents' Cover," *Ottawa Journal* [Ottawa, Canada], July 28, 1980, p. 26.

20. Jeff Stein, "Spooking the Namers," *Village Voice*, November 12–18, 1980, p. 22.

21. *CovertAction Information Bulletin*, no. 2 (October 1978).

22. Andrew and Mitrokhin, *Sword and the Shield*, p. 233.

23. Ibid., p. 234.

24. Ellen Ray, William Schaap, Karl Van Meter, and Louis Wolf, eds., *Dirty Work 2: The CIA in Africa* (London: Zed Press, 1980), p. 3.

25. C. D. Edbrook, "Principles of Deep Cover," *Studies in Intelligence* 5 (Summer 1961): 1–29, https://www.cia.gov/library/readingroom/docs/DOC_0000608982.pdf (accessed April 26, 2018).

26. C. D. Edbrook, "The Principles of Deep Cover," *CovertAction Information Bulletin*, no. 10, August–September 1980, pp. 45–54.

27. Edbrook, "Principles of Deep Cover." *Studies in Intelligence* 5 (Summer 1961).

28. "'Destabilizing' Jamaica," editorial, *Washington Post*, July 28, 1980, p. A18.

29. Louis Wolf, interview by Eyewitness News, WDVM TV, July 10, 1980, Washington, DC; Editorial, *CovertAction Information Bulletin*, no. 10 (August–September 1980), p. 2.

30. Frank Carlucci, CIA deputy director, to Rep. C. W. Bill Young, letter, July 8, 1980, https://www.cia.gov/library/readingroom/docs/CIA-RDP11M01338R000400470010-8.pdf (accessed April 26, 2018); "Passing the Intelligence Identities Protection Act of 1982," *Studies in Intelligence*, approved for release December 29, 2008, https://nsarchive2.gwu.edu/NSAEBB/NSAEBB431/docs/intell_ebb_008.PDF (accessed April 26, 2018).

31. Editorial, *CovertAction*, no. 10 (August–September 1980): 2–3.

32. "The Philip Agees, the Louis Wolfs," *Washington Post*, July 20, 1981, p. A12.

33. Ellen Ray, William H. Schaap, and Louis Wolf, "To Call Us Terrorists Is a Dangerous Flimflam," *Washington Post*, August 29, 1981, p. A21.

34. "Secrecy Is Not the Only Security," editorial, *New York Times*, July 21, 1981.

35. Ibid.

36. Ibid.

37. "A Dumb Defense of Intelligence," editorial, *New York Times*, September 28, 1981, p. A18.

38. Jennifer K. Elsea, "Intelligence Identities Protection Act," Congressional Research Service, April 10, 2013.

39. Naming Names, *CovertAction Information Bulletin*, no. 14–15 (October 1981): 7.

40. "Agee's Passport Revoked," *Washington Post*, December 24, 1979, p. A1.

41. Haig v. Agee, 453 US 280 (1981), https://supreme.justia.com/cases/federal/us/453/280/case.html (accessed April 26, 2018).

42. Bill Schaap, "US Biological Warfare: The 1981 Cuba Dengue Epidemic," *CovertAction* no. 17 (Summer 1982): 28–31.

43. Ken Lawrence, "The History of US Bio-Chemical Killers," *CovertAction*, no. 17 (Summer 1982): 5–7.

44. Robert Lederer, "Origin and Spread of AIDS: Is the West Responsible," *CovertAction Information Bulletin*, no. 29 (Winter 1988)

45. Ibid.

46. Sean Gervasi, "Western Intervention in the USSR," *CovertAction Information Bulletin*, no. 39 (Winter 1991–92): 4–9.

Epilogue

1. Kate Houghton, "Subverting Journalism: Reporters and the CIA," Attacks on the Press in 1996, Committee to Protect Journalists, New York, 1996, https://cpj.org/attacks96/sreports/cia.html (accessed May 25, 2018); CIA's Use of Journalists and Clergy in Intelligence Operations, Select Committee on Intelligence of the United States Senate, One Hundred Fourth Congress, Second Session (US Government Printing Office, 1996); Martha Bayles, Jeffrey Gedmin, "The CIA and Journalists," *Boston Globe*, January 4, 2015, p. 16.

INDEX